D0364116

MITCHELL BEAZLEY

THE TRAVELLER'S GUIDE TO
THE WINE REGIONS
OF
FRANCE

HUBRECHT DUIJKER

The Mitchell Beazley Traveller's Guide to the Wine Regions of France
Edited and designed by
Mitchell Beazley International Limited
Artists House, 14-15 Manette Street, London W1V 5LB

Copyright © Mitchell Beazley Publishers 1989
Some material in this Guide is based upon *The Wine Atlas of France* by Hugh Johnson and Hubrecht Duijker (Mitchell Beazley 1987).

British Library Cataloguing in Publication Data
Duijker, Hubrecht
   The travellers guide to the wine regions of
   France
   1. France. Wine-growing regions. Visitors' guides
   I. Title
   914.4'04'838

ISBN 0 85533 735 4

The author and publishers will be grateful for any information which will assist them in keeping future editions up to date. Although all reasonable care has been taken in the preparation of this book neither the publishers nor the author can accept any liability for any consequences arising from the use thereof or from the information contained herein.

Wine Route contributors Philippa Crawford and Chris Foulkes
Editor Alison Melvin
Editorial Assistant Nicola East
Art Editors Suzie Hooper and Paul Drayson
Senior Executive Editor Chris Foulkes
Senior Executive Art Editor Tim Foster
Production Stewart Bowling
Wine maps Thames Cartographic Services based on the 1988 edition of *The Wine Atlas of France*

Typeset in Spartan
by Bookworm Typesetting, Manchester, England
Produced by Mandarin Offset
Printed in China

CONTENTS

INTRODUCTION

The wine regions of France have many riches — but how easy
it is to miss them. The most rewarding wine routes are often
not signposted; churches and other places of interest are
often hidden in village centres; quiet and hospitable hotels
are harder to spot than the busy hotels along the popular
tourist routes. Equally, the quality and atmosphere of
restaurants may not be obvious from outside appearances,
and it is usually impossible to judge a wine producer on the
basis of the sign outside his premises alone.

This traveller's guide is based on my own careful notes
taken during frequent trips to France. For many years I have
spent an average of three months each year travelling
around the wine regions of the beautiful French countryside.
I have driven thousands of kilometres, slept in a wide range
of hotels and eaten in countless restaurants. I have visited
hundreds of winegrowers, ranging from aristocratic château
owners in the Médoc to small, simple farmers in remote
districts of the southwest and Corsica.

Sometimes my wife and our two children have been able
to accompany me on a so-called "working holiday". They
once spent a hot summer in the sleepy village of St-Romain,
while I toured the vineyards of Burgundy and have probably
seen more of Bordeaux and Alsace than many people do in
a lifetime. They have also shared some of the more
unpleasant experiences. For example, all of us got food
poisoning in a terrible hotel in Rodez in southwest France (it
is no longer in business), and both the children have been
car sick on a particularly bad road. (I cured the car sickness
by offering them five centimes for counting each bend in the
road and was able to make an appointment with a
winegrower on time.)

This pocket guide allows me to share the knowledge I
have gleaned and the wide range of pleasures I have
discovered and enjoyed during my travels around France. To
update my own notes, I have contacted hundreds of serious
and trustworthy wine producers throughout the whole
country. They have been kind enough to check my facts and
to give me additional insider's recommendations for hotels
and restaurants. The names of all those who have helped
are too numerous to mention here, but I am deeply grateful
for all their splendid cooperation. I am also grateful to the
expert team at Mitchell Beazley who have succeeded in
integrating the huge amount of data into this very practical
guide.

Personally, I hope that this book enriches your travels
through the wine regions of France. Bon voyage!

Hubrecht Duijker

HOW TO USE THIS GUIDE

France was the first of the wine-producing countries to map its vineyards. Map them, that is, with the purpose of marking out boundaries that would have legal force and would define status and quality. Today, when every wine nation has a system of mapping of greater or lesser complexity, France still leads the field. It is the country where the place the wine comes from matters most. The better the wine, the more particular are the laws about defining and fixing its home field. In Burgundy the system has reached such a level of sophistication that each plot of vines is named and accorded a status.

The painstaking precision of the French *appellation contrôlée* system has obvious benefits for the wine drinker. It also is of great help to the traveller, who will be able to visit, and gaze upon, the exact vineyards which are home to the most memorable names in wine. Great satisfaction can be had from driving (or walking), map in hand, along the hillside from which comes one of your favourites. Distinctions which were once academic become suddenly clear. It is possible to see how the colour and texture of the soil changes with the slope, how the low gravel dunes of the Médoc quite obviously have better drainage than the land beside the streams, how the best-known sites in Alsace are tucked into the warm, sunny corners.

This Guide attempts to place the many different wines of France within the context of the landscape, the culture and the beauty of the region where they are produced. It is intended to be a practical (and hopefully inspiring) companion both when travelling and when at home.

THE MAPS

The wine maps in this Guide vary in scale and detail depending upon the complexity of the region and the extent of the Wine Route. Beside each map there is a scale bar, key and symbol indicating the direction north. The maps are primarily intended to give the traveller an indication of the direction and complexity of the Wine Route. They also indicate the extent of the vineyards in each wine region. Leading wine châteaux and estates, and individual vineyards in some areas have been marked (or numbered where space is at a premium). The maps are designed to be used in conjunction with the detailed directions given in the text, and you will find it helpful to have a good touring map of the region to guide you to the wine areas.

THE TEXT

Each of the five zones is divided into chapters on the different wine regions and follows a logical progression around the zone. For each wine district there is a wine map with detailed directions for following the Wine Route mapped. The text also contains information on châteaux and other producers as well as useful addresses for both local wine bodies and hotels and restaurants.

HOTEL AND RESTAURANT INFORMATION

This Guide is not intended to provide a comprehensive listing of all hotels and restaurants in each region. All the places described are those which are either known to the author, or which have been recommended by local wine merchants, château proprietors and other knowledgeable people. To a large extent, therefore, the lists are a guide to places local people use and consider worth telling visitors about. In the less important wine regions shortage of space has meant that travel information has been curtailed in some instances.

Hotels and restaurants are graded according to the broad price band, not as the equivalent of a star rating for quality. Remember, too, that ownership, telephone numbers, staff, décor, etc. — and prices — of hotels and restaurants are always subject to change. It is always wise to reserve hotel rooms in advance, and it is preferable to do this by telephone and then confirm by letter.

Hotels, based on the price of an average double room without breakfast, are graded as follows:

Class A, luxury, from 350 francs
Class B, average, from 150 – 350 francs
Class C, simple, up to 150 francs

Restaurants are based on the average price of a meal per person, excluding wine and other drinks:

Class A, luxury, from 250 francs
Class B, average, from 150 – 250 francs
Class C, simple, up to 150 francs

Nearly every wine district in France has some body, usually a Maison du Vin, with the job of publicizing the local wine. It is to these people that it is best to go to enquire about visiting wine châteaux and about places to taste wine. They will have the most up-to-date information. Their addresses are given in this Guide where possible. The address of the Syndicat d'Initiative for almost every town in France is given in the annual Michelin Red Guide. The overseas offices of the French Government Tourist Board should also be able to help.

LOCAL PRODUCERS

A directory which lists the author's selection of local wine producers is featured in some of the wine districts otherwise the main producers are mentioned in the text. There are hundreds of thousands of people making wine in France, and any selection must be to some extent arbitrary. Those chosen stand out as makers of good examples of the wine of their appellation. They are listed in alphabetical order according to their village. As with hotels and restaurants, properties rise and fall. Owners sell, or retire, and the estate may well perform differently in new hands. Recommendations are given in good faith but must be treated with some caution. For an up-to-date assessment of the quality of many French wine châteaux, consult Hugh Johnson's annually updated *Pocket Wine Book* (*Pocket Encyclopedia of Wine* in the USA).

TRAVELLING IN FRANCE

France can be explored with ease and pleasure by road, rail, air or combinations of the three. The road network has been augmented in the last decade by a very good system of autoroutes – superhighways which are run by private concerns and which charge tolls. They are numbered with the prefix A. Roads with the prefix N are the routes nationales, non-toll highways which often date, in alignment at least, from Napoleonic times. Lesser roads are organized on a département basis and carry the prefix D. Study of the maps will show that some D roads provide attractive routes parallel to the main roads.

The French are occasionally disposed to renumber their road system, with consequent confusion as maps and signboards fail to agree. Before planning a journey, invest in an up-to-date single-sheet map of French main roads.

Travel in France becomes very difficult in high summer, especially at the weekends at the start and finish of August. It pays to avoid these periods, but if you have to travel, look out for the specially signposted holiday routes. These are diversions around known traffic black-spots. One runs east of Paris, for instance, taking traffic from the north on its way south around rather than through the capital.

Visitors are often pleasantly surprised by how empty France, and French roads, can seem. It is a large country with a relatively small population, and many roads. Driving in France has a somewhat different flavour. The often straight roads, the fairly long distance between towns and the lack of traffic allows for distances to be covered at a pleasant, rhythmic pace. Many travellers find that a judicious mixture of autoroutes for speed and selected lesser roads for interest is an excellent way of covering distances.

Speed limits are rigorously enforced and police have power to levy on-the-spot fines. The French authorities also take a strict view of drinking and driving. Elect a non-sampling driver – or an on-the-spot fine (or worse) could cast a blight on your holiday. Up-to-date information about speed limits, frontier formalities, road conditions and new roads can be obtained from the French National Tourist Office (offices in many capital cities) and the major motoring organizations.

The maps have marked on them a suggested route around the vineyards. Some districts have formal routes with signposts and even roadside tasting booths. Others are more reticent, or less organized. Often the locals fear that a formal route willl attract too many people (Chablis turned down such a plan for this reason), or local rivalries may make it impossible to agree on a route. In such cases we have suggested a route which takes the traveller through the most interesting and beautiful parts of the district. These routes, be they formal or informal, are marked on the wine maps in black. In several cases the route suggested here does not follow the official signposted route. In general there are no signposted footpaths through the vineyards (except for some in Alsace). However, it is possible to penetrate most vineyards via the tracks used by farmers.

THE VINEYARD VISITOR

For anyone interested in wine, there is no greater pleasure than visiting a wine producer and discussing and tasting the wine with him. There are many wine producers in France where visits of some sort can be made. They vary from impersonal, if fascinating, tours around large factory-like establishments to one-to-one sessions around a farmhouse kitchen or in a cobwebbed cellar. The most rewarding visits are the result of a little pre-planning as the most interesting producers are often the small châteaux and estates where facilities will not be lavish and who will appreciate a prior appointment. A month or so before you leave, speak to your local wine merchant who will be happy to pass a request down the line through the importer to the château or grower concerned. Alternatively, you can approach the importer direct.

If your French is up to it, write direct to the château, or telephone. A call giving a day or so notice will often elicit an invitation. Some larger concerns, such as the champagne houses of Reims and Epernay, have elaborate facilities for visitors and run guided tours. It is nearly always possible to turn up at these places without appointments, although they tend to run tours at fixed times. Signs and notices abound in the wine centres offering such facilities. Beware of those firms where a visit is merely the prelude to an attempt to sell you some wine.

In many areas, châteaux and cellars offer free tastings and direct sales. Not all these by any means are the cynical concerns mentioned above. In remoter districts, many vignerons make a good part of their living by direct sales and are eager to offer a warm welcome to entice winelovers into their cellars.

Before visiting a vineyard, it is good sense (and a courtesy to the host) to do a little background reading about the area and the wines produced. A knowledge of the basics will also highlight the subtle differences that make each wine unique. Is the proprietor using oak ageing in an area which traditionally did not age the wines? Has some new grape variety been tried?

The obvious place to see at a château or estate is the cellar. But try also to visit the *cuvier* or vat-house, and, in large places, the laboratory and the the bottling plant. Take a look too at the vineyards, asking about soil and situation. However, not every wine producer is organized in the same way. The classic château in the midst of its vines is the exception rather than the rule and many winemakers are not winegrowers: they have the press-house and the cellars, but not the vineyards. Cooperatives, which dominate the scene in many parts of southern France, work on this basis.

The most enjoyable time to visit a vineyard district is during the vintage. Bear in mind, however, that the people who make the wine will be at their busiest then and they may not be able to accept visitors. Many places are also closed in August for the traditional holiday. (See the wine calendar overleaf which shows the yearly round of work for the winemaker and also lists some regular wine events.)

THE WINE YEAR

The following calendar lists just some of the wine events that are regularly held in the various wine regions.

JANUARY

Pruning traditionally started on St Vincent's Day (22 January), but nowadays begins in December. Barrels of new wine must be topped up regularly.

Some time in Jan	Fête des Vins Nouveaux in Ampuis (N. Rhône)
Saturday after 22 January	St-Vincent Tournante (the patron saint of winegrowers) festival in the Côte d'Or communes

FEBRUARY

Finish pruning and take cuttings for grafting. Young vines must be trained and tied in to the trellises. New wine is racked in barrels to clear it of sediment.

First weekend	Wine fair in Bourgueil (Touraine)
Second weekend	Wine fair in Saumur (Anjou)
Last weekend	Wine fairs in Azay-le-Rideaux, Vouvray (Touraine)
Late February	Wine fair in St-Pourçain-sur-Sioule (Massif Central)

MARCH

Vines begin to emerge from dormancy. Vineyard is ploughed to aerate the soil and uncover the bases of the vines. The new wine undergoes a second fermentation.

Early March	Côtes du Rhône Villages festival in Vinsobres
First weekend	Wine fair in Le Loroux-Bottereau (Muscadet)
Second weekend	Wine fairs in Durtal (Anjou) and Chinon (Touraine)
Third weekend	Wine fair in Vallet (Muscadet)
Last Sunday	Presentation of new wines in Eguisheim (Alsace)

APRIL

Vines show new leaves, and must be protected against frost. Finish ploughing and plant one-year-old cuttings from the nursery. Topping up of casks continues.

Some time in April	Wine fair in Brignoles (Provence)
Weekend of Palm Sunday	Foire des Vins du Haut Mâconnais in Lugny (Mâconnais)
Palm Sunday	Hospices de Nuits wine auction in Nuits-St-Georges
Easter	Wine fairs in Amboise and Bourgeuil (Touraine)
Around 20 April	Fête de St-Marc in Villeneuve-lès-Avignon (S. Rhône)
Around 25 April	Fête de St-Marc in Châteauneuf-du-Pape (S. Rhône)
Late April	Wine fair in Ammerschwihr (Alsace)

MAY

Danger from frost is at its height. Vines are dusted with sulphur against mildew and sprayed to combat fungus and rot. Suckers must be removed every ten days.

Around 1 May	Wine festival in Bagnols-sur-Cèze (S. Rhône)
Weekend of 1 May	Fête du Crottin de Chavignol in Sancerre (Loire)
Ascension Day	Wine fair in Guebwiller (Alsace)
Saturday nearest 25 May	Fête de St-Urbain in Kintzheim (Alsace)
Late May	Heures Champenoises in Bouzy (Champagne)

JUNE

The vines flower and grapes begin to form. Weather is critical: the warmer and calmer the better. Finish second racking of new wines rack all old wines.

Some time in June	Fête de la St-Bacchus in Perpignan (Roussillon)
Second weekend	Foire de Champagne in Troyes (Aube)

Around 15 June	Wine fair in Pourrières (Provence); and Côtes du Rhône festival in St-Victor-la-Coste (S. Rhône)
Whitsun	Wine fair in Sancerre (Loire)
Late June	World's biggest wine fair, Vinexpo (alternate years, i.e. 1989, 91) in Bordeaux

JULY

The vines are sprayed with "Bordeaux mixture". All efforts are made to keep the cellar cool in hot weather. Bottling can start again.

Some time in July	Fête de Rivesaltes (Roussillon)
First weekend	Fête du Crémant in Orschwihr (Alsace)
14 July	Wine fair in Barr (Alsace); and wine festival in St-Marcel-d'Ardèche (S. Rhône)
Around 14 July	Fête des Vins d'Arbois in Arbois (Jura)
Sunday nearest 14 July	Wine festival in Lisle-sur-Tarn (Gaillac)
Sunday after 14 July	Fête des Guinguettes d'Europe in Husseren-les-Châteaux (Alsace)
Around 15 July	Fête des Côtes du Ventoux in Gordes (S. Rhône); wine festival in Lézignan-Corbières (Languedoc); Fête des Côtes du Rhône Villages in Vacqueyras (S. Rhône); and wine fair in Castillon-la-Bataille (Bordeaux)
Second half July	Wine fair in Duras (Lot-et-Garonne)
Around 20 July	Wine festivals in Buisson and Mondragon (S. Rhône)
Third weekend	Fête du Pinot Noir in Rodern (Alsace); and wine fair in Sigoulès (Bergerac)
Last but one	Fête du Sonnenglanz in Beblenheim; wine fair in Ribeauvillé; Fête du Riesling in Riquewihr (Alsace)
Last weekend	Wine festivals in Kientzheim and Mittelbergheim (Alsace)
Late July	Wine festival in Amarens (Gaillac); Sud-Revermont Wine Fair in Maynal (Jura); Minerve 1210 festival in Minerve (Languedoc); Fête des Vins des Côtes du Rhône Gardoises in Pont-St-Esprit (S. Rhône); Fête des Vins de Cahors in Vire-sur-Lot (Cahors)

AUGUST

There is little to do in the vineyards in this month and traditionally workers take holidays. Equipment is cleaned and repaired ready for the vintage.

Some time in August	Fête du Muscat in Frontignan (Languedoc); and wine festival in St-Tropez (Provence)
Early Augustz	Fête des Vins d'l'Enclave and lavendar parade in Valréas (S. Rhône)
First two weeks	Foire Régionale des Vins d'Alsace in Colmar (Alsace)
First weekend	Fête de la Véraison in Châteauneuf-du-Pape (S. Rhône); and wine festival in Turckheim (Alsace)
First Sunday	Fête du Gewürztraminer in Bergheim and Fête des Amandiers in Mittelwihr (Alsace)
Around 10 August	Fête des Vignerons du Mont Ventoux in Bédoin and Fête des Vignerons Ardèchois in Ruoms (S. Rhône)
First Sunday after 6 August	Fête du Raisin in Fréjus (Provence)
Weekend before 15 August	Cocagne des Vins in Gaillac
Second weekend	Fête du Klevner in Heiligenstein; Fête du Kaefferkopl in Ammerschwihr (Alsace); and wine fair in Cénac (Bergerac)

14 and 15 August	Fête des Vins de France in Dambach-la-Ville (Alsace)
15 August	Wine fairs in Amboise, Chinon, Montlouis and Vouvray (Touraine) and Pouilly-sur-Loire (Loire)
Around 15 August	Wine fair in Chagny (Chalonnais); wine festival in Madiran (Pyrenees); Festival of wines and olives in Mirabel-aux-Baronnies in Séguret (S. Rhône)
Second half of August	Wine festival in St-Chinian (Languedoc)
Last weekend	Foire aux Vins de France in Sancerre (Loire); and wine festival in St-Pourçain-sur-Sioule (Massif Central)
Last Sunday	Fête des Vignerons in Eguisheim (Alsace)
Late August	Wine festival in Visan (S. Rhône)
Late August/early September	Wine festivals in Cogolin and La Motte (Provence)

SEPTEMBER

Before the vintage fermenting vats are filled with water to swell the wood. Vintage begins in about the third week when the grapes are ripe.

Early September	Grape harvest festival in Cassis (Provence); Banée et Trinquée de Meursault in Meursault (Côte d'Or); and Fête du Riesling in Wolxheim (Alsace)
First Saturday	Wine festival in Mont-Brouilly (Beaujolais)
First Sunday	Fête du Bijou in Arbois (Jura); and fêtes des Ménétriers in Ribeauvillé (Alsace)
Second weekend	Wine fair in Bar-sur-Aube (Aube)
Last weekend	Wine festivals in Dahlenheim and Wuenheim (Alsace)

OCTOBER

The vintage continues for perhaps two weeks. Vineyards are prepared for new plantation. New wine is run off into tanks or casks for fermenting.

Some time in Oct	Fête du Vin Nouveau in Béziers (Languedoc)
Early October	Fête des Châtaignes et du Vin in Nantes (Muscadet)
Around 15 October	Fête du Vin Nouveau in Perpignan (Roussillon)
Third Sunday	Grape harvest festivals in Marlenheim and Obernai (Alsace)
Last weekend	Fête Raclet in Romanèche-Thorins (Beaujolais)

NOVEMBER

Vineyard is ploughed to protect the vines from frost. In good vintages, new wine is racked now; in poor ones it is left for another month. Bottling of old wine.

Early November	Show and sale of Beaujolais-Mâconnais Crus
First weekend	Wine fair in Nîmes (Languedoc)
Second Sunday	Wine festival in Juliénas (Beaujolais)
Around 15 November	Fête des Vins Primeurs, Vaison-la-Romaine (Rhône)
Third weekend and following Monday	Les Trois Glorieuses festival in Vougeot, Beaune and Meursault (Côte d'Or)
Fourth Sunday	Fête du Chablis in Chablis

DECEMBER

Pruning the vines may begin in the middle of the month. Older wines are bottled and new wines tested for the first time.

Some time in Dec	Wine market in Cornas (C. Rhône)
First Thursday	Wine fair in Ancenis (Muscadet)
First weekend	Concours des Vins du Beaujolais (Beaujolais)
Second Sunday	Hospices de Beaujeu auction (Beaujolais)
Around 15 December	Wine festival in Aire-sur-l'Adour (Pyrenees)

ORIENTATION MAP

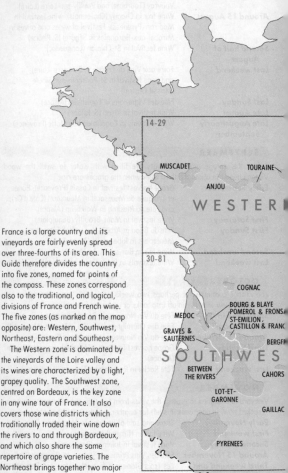

France is a large country and its vineyards are fairly evenly spread over three-fourths of its area. This Guide therefore divides the country into five zones, named for points of the compass. These zones correspond also to the traditional, and logical, divisions of France and French wine. The five zones (as marked on the map opposite) are: Western, Southwest, Northeast, Eastern and Southeast.

The Western zone is dominated by the vineyards of the Loire valley and its wines are characterized by a light, grapey quality. The Southwest zone, centred on Bordeaux, is the key zone in any wine tour of France. It also covers those wine districts which traditionally traded their wine down the rivers to and through Bordeaux, and which also share the same repertoire of grape varieties. The Northeast brings together two major winegrowing areas, Champagne and Alsace, wine regions which solve the conundrums of a cool climate in subtly differing ways. The Eastern zone links Burgundy with the Jura and Savoie, which both have grape varieties and wine styles in common with their famous neighbour. The Southeast zone is dominated by the famous vineyards of the Rhône valley and Provence on the Riviera coast.

MUSCADET

TOURAINE

ANJOU

WESTER

14-29

30-81

COGNAC

BOURG & BLAYE
POMEROL & FRONS
ST-EMILION
CASTILLON & FRANC

MEDOC

GRAVES & SAUTERNES

BERGE

BETWEEN THE RIVERS

SOUTHWE

CAHORS

LOT-ET-GARONNE

GAILLAC

PYRENEES

N

82-99

PARIS

CHAMPAGNE

N O R T H E A S T

THE AUBE

ALSACE

CHABLIS

100-143

SANCERRE &
POUILLY

COTE D'OR

CHALONNAIS

JURA

E A S T E R N

MACONNAIS

BEAUJOLAIS

MASSIF
CENTRAL

SAVOIE

NORTHERN &
CENTRAL
RHONE

144-171

S O U T H E A S T

SOUTHERN
RHONE

CHATEAUNEUF-
DU-PAPE

LANGUEDOC

PROVENCE

ROUSSILLON

CORSICA

0   40   80   120   160   200 KM

40   80   120 MILES

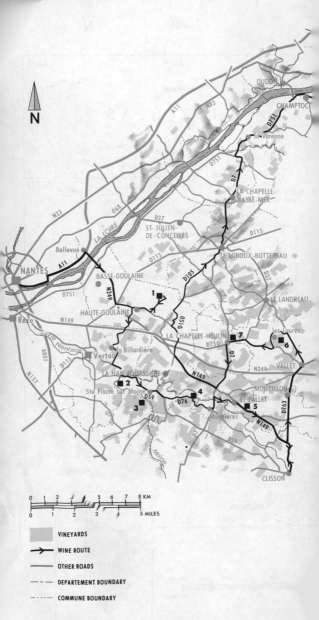

The Muscadet appellation covers a wide area and is divided into several sub-zones, of which the most interesting, both from a wine and a travel point of view, is the Sèvre-et-Maine.

The best Muscadet vineyards lie in the undulating countryside southeast of Nantes between and beside the Sèvre and Maine rivers. The city itself, although the capital of the region has little to offer the wine tourist.

There is no real centre to this countryside, just a collection of villages and small towns set amid fields and vineyards. The land is owned by thousands of small farmers, many of whom make their own wine. There are relatively few showpiece châteaux, although those that do exist are interesting to visit

THE WINE ROUTE

This Wine Route starts from the north and covers both the Muscadet country and the Coteaux d'Ancenis, a red-wine district which runs along the Loire banks.

The best way to reach the Route is to cross the Bellevue bridge over the Loire. The bridge approach branches off the A11 autoroute onto the N249.

First visit, or at least look at, the splendid Ch de Goulaine **1**, the property of the Marquis de Goulaine. The château lies E of the hamlet of Haute-Goulaine, which is itself E of the N249.

Ch de Goulaine is a stately home and architectural showpiece, and good Muscadet is made from the estate vineyards. Leaving the château, return to Haute-Goulaine and follow the D105 (south), crossing the N249 by a bridge. Past La Billadière turn left, soon turning left again to join the D59. This road crosses the Sèvre close

to its confluence with the Maine. Where the rivers meet, and visible to your right, is the beautiful and secluded Ch du Coing de St-Fiacre **2**, one of the Chéreau family estates. The village of St-Fiacre is at the heart of the Sèvre-et-Maine, home of many growers. Close by are châteaux such as de Chasseloir **3**, (to the south on the Maine).

Continue along the D59, branching left onto the D76 through La Févrie (headquarters of the well-known Louis Métaireau concern) **4** to Monnières, another vignerons' village. Turn left, crossing the river Sèvre and bearing right to Le Pallet, where the Domaine de l'Hyvernière **5** is the headquarters and chief estate of the Sautejeau négociant firm. Turn right, following the N149 (southeast) to the town of Clisson. All the way along this 5km stretch the river Sèvre is to the right. Clisson has a notable church and a market on Tuesday and Saturday: an opportunity, with its shops, for the purchase of a picnic. The castle dates from the 14th century and has a wine-tasting hall.

Leave Clisson following the road you arrived by, but branch right on the D763 through Mouzillon and Vallet. In Vallet take the second left signposted Le Landreau. In a km, the impressive neo-classical Ch La Noë **6** appears on the left. Built in 1836, Jean de Malestroit now produces attractive wines at this graceful mansion. Turn left immediately after the château, curving round to its N and W on your way through the hamlet of Les Laures. At a crossroads turn right on the D756 for La Chapelle-Heulin. To the right just before the village is the noted Ch de la Cassemichère **7**, headquarters of Donatien-Bahuaud. In the village turn left and follow the D7 (south) to the junction with the N149. Turn right, onto the N149 passing the Maison des Vins, at the roadside near La Haie-Fouassière, where wine can be tasted and literature obtained. This is the place to arrange visits to winemakers, as this village claims fame as "the birthplace of Muscadet".

Take the D74 from La Haie-Fouassière and continue until it meets with the D105. Turn left and take the D105 to Le Loroux-Bottereau. From the town pick up the D7 to La Chapelle-Basse-Mer and continue N to La Varenne. Here the road twists and turns through hills and valleys covered with farmland, forest and vineyards, providing a lovely view of the La Varenne château off to the right.

Take the D751 through the wine villages of Champtoceaux and Drain to Liré. Once in Liré, turn left on to the D763 and cross the Loire by the suspension bridge to Ancenis. This ancient little town has long been important because of its defensive position over the river and it is worth making a stop in the city to look at the remains of the 15th-century castle which dates from Louis XI.

To continue a tour of the Loire, head E from Ancenis towards Angers, where you can join the Wine Route covering the Anjou district, which in turn ends at Saumur (see page 18).

A far less frequented countryside runs S and W from Nantes (off the map). This is still within the Muscadet appellation, but "simple" Muscadet, not the more closely-defined AOC Sèvre-et-Maine. The wide, flat landscape spreads W to the Baie de Bourgneuf, a great inlet sheltered by the Noirmoutier peninsula. The seaside resorts on the Baie constrast with the sophisticated town of La Baule on the northern side of the Loire estuary, accessible via a giant suspension bridge at St-Nazaire.

The western Muscadet vineyards are also the countryside of the Vin de Pays de Retz, which has a more liberal set of regulations than Muscadet and can, therefore, use non-traditional grapes like Chardonnay. Here too, is the Lac de Grand-Lieu, a wide expanse which provides freshwater fish as a change from the abundant seafood of the Pays Nantais.

LOCAL PRODUCERS

LA CHAPELLE-HEULIN

Donatien Bahuaud: Négociants marketing the carefully selected Le Master de Donatien, Château de La Cassemichère and other brands.

LA HAYE-FOUASSIERE

Domaine de la Louveterie: The Landron family makes very pure wines, including a Cuvée Prestige.

MOUZILLON

Michel Chiron: Excellent Clos des Roches Gaudinières.

Marcel-Joseph Guihoux

Guilbaud Frères: Energetic small firm with wines that include a number of good ones from its own estate.

ST-COLOMBAN

Château de la Roulière: Fine Muscadet and Gros Plant.

ST-FIACRE-SUR-MAINE

Chéreau-Carré: Distributes the estate wines from the Chéreau and Carré families. Among them are the Muscadets from Domaine du Bois Bruley, Château de Chasseloir, Château du Coing de St-Fiacre and Grand Fief de la Cormeraie.

Domaine de Gras-Moutons/

Jean Dabin
Louis Métaireau: Louis Métaireau
has brought together a group of
like-minded growers who select and
sell their wines under the Métaireau
brand name. They also bought
Domaine du Grand Mouton. For sheer
class, Métaireau wines are
outstanding.
ST-GEREON
Domaine Guindon
VALLET
Joseph Hallereau
Château la Noë: One of the few
châteaux in Muscadet, a graceful
mansion built in 1836, where Jean de
Malestroit produces attractive wines.
**Sauvion & Fils/Château du
Cléray**: The Sauvion family produce
their own elegant château wine. They
also market very pure, lively
Muscadets from individual estates
(Les Découvertes, Lauréat, Cardinal
Richard). The Sauvion Muscadets are
of a very high average standard.
(Another Sauvion product is Les
Geneviève: Muscadet grapes soaked
in *eau-de-vie* and coated in
chocolate.)
VIX
**Domaine de la Chaignée/
Mercier Frères** (Fiefs Vendéens).

WINE INFORMATION

LA HAIE-FOUASSIERE
Maison des Vins

HOTELS AND RESTAURANTS

ANCENIS, 44150
Auberge de Bel Air (B)
tel: 40 83 02 87
Pleasant restaurant with good serv⋯
on the road to Angers. Fish
specialities.
BASSE-GOULAINE, 44115
Mon Rêve (A)
La Divatte, tel: 40 03 55 50
Restaurant by the river with excellent
pike.
La Bonne Auberge (B)
tel: 40 54 01 90
Inventive dishes and inexpensive lunch
menu on weekdays.
NANTES, 44000
Le Mangeoire (B)
16 Rue des Petites-Ecuries,
tel: 40 48 70 83
Sturdy cooking and regional wines.
Les Maraichers (B)
21 Rue Foure, tel: 40 47 06 51
One of the best seafood restaurants in
Nantes.
PONT DE BELLEVUE, 44470
Delphin (B), tel: 40 25 60 39
Highly regarded restaurant on the
Loire. Extensive wine list.
**ST-SEBASTIEN-SUR-LOIRE,
44230**
Le Manoir de la Comète (A)
tel: 40 34 15 93
Excellent top class restaurant in a
large 19th-century manor with park
and terrace.
LES SORINIERES, 44400
Abbaye de Villeneuve (A)
tel: 40 04 40 25
Luxurious hotel in former 18th-
century abbey with a swimming pool.
Good cooking in restaurant (B).
VALLET, 44330
**Hotel-Restaurant du Don
Quichotte (B)**
tel: 40 33 97 67
A modern motel (opened in 1988) with
a dozen rooms. Next door one finds a
pleasant restaurant (C).

ANJOU

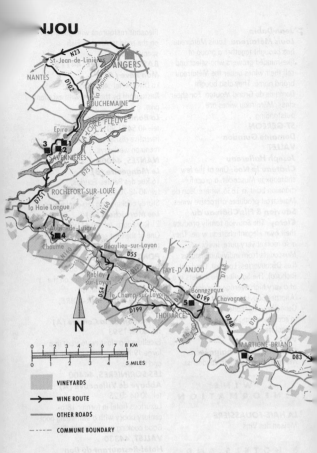

Anjou offers the widest choice of wines in the Loire region. In all there are some 25 appellations, most of them south of the river Loire and the capital Angers. The countryside is as varied as the wines: pleasant hills alternate with green pastures, vineyards, orchards and woods. In terms of volume, the semi-sweet Rosé d'Anjou is the most important still wine. The region also produces considerable quantities of classic light Anjou Blanc and there is a growing interest in red Anjou.

The speciality of the Coteaux du Layon is naturally sweet wines from overripe grapes, these wines however, are not as rich and creamy as those of Sauternes (Bordeaux). In the area around Saumur there are a great number of wine firms, most producing exclusively sparkling wines. Their caves are particularly popular with visitors.

THE WINE ROUTE

Angers, with its brooding grey castle housing a magnificent collection of tapestries, demands a visit. Call in at the Musée du Vin in the 12th-century cellars of the Musée Jean Lurçat (north bank of the river Maine, at 4 Boulevard Arago).

To start the wine tour, leave Angers on the N23 westward (Michelin exit 5). Ignore the signs for the A11 autoroute and turn left off the N23 in the village of St-Jean-de-Linières. Follow the D102 to Bouchemaine, turning right on the D111, past the confluence of the Maine and the Loire and along the north bank of the Loire to Epiré, the beginning of the noted white wine commune of Savennières.

The vineyards extend N and W away from the river, interspersed with woods. Just past Epiré, on the left, is the Ch de Champboureau **1**, centre of a wine

the Coteaux du Layon. Turn right in the village, following the corniche road (D751) with its fine views across the wide, marshy valley. Just past La Haie Longue take a sharp left through St-Aubin-de-Luigné, a wine village on the river Layon. The vineyards of this steep-sided little valley cluster on sheltered slopes and produce sweet, white wines. The growers hope for warm, moist autumns and the consequent "noble rot". Turn left in St-Aubin, on the D106, turning right at Bellevue and immediately right again to Chaume, a hamlet at the centre of the 40ha Quarts de Chaume vineyard **4**, where the white wine is sweetest and finest of all.

There is no bridge across the Layon here, so retrace your steps to the ridge-top road and turn right to Beaulieu-sur-Layon, a wine village offering opportunities to taste and

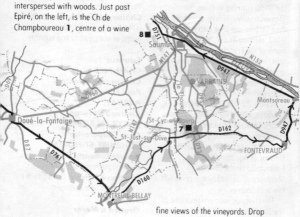

estate owned by the Soulez family. Just beyond is the tiny Coulée de Serrant vineyard **2**, a Savennières Cru owned by the Joly family. At the next crossroads turn left towards the river. The road crosses La Roche-aux-Moines vineyard **3**, another Savennières Cru.

Turn right beside the railway station, then left over the Loire to Rochefort-sur-Loire, the gateway to

fine views of the vineyards. Drop down the hill to cross the river at Rablay-sur-Layon, another wine village, continuing on the D54 to Le-Champ-sur-Layon.

Now take the D199, with views of the Layon vineyards to your left, to Thouarcé. Leave this village on an unnumbered road leading E along the river bank. To your left is the 160ha Bonnezeaux district **5**, noted for sweet white wine. Turn left up the hill (D114), and left again on the D199, encircling the Bonnezeaux vineyard.

From the village of Bonnezeaux, either return on a leisurely route through Faye-d'Anjou and back through Beaulieu to Rochefort, or continue along the D199. The Wine Route continues through the vineyards of the upper Layon valley and to Saumur, passing several features of historical interest.

THE UPPER LAYON AND SAUMUR

Follow the D199 to Chavagnes, then the D748 to Martigné-Briand. Turn left past the ruined château **6** onto the D83, which runs through vineyards and woods to Doué-la-Fontaine, a small town with some attractive old turreted houses and a network of *caves*.

Drive on SE along the straight D761 to cross the river Thouet at Montreuil-Bellay, a walled town with a moated castle. Leave the town by the D160, running NE along the Thouarcé valley with its vineyards. Past St-Just-sur-Dive turn right on the D162, skirting St-Cyr, famous as the home of the French cavalry school as well as an important cooperative with various types of Saumur. It offers guided tours of its impressive underground cellars **7**.

Follow the D162 to Fontevraud-l'Abbaye, where the enormous abbey shelters the tombs of the Plantagenets, including Henry II, Richard the Lionheart and Queen Eleanor of Aquitaine. Leave Fontevraud on the D947 to Montsoreau on the Loire, turning left towards Saumur.

The riverside road passes some of the Saumur sparkling wine firms, others are at St-Hilaire-St-Florent **8** to the west of Saumur (south bank). Many of the firms offer tours of their *caves*: a good chance to see the sparkling-wine process in operation.

LOCAL PRODUCERS

Anjou
DOUE-LA-FONTAINE
Vignobles Touchais: Mature white Anjou, including legendary Moulin.

MOZE-SUR-LOUET
Domaine Richou
LE PUY-NOTRE-DAME
Henri Aupuy/Clos de l'Abbaye

Coteaux du Layon
BEAULIEU-SUR-LAYON
Domaine Pierre-Bise
Domaine de la Soucherie
CHAVAGNES-LES-EAUX
Domaine du Petit Val: Excellent Bonnezeaux.
ROCHEFORT-SUR-LOIRE
Domaine des Baumard: Biggest producer of Savennières. Also the excellent Coteaux du Layon Clos Ste-Catherine and a beautiful Quarts de Chaume.
Château de Belle Rive: Leading Quarts de Chaume.
Château de la Guimonière
Domaine de la Motte
THOUARCE
Domaine la Croix de Mission: Very good Bonnezeaux.
Château de Fesles: Jacques Boivin is the driving force of Bonnezeaux in terms of both quality and quantity.

Saumur
CHAINTRES
Château de Chaintres
Paul Filliatreau
PARNAY
Château de Targé
ST-CYR-EN-BOURG
Cave Coopérative
ST-HILAIRE-ST-FLORENT
Bouvet-Ladunay: Owned by the Champagne firm Taittinger.
Langlois-Chateau: Owned by the Champagne firm Bollinger.
SAUMUR
Gratien & Meyer
VARRAINS
Claude Daheuiller/Domaine des Varinelles
Domaine des Roches-Neuves

Savennières
SAVENNIERES
Domaine de Bizolière
Château de Chamboureau
Domaine du Closel
Clos de Coulaine
Clos de la Coulée de Serrant: In a lovely situation on north bank of the

Loire. Whites need to mature 5-10 years.
Château d'Epiré

Other Areas
NEUVILLE-DE-POITOU
Cave Coopérative: This excellent cooperative produces almost all the wines of Haut-Poitou.
OIRON
Michel Gigon: The best and most energetic producer of Vins du Thouarsais. The Chenin Blanc is the highest quality in the range.

WINE INFORMATION

ANJOU
Maison du Vin de l'Anjou
5bis Place Kennedy
SAUMUR
Maison du Vin de Saumur
25 Rue Beaurepaire

HOTELS AND RESTAURANTS

ANGERS, 49000
Hotel d'Anjou (A/B)
1 Boulevard Foch, tel: 41 88 99 55
Modern and centrally located. Fish dishes and a wide range of regional wines in restaurant (B).
Le Quéré (B), 9 Place de Ralliement, tel: 41 87 64 94
The best restaurant in Anjou, named after its owner/chef. His wife is responsible for the excellent wine list.
Le Toussaint (B)
7 Rue Toussaint, tel: 41 87 46 20
Recommended for regional cuisine at its best. Good choice of wines.
BAGNEUX, 49400
Campanile (B), tel: 41 50 14 40
Straightforward comfortable hotel. Restaurant.
CHACE, 49400
Auberge du Thouet (B/C)
tel: 41 50 12 04
Rural simplicity in a wine village near Saumur.
CHENEHUTTE-LES-TUFFAUX, 49350
La Prieuré (A), tel: 41 50 15 31
Luxury hotel a few kms northwest of Saumur via D751 and D161. Pleasant

views of river and surrounding countryside. Cheerful rooms in the old priory. Excellent but expensive cuisine.
FONTEVRAUD L'ABBAYE, 49590
Auberge de l'Abbaye (C)
tel: 41 51 71 04
Traditional cooking and surprisingly agreeable prices.
La Licorne (A), tel: 41 51 72 49
Small restaurant offering sophisticated dishes.
MONTREUIL-BELLAY, 49260
Hostellerie de la Porte St-Jean (C), tel: 41 52 30 41
Regional dishes and wines.
Relais du Bellay (B)
tel: 41 52 35 50
Comfortable hotel with a swimming pool.
MONTSOREAU, 49730
Le Bussy (B), tel: 41 51 70 18
Pleasant place to stay; many rooms look out on the local château.
ROCHEFORT-SUR-LOIRE, 49190
Grand Hotel (B), tel: 41 78 70 06
Pleasant but certainly not grand. A good base from which to visit the Coteaux du Layon and Savennières vineyards.
LES ROSIERS-SUR-LOIRE, 49350
Jeanne de Laval (A/B)
tel: 41 51 80 17
Very good regional dishes and a brillant range of wines. Garden and terrace. Also a deluxe hotel (A).
La Toque Blanche (C)
tel: 41 51 80 75
Typical French restaurant where you can eat well quite cheaply.
SAUMUR, 49400
Anne d'Anjou (B)
31 Quai Mayaud, tel: 41 67 30 30
Comfortable fairly recent hotel in a beautiful building.
Le Gambetta (C), 12 Rue Gambetta, tel: 41 67 66 66
Good food and fresh ingredients. The menu usually has dishes prepared with wines of the region.
Le Pullman (C), 52 Rue d'Orléans, tel: 41 51 31 79
Restaurant amusingly fitted out as a railway carriage. Plenty of fish on menu.

TOURAINE

Vines have been grown for a long time in the green valleys and fertile fields of Touraine, which is also known as the "garden of France". Today the area has some 11,500 hectares (28,400 acres) of vineyards and more than a third of the vineyard area produces the local Touraine wine. The most important and usually the best is the white Sauvignon, whereas red wines vary greatly in quality.

The most westerly districts of the appellation are Bourgueil, St-Nicolas-de-Bourgueil and Chinon. They produce a red wine that is comparable with a simple Médoc. The area a few kilometres east of Tours is of particular interest to the wine visitor. Growers in Vouvray and Montlouis produce a range of dry and sweet white wines, with about three-fifths of the vintage processed into sparkling wine using the champagne method.

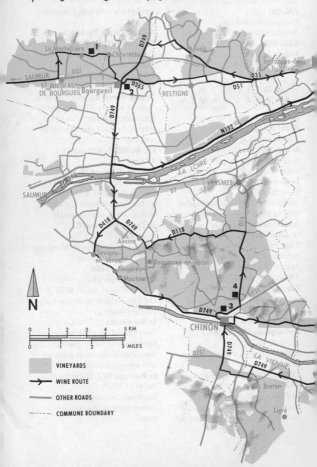

THE WINE ROUTE

The broad province of Touraine has many vineyards, but the two areas which most repay a visit are Vouvray and the district around the red wine towns of Bourgueil and Chinon. These areas are about 50km apart but can be visited in a day. In between lies the city of Tours, with its restored medieval quarter, cathedral of St-Gatien, many museums and basilica.

The Route runs from w to e. Start on the D35, which branches off the N147 N of Saumur. Pass through Allonnes to St-Nicolas-de-Bourgueil, the first wine village on the Route. The appellation produces red wine from Cabernet Franc and a little Cabernet Sauvignon. The wines of St-Nicolas are considered lighter than those of Bourgueil, the adjoining village. In St-Nicolas, turn left up the hill to view the vineyards on the south-facing slope, with its clay soil over tufa limestone. At a T-junction turn right, passing through la Martellière to Chevrette (where there is a *cave* **1** offering tastings). Turn right here, go over a crossroads and on to Bourgueil. The wines made here are more robust, and in warm years they can age suprisingly well. Several producers in the village open their cellars to visitors. Leave Bourgueil on the D365 past the ruins of the medieval abbey **2**, passing through the wine hamlet of Restigné and on, via the D51, to Ingrandes-de-Touraine. Turn back at this point, following the D35 with more hillside vineyards, still in the Bourgueil AOC on the right. At a signpost, turn right to Benais, a wine hamlet which is the home of several wine producers. Continue up the D469 beside the vineyards, which here face sw. Turn left to cross the valley to join the D749 back to Bourgueil.

Continue s on the D749 towards the river. To your left, vines stretch along the riverside gravel terraces. The wine from here is lighter and less long-lived than that of the slopes away from the river. Cross the Loire past the giant atomic power station on the south bank. Vineyards line the river to the east and west: these, also on riverside gravel, are part of the Chinon AOC. Most of the vineyards are to the south of a low ridge which here divides the Loire valley from that of its tributary, the Vienne. Chinon's best wine comes from these slopes,

...are the same soil and
...y as Bourgueil.
...n right onto the D418 to
...gny-en-Véron, continuing on
...rough Fougères and Montour. On
the left are south-facing slopes of
Cabernet Franc vines, on the right the
river Vienne. Enter the town of Chinon,
where the old centre, the medieval
bridge and above all the castle **3**
deserve attention. Several wine
merchants have premises in the town,
and there is a museum of winemaking and cooperage housed in a
cave which has some interesting
coin-operated models.

Leaving Chinon, follow the D21
(east), passing along a belt of
vineyards sloping down from the
wooded slopes to the left. At Cravant,
turn left to visit Le Vieux Bourg, a
wine hamlet, returning to the D21 and
continuing E through Panzoult,
another winegrowers' village, to l'Ile
Bouchard where you cross the river
Vienne. Return along the south bank
(D760), with a view across the river to
the vineyards. Vines are planted
around Ligré and Le Vau Breton
opposite Chinon. Divert left up a
minor road to this hamlet, rejoining
the Chinon road just short of a
crossroads s of the bridge. Return to
Chinon, passing around the town to
the west and follow the D751, soon
branching off left on the D16. This
road runs through the heart of the
Chinon vineyard, passing the noted
Clos de l'Echo **4** (left immediately
after joining the D16). Turn left off the
D16 onto the D118, then right at
Avoine (D749) back to the bridge over
the Loire.

FROM CHINON TO TOURS

Once over the bridge, turn right onto
the N152 which follows the north
bank of the Loire to Tours.

VOUVRAY AND MONTLOUIS

Leave Tours by the N152 (Michelin
exit 4) along the north bank of the
Loire. At Rochecorbon turn left to
begin a tour of the Vouvray vineyards,
which are mostly on a limestone
plateau, whose *caves* both man-made
and naturally provide ample cellars
for the growers. From the north end
of the strung-out village of

Rochecorbon turn right along an
unclassified road to Les Bas Closeaux,
passing Chenin Blanc vines on the
way. Turn right, joining the D76,
passing through Vaugondy and on,
via the D46, across the stream to
Vernou-sur-Brenne. The hill behind
the village has some finely-placed
vineyards: in warm years Vouvray
growers make a sweet wine,
sometimes, if autumn conditions are
perfect, with "noble rot". Recross the
stream by the southern bridge, joining
the D46 which runs in the direction of
Vouvray. On the right are vineyards
such as Les Bidaudières **5**, source of a
number of single-vineyard Vouvrays.
Turn right at a crossroads about 2km
after the bridge, passing two
junctions then turning sharp left to
pass the noted Haut-Lieu vineyard **6**
and into the village of Vouvray past
La Vallée de Nouy and Bel-Air.

After visiting the village itself,
return along the D4, passing Le
Bois-Rideau and branching left along
an unclassified road into La Vallée
Coquette. Return to the Loire-side
road (N152) at Vauvert.

MONTLOUIS

There is no bridge between Vouvray
and Montlouis, so either return to
Tours, or cross the river at Amboise,
taking a look at the superb château in
passing. The following Route assumes
arrival from the direction of Amboise.

Leave Amboise on the D751
(Michelin exit 5). At Lussault-sur-
Loire fork left in the village along an
unnumbered road through Husseau
and La Bare, with vineyards on the
left and the river plain to the right. As
in Vouvray, the Chenin Blanc vines
here are mosly grown on the
limestone plateau. Montlouis-sur-
Loire, set between river and
vineyards, has a *cave touristique* **7**
where wine can be tasted and
growers' premises visited. Leave
Montlouis via an unnumbered road to
the east through vineyards to Le
Cormier, turning right onto the D40 at
La Milletière. Take the first left turn,
signposted Husseau, and pass
through vineyards until the outskirts
of the town, where you turn right and
right again to skirt the Clos de Mosny

8 and return to the D40. Continue to
St-Martin-le-Beau where you turn
left, taking the D83 and then the D283
northwards to rejoin the Loire at
Lussault, where the Route started.

LOCAL PRODUCERS

Touraine-Mesland
BOURGUEIL
**Clos de l'Abbaye/GAEC de la
Dîme**: The vineyard that belonged to
the old abbey at Bourgueil.
**Domaine des Galluches/ Jean
Gambier**: Family firm handling
excellent wines from Bourgueil, St-
Nicolas-de-Bourgueil and Chinon.

Chinon
CHINON
Couly-Dutheil: This family firm has
made an important contribution to
establishing the reputation of Chinon.

Vouvray
VOUVRAY
Domaine Huet: Vouvrays of very
highest quality and splendid cellars.
Prince Poniatowski: One of the
best and most conscientious
producers in district with a famous
Vouvray Clos Baudoin.

WINE INFORMATION

BLOIS
Maison des Vins de Blois
84 Avenue de Verdun
CHINON
Musée du Vin et de la Tonnellerie
TOURS
Comité Interprofessionnel des Vins
de Touraine
19 Square Prosper-Mérimée
Musée des Vins de Touraine
16 Rue Nationale

HOTELS AND RESTAURANTS

AMBOISE, 37400
Le Mail St-Thomas (B)
tel: 47 47 22 52
Traditional cooking in a villa near the
château. Excellent wine list.

CHINON, 37500
Chris' Hotel (B), tel: 47 93 36 92
Attractively furnished hotel in a
beautiful building.
Le Plaisir Gourmand (B)
tel: 47 93 20 48
The best restaurant in Chinon, in a
17th-century building with walls of
tufa (volcanic rock).
La Ste-Maxime (C)
tel: 47 93 05 04
Simple, good food.
MARCAY, 37500
Château de Marçay (A)
tel: 47 93 03 47
Beautifully-restored 15th-century
castle where the cooking is
outstanding.
MONTBAZON, 37250
Château d'Artigny (A)
tel: 47 26 24 24
Luxurious hotel serving fine cuisine.
La Chancelière (A)
tel: 47 26 00 67
Inspired cooking. Lunch menu with
lower prices on weekdays.
Domaine de la Tortinière (A)
tel: 47 26 00 19
Small château on hill overlooking
valley. Restaurant in orangery (B).
Le Moulin Fleuri (C)
tel: 47 26 01 12
Restored 16th-century mill by the
Indre with good restaurant. *Demi-
pension* in season (Hotel B/C).
Le Relais de Touraine (B)
tel: 47 26 06 57
Good rooms, a restaurant and a park.
**MONTLOUIS-SUR-LOIRE,
37270**
Roc en Val (B), tel: 47 50 81 96
Modern cooking is capable. Park and
a terrace.
TOURS, 37000
Le Bordeaux (B)
3 Place du Maréchal-Leclerc,
tel: 47 05 40 32
Centrally located, comfortable hotel
with restaurant (C).
Les Jardins du Castel (A)
10 Rue Croison, tel: 47 41 94 40
Fine restaurant with a garden and 10
rooms. Restaurant (B).
La Renaissance (C)
64 Rue Colbert, tel 47 66 63 25
Good value restaurant.

SANCERRE AND POUILLY

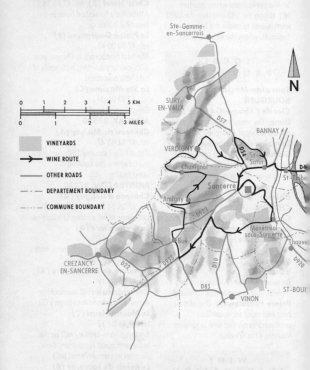

Vineyards are more scarce along the upper reaches of the Loire, but this is also where Sancerre and Pouilly-Fumé, the best-known white wines of the entire valley have their origin. Both are made from the Sauvignon Blanc grape which is only grown so successfully in a few other places in the world. The attractive hilltop village of Sancerre is interesting to visit with the remnants of a tenth century castle. Fourteen wine communes make up the Sancerre appellation and there are many impressive vineyards to visit, particularly in the communes of Bué and Verdigny.

Pouilly is a smaller wine district with some some 600 hectares (1,500 acres) compared to Sancerre's nearly 1,600 hectares (4,000 acres). The best vineyards lie in a band some 6 kilometres (4 miles) to the north of Pouilly-sur-Loire and most of the growers are based in the hamlets of Les Loges and Les Berthiers, where wine can be tasted in nearly all the houses.

the D125, past Ch de Fargues on the left which has belonged to the Lur Saluces since 1472, and prior to that, to the family of Pope Clement V.

Follow the road through wooded and hilly countryside, and after crossing the D8; you will see Ch Guiraud **20** over to your right. At the crossroads leading into Sauternes, turn left, then right, and you come upon the large estate of Ch Filhot **21**, with its particularly fine château and park. At Pineau turn right towards Sauternes and just before the village, off the D125 to the left is Ch Lamothe **22** perched on a hill.

Continue through Sauternes enjoying the lovely undulating countryside past the Deuxième Cru Ch d'Arche **23** and further to the west, the Premier Cru Ch La Tour Blanche **24** (now a school for winemakers).

Surrounded by Ch d'Yquem and other Grand Crus is Clos Haut-Peyraguey **25**. Its more illustrious neighbours are Premiers Crus Ch Lafaurie-Peyraguey **26**, very ancient and spectacular, and Ch Rayne-Vigneau **27**.

Turn left along the D116 E1 and follow the descending road to a crossroads. Turn right, parallel to the river Ciron whose cold waters, when they flow into the warmer Garonne, create the morning mists which encourage *Botrytis cinerea* and create the "noble rot" which distinguishes the wines of the area.

Turn right on the D116, with Ch Sigalas-Rabaud **28** on the right Ch Rabaud-Promis **29** on the hill further in the distance.

At Boutoc turn left, returning to the flatter countryside of Barsac; left on the D109, then right on the D114. Just after the road has crossed the autoroute you enter La Pinesse – the right-hand fork leads to Ch Doisy-Védrines **30**, the left-hand fork continues the Route.

At the next junction turn right: Ch Climens **31** just after the turn; Ch Doisy-Dubroca **32** on the left and down the right-hand fork, Ch Doisy-Daëne **33** followed by Ch Coutet **34**. The road then bends sharply to the right, crosses the D114, the railway

line, and returns to the N113. Turn left to return to Bordeaux.

WINE INFORMATION

PODENSAC
Maison des Vins de Graves
SAUTERNES
Maison du Vin

HOTELS AND RESTAURANTS

L'ALOUETTE, 33600
La Réserve (A), Avenue Bourgailh, tel: 56 07 13 28
Luxury hotel and restaurant near exit 13 on Bordeaux ring road.
CERONS, 33720
Grillobois (B), tel: 56 27 11 50
Simple hotel and restaurant on busy N113. Also small wine museum.
LANGON, 33210
Claude Darroze (A), 95 Cours Général Leclerc, tel: 56 63 00 48
The best restaurant of the district. Extensive wine list. Pleasant rooms.
Le Grangousier (B), tel: 56 63 30 59
An old manor house on the D10 to Auros. Regional cuisine.
Hotel Le Midi-Modern (B), Place Général de Gaulle, tel: 56 63 06 65
Hotel belonging to a brasserie.
MARTILLAC, 33650
Hostellerie Lou Pistou (C)
tel: 56 23 71 02
Good value.
PREIGNAC, 33210
Restaurant du Cap (B)
tel: 56 63 27 38
Mainly regional dishes.
SAUTERNES, 33210
Château de Commarque (B)
tel: 56 63 65 94
Charming hotel with extensive grounds. Restaurant.
Le Sauternais (B)
tel: 56 63 67 13
In a former annex of Château Guiraud. Interesting wines by glass.
Les Vignes (C), tel: 56 63 60 06
Inn serving regional dishes with few trimmings. Wines served by glass.
TOULENNE, 33210
Maeva (C), tel: 56 62 38 77
Good wine list and regional dishes.

BETWEEN THE RIVERS

The "land of the two rivers" stretches between the Dordogne, the Garonne and the département's eastern boundary and is the biggest wine district in Bordeaux. The area is made up of several districts with Entre-Deux-Mers by far the most important in area and scale. The appellation is now used for dry white wine.

The Premières Côtes de Bordeaux is a narrow, hilly stretch on the right bank of the Garonne. The best red wines come from the northern half of the Côtes; whereas largely sweet white is produced in the south.

THE WINE ROUTE

To discover the many aspects of this large region, including most of the wine districts, try the following Route starting and ending in Bordeaux.

From the eastern side of Bordeaux

take the D10 SE along the Garonne. The first village you come to is Floirac where an observatory is open to visitors. Stay on the D10 to Bouliac, the next village which is well worth visiting for its restaurants.

Keep on the D10 to Latresne where you make a detour off the main road

by turning left into the village, through and over the crossroads and head roughly NE beside a small river and the railway line. Turn right at the T-junction with the D10E and follow that to a junction with the D115. Turn right and continue through Lignan-de-Bordeaux to Sadirac, which is the

home of Ch Le Grand-Verdus, a fortified 16th-century manor house. The 22ha vineyard is planted with Merlot and Cabernet Sauvignon.

From Sadirac take the road s to the D14 (linking Créon and Camblanes-et-Meynac). Turn immediately left down the D115, and then continue on the D121 until you reach the D10 again at Cambes.

Follow the road through Baurech at the foot of some steep hills in the Premières Côtes until you reach Langoiran, the site of an ancient fortress and medieval keep.

Take the D13 out of Langoiran past the Parc de la Peyruche (caves and a zoo) **1** and then follow the left-hand fork which is the D20 heading for Créon.

The road follows a tributary of the

Garonne and about halfway to Créon you pass through St-Gènes-de-Lombaud whose church is said to be built on the site of a Roman villa.

Still on the D20 you enter Créon, the capital of the region, whose cooperative vinifies much of the area's crop. In the centre of Créon turn right along the D671 heading E and it is only a few kms to La Sauve, home of Ch Thieuley **2**. Look out for the magnificent ruins of the Benedictine abbey of La-Sauve-Majeure. Keep on the D671 until you come to the intersection with the D11 and then go s to the wine village of Targon, with its Romanesque church. The region is rich in historical remains, Gallo-Roman and medieval reminders of a turbulent past. The D11 heads E for a short distance out of Targon before continuing its winding route southwards towards Cadillac through some lovely hilly countryside, where vineyards abound.

Drive through Escoussans into Cadillac overlooking the Garonne from behind the remains of its medieval walls, its two fortified towers once defensive positions when this area was at the frontier between the warring English and French. Don't miss the impressive 17th-century Ch des Ducs d'Epernon **3**, built on the orders of Admiral Jean-Louis de Nogaret de Lavalette (the same admiral who built Ch Beychevelle).

This is principally sweet white wine country, and as you follow the river route upstream along the D10, the next village, Loupiac, is no exception. This is the home of Ch du Cros **4** built on a 300ft sheer rock, it dates back to the 13th century and the vineyard itself commands spectacularly panoramic views. In the village itself there is a Romanesque church which is an historical monument.

Continuing on the D10 the next stop is Ste-Croix-du-Mont, a sweet white wine appellation. Turn off the main road into the hills where Ch Loubens **5** is situated whose cellars, dug deep into the clay-limestone soil and rock are formed from beds of fossilized oysters from the Tertiary period. A château visited by Richelieu and Louis

SW

XIII, the nearby Ch de Tastes **6** is also worth attention.

Turn right onto the D117 and follow it into Verdelais. In the 17th-century basilica of Nôtre Dame is a 14th-century wooden carving of the Virgin Mary above the high altar. Follow the road beside the church to the cemetery where the Impressionist painter, Henri de Toulouse-Lautrec, is buried. He lived at Ch Malromé **7** in St-André-du-Bois, a few kms to the north; the meticulously maintained château can be visited.

For the next village on the route, take the D672 to St-Macaire ovelooking the Garonne. A medieval village, perched on a cliff, it is well worth a leisurely stroll to visit the Aquitaine Postal Museum.

Take the N113 out of St-Macaire running beside the river to La Réole, one of the oldest towns in the southwest and a real mixture of architectural styles: from medieval houses to an 18th-century Benedictine monastery on the waterfront, to the Town Hall originally Roman and Gothic and added onto in the 14th and 15th centuries.

Take the D668 out of the town, past, to your right, the Signal du Mirail viewpoint. Follow the road to the Roman town of Monségur. Turn left to Bordepaille, then left onto the D21E to the fortified village of Castelmoron-d'Albret, the smallest commune (only 4ha) in France. Follow the road (now the D14) to the D670 and turn right into Sauveterre-de-Guyenne, dating back to the 13th century. Four gates remain from the original fortifications and the central square with its four arcades is worth visiting.

From here take the D672 turning right onto the D131 through St-Sulpice-de-Pommiers, then right, on the D11E into Castelviel. The Romanesque church on the hill has a marvellous porch with carvings which illustrate early viticulture. Head north out of the village along the D123 and follow the road, turn northwards, through St-Brice and Daubèze, then turn right on the D123E into Blasimon with its fine Romanesque monastery.

Head NW along the D127E out of Blasimon and at the D670 turn into Rauzan, home of the magnificent ruined Ch de Duras **8**, a fortress dating back to the 13th-century.

Go out of Rauzan on the D128 through the villages of Jugazan, Naujan-et-Postiac and Guillac. In the next village, Bonnet, turn up the D11E to Grézillac where Ch Bonnet **9** is situated. The original 17th-century château was demolished and a splendid building erected in its place in the late 18th century by M. de Chillaud. In the 19th century limestone quarries were in operation which made excellent cellars.

Turn left along the D936 heading back into Bordeaux, across the river Estey. Turn right on the D20 towards Goudon and just through Beaupied turn left on the D120 to Ch du Grand-Puch, a 14th-century fortified castle.

Retrace your steps to the D20 which takes you N towards Libourne and St-Emilion. (By turning right at Goudon onto the N09 you can go straight into Libourne where you are able to join the Wine Routes for St-Emilion and Castillon as well as Pomerol and Fronsac.) To continue this Route, cross the N89 onto the D20E into Vayres, right on the Dordogne, where the castle is a tourist attraction. Gardens and terraces run down to the river and there is an enormous *colombier* housing up to 2600 pigeons.

Return to the N89 and continue in the direction of Bordeaux, to Beychac where Ch La France **10** is situated with its Restoration château built on the site of a Gallo-Roman villa. At Beychac turn left on the D13 to Salleboeuf, dominated by the 13th-century castle of Ch de la Tour. Take the D120 to Pompignac and then join the N89 back into Bordeaux.

WINE INFORMATION

CADILLAC
Maison du Vin
Château des Ducs d'Epernon
STE-CROIX

Tasting cellar nr Château de Tastes
BEYCHAC-ET-CAILLEAU
Maison de Qualité
(Also tasting room and information
office)

HOTELS AND RESTAURANTS

BOULIAC, 33270
Auberge du Marais (B)
tel: 56 20 52 17
Seasonally based cuisine. Servings
are generous and so are the agreeably
priced lunch menus through the week.
Le St-James (A), tel: 56 20 52 19
Chef and owner, Jean-Marie Amat's
excellent cooking makes this one of
the best restaurants of Gironde. Good
wine list. Also a hotel.
BRANNE, 33420
Hotel de France (B)
tel: 57 84 50 06
Country hotel on the banks of
Dordogne.
CAMBES, 33880
Auberge André (B)
tel: 56 21 31 08
Friendly riverside restaurant,
furnished in country-style with a
talented young chef.
CREON, 33670
Le Prévôt (B), tel: 56 23 08 08
Village restaurant with an excellent
reputation. Regional cuisine.
ESCONSAC, 33880
A la Varenne (B), tel: 56 21 31 15
Restaurant with park and terrace
situated by the Garonne between
Quinsac and Cambes. Rooms.
FONTET, 33190
La Fontine (C), tel: 56 61 11 81
Large farm on the D9, just south of La
Réole. Friendly service.
JUILLAC, 33890
La Belvédère (C), tel: 57 40 40 33
Restaurant with terrace and pleasant
views over Dordogne. Good cooking at

reasonable prices.
LANGOIRAN, 33550
Hotel St-Martin (C)
tel: 56 67 02 67
Simple hotel by the river. Restaurant.
MONSEGUR, 33580
Le Grand Hotel (C)
tel: 56 61 60 28
Family hotel serving authentic
regional dishes in restaurant.
MONTUSSAN, 33450
Le Commerce (B)
tel: 56 72 96 72
Alongside busy N89 but the cooking is
talented. Rooms.
QUINSAC, 33360
Hostellerie Robinson (B)
tel: 56 21 31 09
A trusted address, right on the river
Garonne. Dishes are strictly regional.
Try the Clairet (rosé) from the local
cooperative.
LA REOLE, 33190
Hotel du Centre (C)
tel: 56 61 02 64
Also a hotel. Excellent oysters.
ST-MACAIRE, 33490
Café des Arts (C)
tel: 56 63 07 40
Restaurant and also a hotel.
STE-FOY-LA GRANDE, 33220
Grand Hotel (B), 117 Rue de
République, tel: 57 46 00 08
Well-situated hotel with character.
Restaurant.
TARGON, 33760
Auberge du Lion d'Or (C)
tel: 56 23 90 23
Popular, serving local dishes.
VAYRES, 33870
Le Vatel (B), tel: 57 74 80 79
Regional cooking.
VERDELAIS, 33490
Hostellerie St-Pierre (C)
tel: 56 62 02 03
Rooms without private facilities.
Restaurant.

SW

POMEROL AND FRONSAC

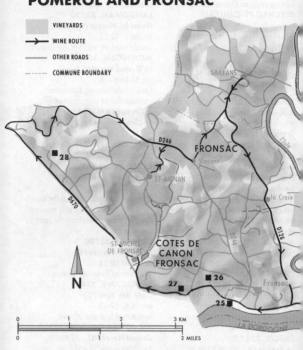

VINEYARDS
→ WINE ROUTE
OTHER ROADS
---- COMMUNE BOUNDARY

SAILLANS

D246

FRONSAC

Vincent

ST-AIGNAN

la Croix

D670

■ 28

D126

ST-MICHEL
DE FRONSAC

D246

COTES DE
CANON
FRONSAC

N

Fronsac

■ 26

27 ■

25 ■

LA DORDOGNE

```
0       1         2        3 KM
|---|---|---|---|---|---|---|
0         1                 2 MILES
```

The little wine district of Pomerol fans out from the port of Libourne on the north bank of the Dordogne, bisected by the N89 that links Bordeaux with Périgueux. The commune is made up of a number of small hamlets, each with the name Pomerol preceeding its own. The typical château is modest and as there are some 180 growers in the district, most of the estates are small. The leading estate, Château Pétrus has only 11.4 hectares (28 acres) and Château de Sales is the largest property with 47.5 hectares (117 acres). The homogenous standard of wines produced in Pomerol contrasts with the variation of wines from nearby Fronsac.

THE WINE ROUTE

This Wine Route begins and ends in Libourne on the banks of the river Dordogne, a beautiful valley much-loved by tourists for holidays and second-homes.

Pomerol as a wine-growing region dates back to the Romans, but the vineyards were wiped out during the Hundred Years War. Restoration took place in the 15th and 16th centuries, but the area only really acquired its own identity with the first *appellation contrôlée* in 1936. Nowadays prices

paid for the top growers can be astronomical.

The best wines (headed by Ch Pétrus) are made from vines grown on a clay plateau at the heart of the region. The grape that succeeds on clay is Merlot, which makes up 75% of the vines and contributes to the soft, generous character of the wines.

Head from Bordeaux to Libourne on the N89 crossing the river Dordogne by the 19th-century bridge.

as the road climbs slightly, over to the left is Ch Moulinet **3**. This estate is a third of the size of de Sales and surrounded by trees.

The road now swings away up the hill past Ch Grand-Moulinet on the left and Ch L'Enclos **4** to the right. Follow the road until it meets the N89 and turn left. At the next crossroads turn right, following the road as it climbs to the gravel plateau on which the major growths are situated.

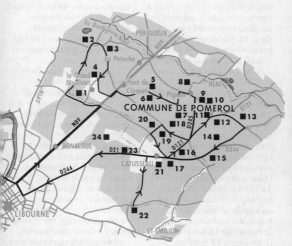

Libourne itself dates from the 13th century and was founded by an Englishman, Roger de Leyburn.

Head out of Libourne on the N89 through the town, crossing the railway line and the Ruisseau du Mauvais Temps. Travelling NE out of Libourne takes you along a straight road through the hamlet of Bonalgue and passing Ch Cantereau on the left. Take a left turn at the crossroads and on the right is Clos René **1**. At the next crossroads turn right and head N again and you will be in the midst of the vineyards which surround the road and run parallel to the railway. Watch out for the left-hand fork leading to the resplendent Ch de Sales **2**, set off the road and surrounded by lawns and an extensive park.

Travelling away from the château

First on the left is Ch Latour à Pomerol **5** next to the little church and opposite Ch Feytit-Clinet. Further up the hill to the right in the centre of the commune of Pomerol is Ch La Cabanne **6**. The commune revolves around the parish church of St-Jean which is very close to Ch Lagrange, rebuilt in the late 19th century on the site of a church used by the Knights of St John who most likely encouraged the cultivation of vines in Pomerol.

As you take the left-hand bend, Ch l'Eglise-Clinet **7** is on your right. This was created from the amalgamation in the 1880s of Clos de l'Eglise and Domaine de Clinet. At the T-junction with the D245 turn right, and having made the turn you can see to the left on the slopes of the plateau a long shuttered house, smothered in ivy

which is Ch Rouget **8**. Follow the contours of the hill and then take the D245 through a clutch of châteaux close to the church.

To the left is Ch La Croix-de-Gay **9** four-square behind its railings and further to the east, Ch Lafleur **10**, followed by Ch Vray-Croix-de-Gay in the middle of this important winemaking area. Just to the right, is Ch Lagrange with the parish church behind.

Follow the D245 to the crossroads with the D121 and turn left across the plateau to the château and estate that dominates the area of Pomerol. Ch Pétrus **11** is an exceptionally fine and intense wine, with its unique class reflected by its price. Across the road is Ch La Fleur-Pétrus **12** and down the D121, straight over at the next crossroads, is Ch Lafleur-Gazin. Turn right at the crossroads and Ch Gazin **13**, once the property of the Templars, is on your left.

Turn right at the next crossroads to pass Ch l'Evangile **14** on your right. Take the right-hand fork as the road joins the D244 heading back to Libourne, passing Ch La Conseillante **15** on the St-Emilion – Pomerol boundary which has belonged to the same family for more than a century. Keep on this road and you will pass Ch Petit-Village **16** to the right and Ch Beauregard **17** to the left.

Immediately afterwards take a sharp right-hand turn (the D121) past Chx Grate-Cap and La Croix St-Georges. Turn left just before the crossroads with the D245 passing Chx Clos du Rocher **18** and La Violette **19**. To the southwest is Ch Trotanoy **20**, a small estate producing a magnificent wine.

Return to the D244 and turn right towards Libourne, driving through Catusseau and leaving Ch La Croix **21** to your left.

Take a short detour off the main road by turning left by Ch Le Caillou to see the following châteaux: Ch La Cailloi, Ch La Commanderie (once the home of the Knights Templar), Ch La Croix Taillefer, and across the road to Ch Taillefer **22**.

Retrace your steps to the the D244

and turn left to pass Chx Nenin **23** and La Pointe **24**. Follow the main road for Libourne and just before the railway line turn right to cross over to the N89. Turn left and follow the road into Libourne, then turn right to cross the River Isle in the direction of Fronsac.

The river forms the boundary between Pomerol and Fronsac and the countryside changes from the gentle plateau of Pomerol to Fronsac's landscape of hills. The river is dominated by the "Tertre de Fronsac", a hillside used from the Gauls onwards for military defensive purposes. The best area is the hilly Canon Fronsac in the south, with its south-facing slopes.

Cross the river and join the D670 travelling alongside the river Dordogne towards Fronsac itself. Following the road you pass Ch de la Dauphine **25**, then at the next T-junction turn left away from Fronsac past Ch Junayme **26** and as the road bends you will find Ch Canon **27** on the right. Follow the road as it passes along the edge of the appellation Canon Fronsac to St-Michel. To the right is Ch de la Rivière **28**, the showpiece of the whole district and essential visiting. Just over a km further on, turn right, then right again at the T-junction, along a winding road through hilly countryside to the junction with the D246. Turn right and follow the road as it heads back towards Fronsac, but be sure to make a detour in St-Aignan to see its Romanesque church and the excavated Gallo-Roman villa.

Turn left to visit Saillans, then return along the D128 towards Fronsac to pick up the D670. Turn left to return to Libourne.

LOCAL PRODUCERS

Pomerol
Château Le Bon Pasteur
Modest estate in the NE corner of the district producing high quality wines.
Château Certan (De May de Certan)
Estate opposite Vieux Château Certan.

Château La Conseillante
Estate producing one of the finest
wines of the district.
Château la Croix de Gay
A *supérieur* selection from a small
plot is sold as Ch La Fleur de Gay.
Château l'Eglise-Clinet
Vital, stylish wine with balance.
Château l'Evangile
The vineyard borders on Ch Pétrus.
Château La Fleur-Pétrus
Château with distinguished wines.
**Château la Grave Trigant de
Boisset**
Consistent wine marked by good deal
of tannin.
Château Lafleur-Gazin
Carefully made and generous wine.
Château Latour à Pomerol
Mouth-filling and fruity Pomerol.
Château Petit Village
Excellent wine that is not *petit*.
Château Pétrus
Not a grand château, but Pétrus is an
exceptionally rich wine in a class of
its own. A Moueix team looks after
the vineyard and makes the wine.
Other Moueix properties in Pomerol
include Feytit-Clinet, La Fleur-Pétrus,
La Grave Trigant de Boisset,
Lagrange, Latour à Pomerol and
Trotanoy.
Château Trotanoy
The wine is more grand than the
château, and if Pétrus is the emperor
of Pomerol, Trotanoy is the king.
Vieux Château Certan
Belgian owners produce a charming
wine. Bottle recognized by pink cap.
Château La Violette
Graceful with perfume of violets.
Château Vray Croix de Gay
Age of vines makes this a good
Pomerol.
**Fronsac
(Appellation Canon-Fronsac)**
Château Canon
If Fronsac had a first-growth, this
would be it.

WINE INFORMATION

FRONSAC
Les Gentilshommes du Duché de
Fronsac
Maison du Vin

LIBOURNE
Maison du Tourisme
Many of the châteaux in Pomerol
welcome visitors (with advance
warning) incl, Beauregard, La
Conseillante, La Croix de Gay, Nenin,
La Pointe, De Sales and Vieux Château
Certan.

HOTELS AND RESTAURANTS

ARVEYRES, 33500
Hotel Climat de France (B)
Port du Nouguey, tel: 57 51 41 41
Modern hotel with restaurant across
the bridge from Libourne.
GALGON, 33133
Clo-Luc (C), tel: 57 84 36 16
Beside the D18 on road into Galgon
from the south.
LIBOURNE, 33500
Hotel Backgammon (B), 16 Quai
de l'Isle, tel: 57 74 06 06
Acceptable rooms but the restaurant
is expensive.
Le Chai (C), tel: 57 51 13 59
Formerly elegant establishment now a
simple restaurant with good food at
reasonable prices.
Hotel de la Gare (C)
43 Rue Chanzy, tel: 57 51 06 86
Decent and simple hotel with
restaurant.
Hotel Loubat (B), 32 Rue Chanzy,
tel: 57 51 17 58
Best-known hotel in town. Restaurant
with good local wines and dishes.
Hotel Le Petit Duc (B), 22 Place
Decazes, tel: 57 51 03 39
Modern, friendly hotel.
La Ripaille (B), 15 Rue des Treilles,
tel: 57 74 07 40
This restaurant used to belong to
Hotel Loubat (around the corner) but
now independent. Good regional food
with meals served outdoors in
summer.
SABLON-DE-GUITRES, 33230
Auberge de l'Isle (C)
tel: 57 69 22 58
To the north of Libourne on D910,
good cooking and reasonable prices.

ST-EMILION, CASTILLON AND FRANCS

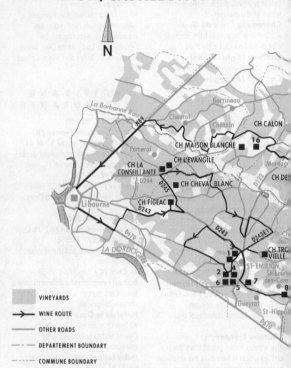

VINEYARDS

→ **WINE ROUTE**

—— **OTHER ROADS**

—·—· **DEPARTEMENT BOUNDARY**

------ **COMMUNE BOUNDARY**

The St-Emilion appellation covers eight communes, a part of Libourne and five "satellite" communes. It is one of the most intensively cultivated areas in the Bordeaux region and the average estate is comparatively small. There are two official appellations: St-Emilion for the basic wines of the region and St-Emilion Grand Cru for the 90 best vineyards. Immediately to the east is the appellation Côtes de Castillon. This neighbours the upcoming district of Côte de Francs, the highest in the Gironde département.

THE WINE ROUTE

The wine tour around St-Emilion and Castillon is full of hidden treasures, not least the charming town of St-Emilion itself, perched on a hillside. The local museum in the Logis de Malet contains artefacts, documents and gives an overall view of the remarkably varied history of St-Emilion.

The tour begins and ends in Libourne (also the starting point for the wine tour of Pomerol and Fronsac).

Take the D670 as it heads straight out of the town towards Castillon.

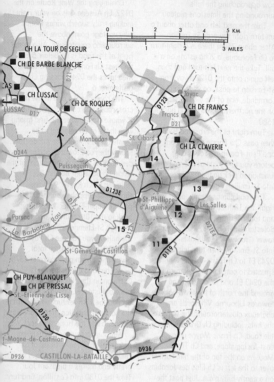

Just under 2km out of the town take a left turn at the crossroads opposite Ch Martinet, over the next crossroads, then turn right joining the D243 before it crosses the railway line beside Ch du Tailhas in Pomerol. Crossing the Ruisseau du Tailhas will take you into St-Emilion.

As you follow the D243 you pass over layers of gravel, which, together with the limestone plateau, produce the best wines of the area. To your left is the road to Ch Figeac which used to be part of the same estate as Ch Cheval Blanc, and shares the same gravelly soil as its illustrious neighbour.

Retrace your steps to the D243 and turn left then left again, almost back on yourself along the D245, across

the slope of the hill. A little over a km down the road to your right is a turning to Ch Cheval Blanc, one of the two Premiers Grands Crus Classés "As" (along with Ch Ausone) of St-Emilion. To the left of the D245 is Ch la Tour du Pin Figeac. Turning right at the next crossroads you slip back briefly into Pomerol with, to your left, Ch La Conseillante, and at the fork in the road, Ch l'Evangile.

Now on the D244, the soil is a mixture of gravel and sand. To the left is Ch Croque-Michotte, before a right turn takes you past Ch Corbin-Michotte and Ch de Grand Corbin.

The road descends: take the first sharp right-hand turn and then first left following the contours of the hill briefly before crossing over the next

road and starting to climb. You are now approaching the hills surrounding the limestone plateau.

Take the next left and after about a km turn right towards St-Emilion. After about 750m there is a right turn to Ch Fonroque, a 20ha estate on a hill. Take the next left turn and then left again onto the D122 away from St-Emilion to pass, on your right, Ch Larmande, one of the oldest estates on the northern slopes dating back to 1580.

Turn right at the crossroads and then pass Chx Faurie de Souchard and Petit-Faurie-de-Soutard before you turn right at the next junction to pick up the D243 heading into St-Emilion.

The road climbs steeply past, to the right, the 18th-century Ch Soutard, and to the left, the much older Ch Balestard-la-Tonnelle, where the old tower ("tonnelle") still exists. Continue into St-Emilion, then turn left on the D243 E1 to Ch Trotte-Vieille, well-situated to catch the sun. Return to the D243 E1 and follow the road around the north of the town back towards Libourne. Vineyards and châteaux cluster around the slopes of the hills, including Ch Grand Pontet by the road, Ch Franc-Mayne on an east-facing slope, and Ch Trois Moulins on the top of the hill. Further over to the left is Ch Clos des Jacobins on a gently hilly plain. Just past the château turn left taking you past Ch Laroze back to the St-Emilion road. Turn left, the road climbing as you travel eastwards, and passing to your right, Ch l'Angélus.

The road curves upwards through the hamlet of St-Martin where Ch Canon **1** is situated behind the church. Its name derives from its original owner, M. Kanon.

Head s from St-Martin following the road as it curves to the left and Ch Magdelaine **2** is situated on a plateau overlooking the Dordogne. Take the left turn passing along the edge of St-Emilion, and with Clos Fourtet **3** on your left. At the junction take the right-hand road back on yourself into the town itself which, with its rich history and panoramic views, is well-worth visiting.

Continuing the Wine Route on the D122, Ch Ausone **4** is on your right making truly superb wines from a hilly vantage point above the surrounding countryside. Also to the right of the road is Ch Belair **5** and to the west Ch Fonplégade. The Route then takes the D245 passing Ch la Gaffelière. **6**

The road heads E and at the first crossroads you come across Ch Pavie **7** whose slopes were the first (along with those of Ch Ausone) to be planted with vines in the 4th century. Follow the road towards St-Laurent-des-Combes passing at the foot of the slope, Ch Bellefont Belcier **8**, followed by Ch Rozier **9**. Drive through St-Hippolyte on the D130 past Ch Capet-Guillier **10**, dating back to the 18th century, and then through St-Etienne behind which on the hillside you can see Ch Puy-Blanquet, replanted after total devastation from phylloxera in 1878.

As the road curves towards Castillon on the hills to your left is a piece of history: Ch de Pressac, dating back to the 13th century where, after the battle of Castillon, the treaty was signed to end the Hundred Years War.

Although the wines of Castillon lack the distinction of those of St-Emilion, the hilly countryside is very pretty and makes a pleasant tour. Take the D130 into Castillon, and turn left onto the D936, following the road through this little river town which commemorates the battle that returned Aquitaine to the French in 1453. Turn left up the D21, then left up the hill where the twisting and turning road meets the D119. Continuing on the D119 will take you to the quality-orientated wine district of Côtes de Francs. Pass Ch La Fourquerie **11** and shortly afterwards turn left on the D21 E4 past Ch de Clotte **12** and Ch de Belcier **13**. Turn left along the D123 and take the left turn onto the D21, turn right, then right again through St-Cibard. Meander along back to the D123. Turn left, then take the right turn, past Ch Puygueraud **14**. At the next crossroad turn right again to return to the D123

at St-Philippe-d'Aiguilhe. Leave Ch d'Aiguilhe **15** to your left (now back in Côtes de Castillon) and continue along the D123 E towards Puisseguin, and the peaceful countryside of the "satellites". In Puisseguin turn right onto the D17 and stay on this road, passing on the right the D21 and Ch de Roques, dating back to the 15th century. Where the D17 forks to the left towards Lussac, take the right-hand road crossing the D122 to visit Chx de Barbe Blanche and La Tour de Ségur. Take the next left-hand turn, past Ch Lucas dating from the 16th-century, then right into Lussac, passing Ch Lussac on the left.

Take the D122 out of Lussac, crossing from the commune of Lussac into that of Montagne. Over to the right is Ch Calon, commanding panoramic views of the countryside.

In Montagne turn right along the D244, however if you wish to make a detour, turn left instead and then right, to one of the loveliest châteaux of the region: Ch des Tours. Return to the D244 and drive past Ch Corbin **16**, then take the first road on the left. Follow this road until you come to the large and lovely estate of Ch Maison Blanche. Turn right, crossing the D121 and keep on this road as it winds to a left turn, near Châtain, followed shortly by a right turn where the road runs parallel to the Barbanne Rau before entering Chevrol. Turn left out of the village, close to the river and take a left at the next T-junction, which will bring you to the N89. Turn left onto the road heading back into Libourne.

WINE INFORMATION

CASTILLON-LA-BATAILLE
Maison du Vin

ST-EMILION
Maison du Vin
Cloître de la Collégiale
Office du Tourisme

HOTELS AND RESTAURANTS

CASTILLON-LA-BATAILLE, 33350
La Bonne Auberge (C)
tel: 57 40 11 56
Reasonable comfort and prices. Regional dishes. Restaurant (B).
ST-EMILION, 33330
Logis de la Cadène (C)
Rue de la Cadène, tel: 57 24 71 40
Family cooking, excellent lunches.
Cloître des Cordeliers
Not a restaurant, but you can enjoy a glass of Clos des Cordeliers here.
Auberge de la Commanderie (B), Rue des Cordeliers, tel: 54 24 70 19
Middle-range hotel with simple restaurant.
Chez Dominique (C), Rue de la Petite Fontaine, tel: 57 24 71 00
Local dishes as well as pizzas.
Goullée Francis (B), Rue Guadet, tel: 57 24 70 49
Elegant decor and often fine dishes.
Chez Germaine (B), Place du Clocher, tel: 57 24 70 88
Traditional dishes based on local ingredients.
Auberge de la Monolithe (B)
Place du Marché, tel: 57 24 47 77
Attractively situated and dinner served alfresco if fine.
Hostellerie de Plaisance (A)
Place du Clocher, tel: 57 24 72 32
Comfortable rooms named after wine estates and the best restaurant (B) in town.
Logis des Remparts (A)
Rue Guadet, tel: 57 24 70 43
Comfortable, well-furnished rooms.

COGNAC

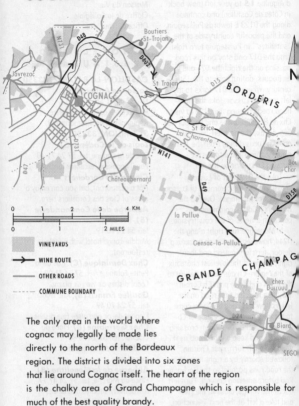

The only area in the world where cognac may legally be made lies directly to the north of the Bordeaux region. The district is divided into six zones that lie around Cognac itself. The heart of the region is the chalky area of Grand Champagne which is responsible for much of the best quality brandy.

THE WINE ROUTE

Many of the well-known cognac houses have their headquarters in the town of Cognac and welcome visitors. The Office de Tourisme in the Place J.-Monnet will advise on visiting the *chais*, or just follow the signs on the premises of the larger concerns, which have organised tours. It is increasingly possible to buy cognacs made and distilled on farms. So watch out for signs along the Route.

The Cognac appellation covers a very large area, from well E of the town to as far W as the Atlantic. The

Wine Route given here passes through the Grande Champagne region, the heart of the appellation and the location of the most prestigious vineyards.

Leave the town via the main bridge on the N141, the road to Saintes. Note the big *chais* on either side of the river, with those on the west bank belonging to Hennessy. Turn right at the first major junction onto the D48, which follows the river Charente through low-lying wooded country. Cross the D24 and take an unclassified road into the village of Boutiers-St-Trojan. From the latter continue along the D402 to St-Trojan,

leaving the village over a bridge across a stream and immediately turning left along a minor road past the Ch de la Solaire. Turn left at the top of the hill, driving along the D15 for a short while until a signpost shows the road into St-Brice on the left. Leave the village on the D15, turning right almost immediately onto

a minor road which runs close to the river and passes through La Maurie and on to Margonet. Once through the village, go left at the junction with the D158 and then right, passing through La Touche on a road which leads into Jarnac.

Jarnac is home of several famous firms such as Delamain, Hine and Courvoisier. At the first major crossroads coming into the town, turn right, driving down to the riverside where the cognac houses have their premises. Drive along the quay and turn right over the bridge, joining the main N141 for a short, straight stretch across the flood-plain. Follow the N141 as it curves right and begins to climb, but look out for a sharp left

turn up a wooded hill, the D736. Take this road, turning left again at the first crossroads onto the D10. Here you are in the heart of the Grande Champagne country. Turn right on the edge of the hamlet of Le Four à Chaux, following a minor road to Mainxe, after which you turn left at a crossroads, joining the D736. Continue s to Segonzac, noting the increasingly hilly chalk country on the left. These hills are capped with the fine, hard chalk which gives so much quality to the wine made here. Experienced blenders say that Grande Champagne, with its chalk, is responsible for 90% of the best cognac.

Segonzac is a small town, site of several distilleries and *chais*. Leave the town in a NW direction on the D49, forking right in 2km to chez Barraud, taking a right turn then a left through this hamlet onto the Tilloux road. Pass through Tilloux, over the railway and then turn right to Veillard, crossing the main road to continue N to Bourg-Charente. Turn left along the riverside, pass the end of the bridge then bear left again up the hill through the vineyards. Cross the N141, continue along the D158 across the railway to Gensac-la-Pallue, where you turn right onto the D49, which rejoins the N141. Follow the main road back to Cognac.

HOTELS AND RESTAURANTS

COGNAC, 16100
Le Coq d'Or (B), 33 Place François 1er, tel: 45 82 02 56
Excellent oysters.
l'Auberge (B), 13 Rue Plumejeau, tel: 45 32 08 70
Central but quiet restaurant.
La Halle aux Vins (C), 7 Place François 1er, tel: 45 32 07 51
Honest cooking and regional wines.
Mapotel Le Valois (B), 34 Rue du 14-Juillet, tel: 45 82 76 00
Businesslike comfort.
Les Pigeons Blancs (B), 10 Rue Jules-Brisson, tel: 45 82 16 36
Good cooking based on market-fresh produce. Also a hotel.

BERGERAC

Winegrowing in the Dordogne is concentrated around the town of Bergerac in the southeast of the département. Traditionally the region has produced sweet white wines, but at present red wine represents about half of production with the best reds coming mainly from the little district of Pécharmant. Among the white wines, the drier styles are gaining ground but Monbazillac to the south continues to produce good, sweet white wines.

THE WINE ROUTE

Whilst other Wine Routes in the southwest are relatively undiscovered, that of Bergerac in the picturesque Dordogne is very well-known to visitors. (There is a signposted *Route des Vins*.)

The tour starts in the town of Bergerac itself which is the centre of the winegrowing district. Take the D32 (west) out of Bergerac through the wine villages of Prigonrieux and then Le Fleix (with its cooperative). Keep on the D32 heading NE towards St-Méard-de-Gurçon where you will find Domaine du Gouyat.

In the village pick up the D708 and head N to St-Rémy where you turn left onto the D33 to St-Martin-de-Gurçon

and then on to Villefranche-de-Louchat. Take the D9 southwards as it passes through the village, then turn off left, through Pont Lapeyre, left at the next crossroads, right and into Montpeyroux.

Drive s out of the village, through St-Claud and turn right at the first crossroads to Pombazet, close to the river Lidoire. Follow the road into St-Michel-de-Montaigne, famous for its château and where red Bergerac is produced.

Follow the road s towards Lamothe-Montravel. Turn left onto the D936 and follow the road to Tête-Noire where you turn left into Montcaret. This is the area of Montravel, offering white wines ranging from dry to sweet made from a variety of grapes. From Montcaret

APPELLATION
CONTROLEE AREA

→ WINE ROUTE

— OTHER ROADS

– – – DEPARTEMENT BOUNDARY

0 2 4 6 8 10 KM

0 5 MILES

continue to travel N, turning NE onto the D10E and then right on the D10 into Bonneville-et-St-Avit-de-Fumadières. The Ch du Bloy here produces mostly red Côtes de Bergerac, but also some dry white Montravel. Return to the D10e and continue into St-Vivien, where you turn SE to Le Brunet and onto the D11 to Vélines where you will find Ch La Raye, the producer of an excellent red Bergerac and white Côtes de Montravel. Vélines is also the main wine village in the Montravel district.

From Vélines return to the D936 and follow the road to Port-Ste-Foy-et-Ponchapt and Ste-Foy-la-Grande. This marks the eastern boundary of the Montravel district which is divided into several appellations: namely, Haut-Montravel, and Côtes de Montravel. Take the D8 (southeast) from Ste-Foy to St-Philippe-du-Seignal which becomes the D18, then turn off left to Razac-de-Saussignac which takes you into the Saussignac district. The wines are a minimum 12.5% alcohol, usually dry and rarely seen. Razac-de-Saussignac has a modern winery at Ch Court-les-Mûts. Continue through the village to

Saussignac with its impressive Ch de Saussignac. Head s from Saussignac, turn left to Gageac-et-Rouillac and then s and w to Monestier.

Take the D16 (northeast) to Cunèges, then turn right heading SE on the D15 through Lastignac and Blazy to Sigoulès. The D17 (north) takes you across the river Cardonnette into the main Monbazillac appellation. The first stop is Pomport which is the centre for a number of producers.

Stay on the D17 (northeast) and follow it as it curves eastwards to join the D933. Turn right then left on the D14E to Monbazillac. Here the obligatory visit is to the Ch de Monbazillac (on the D13). The château is owned by the cooperative which produces Monbazillac in sizeable quantities. You can buy the château wine (not readily available elsewhere) at the entrance.

From Monbazillac take the D13 back into Bergerac, and then, to visit the Pécharmant district (just NE of the town) where the best red wines of the area are made, head N through Gravouse to Ste-Foy. From here turn right and E in the direction of Jaure and turn right again onto the D107 which takes you onto the N21. Turn right towards Bergerac, then left at Pombonne along a winding road to the wine village of Peyrelevade. To complete the wine tour, turn right on the D32 to return to Bergerac.

LOT-ET-GARONNE

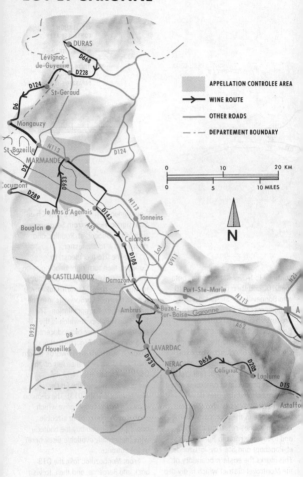

If Tuscany were to have a successor then the undiscovered countryside of the Lot-et-Garonne would provide the ideal country retreat. The scenery here is varied: in the east it is hilly and a large part of the west is woodland, with in between the broad flat valley of the Garonne, fed by its many tributaries including the Lot which flow down from the Massif Central. The fertile Garonne valley has a rich history with many old villages, castles and churches. Since the 1970s four districts have gained recognition. From north to south they are the Côtes de Duras, Côtes du Marmandais, Buzet and the Côtes du Brulhois.

THE WINE ROUTE

Travel s on the D933 from Bergerac through Eymet and then turning right into La Sauvetat-du-Dropt. From here take the D134 right and head NW into the Côtes de Duras on the D13. This area has red and white AOC wines.

Continue on the D13 through the village of St-Jean-de-Duras, past the Ch de Puychagut. Turn left at the crossroads and take the D244 through St-Astier, around a sharp right-hand bend to a T-junction with the D708. Turn left and continue on the main road which runs parallel with the river Dourdèze, cross the river immediately before turning right and then take the right-hand fork. At the next crossroads turn right, and N onto the D203 to Landerrouat, the base of a good cooperative. In the village, head s on the D139E (becoming the D312) to Esclottes where several producers are based.

Continue on the D312, past the villages of Les Pastureaux and Les Riquets then turn right to Ste-Colombe-de-Duras where the Lusoli family make Côtes de Duras wines.

Return to the D312, turn left onto the road then take an immediate right through Baleyssagues onto the D134 and left into Duras itself before crossing the Dourdèze river again. The local cooperative, just outside the town, produces splendid wines.

Take the D708 (south) out of Duras then head E on the D668 towards Miramont. Drive through Auriac-sur-Dropt and turn right towards the village of Monteton, off the main road and from which there is a splendid view. Return to the D423 and head s, turning right at the T-junction with the D228 towards Lévignac-de-Guyenne. Cross the D708, keeping on the D228, then turn left to St-Géraud. Go through the village crossing the D303 towards St-Vivien-de-Montségur. Turn left to St-Michel-de-Lapujade where the Domaine des Geais produces Côtes du Marmandais wine.

Almost all the wine produced is red and two cooperatives make nearly all

the wine. The better and the more progressive is the one at Cocumont and the other is at Beaupuy.

To reach Cocumont take the D129E and when you reach Mongauzy turn left on the N113. To the right of the road is the river Garonne. At Ste-Bazeille turn right to cross the river on the D3 and then under the A62. From Cocument take the D289 eastwards to Samazan, and keep following the road until you reach the D933. Turn left to Marmande and having crossed the Garonne follow the D708 (north) to Beaupuy.

Now retrace your route back into Marmande where you take the N113 eastwards as far as Fauguerolles when you turn right on the D6 to cross the Garonne at Le Mas d'Agenais. Just over the bridge turn left on to the D143 to Calonges and follow the road running parallel to the canal on the left and the autoroute (A62) to the right.

Here you enter the Buzet appellation, and joining the D300 from the left the first centre of production you come to is Damazan. SW Granted full AOC status in 1973 as Côtes de Buzet, the wines are now known simply as Buzet. Nearly all the wine produced is red and ageing in oak produces successful wines.

Continue through Damazan crossing the D8 on the D108E to Buzet-sur-Baïse where almost the entire production of the appellation is handled by the local cooperative. Take the D108 to Ambrus where wine is produced by a Beaujolais grower at the Ch de Padère. Head s from Ambrus to Xantrailles and then take the D108 to Lavardac followed by the D930 to Nérac. Out of Nérac on the D656 zigzagging eastwards towards Agen, but turn onto the D208 to Laplume and then follow the D15 (east) to Astaffort.

At Astaffort join the N21 and follow the road N as far as Goulens where the important Côtes du Brulhois cooperative is based. Continue through the Gers valley to Layrac on the N21 and then take the D17 to Agen.

CAHORS

The ancient town of Cahors was founded by the Gauls and has a winemaking tradition that dates back to the seventh century. However, it was not until 1971 when this wine region was given its *appellation contrôlée*. The wines of Cahors have gradually been undergoing a rejuvenation, largely due to the forward thinking and activity of the cooperative at Parnac to which almost half the growers are affiliated. Classis Cahors is dark red and distinguished by an intense taste, rich in tannin.

SW

THE WINE ROUTE

This Wine Route follows the course of the Lot Valley as the river loops between Cahors and Fumel in the west. It begins in Cahors, a very old town which was historically an important trading place, occupying a spectacular site in a loop of the river Lot. Visit Mont St-Cyr for glorious views of the town and the Pont Valentré across the river on the western side of the town. Take the D911 heading N out of Cahors close to the river and at Mercuès, you will find the expensive château-hotel, the Ch de Mercuès. Turn left on the D145 past Caillac on your left to Lapoujade. Take the D23 up the hillside to Crayssac. From the village turn left onto the D9 and follow the road around the loop of the river past the 17th-century Ch de Caix which is owned by the Danish Royal family. Continue into Luzech, a village characterized by its feudal castle.

Return to the D9 travelling W

parallel to the river's curving course. Don't take the road to the bridge opposite Albas, but turn off right and follow the road to Castelfranc. The countryside here is characterized by steep hillsides where vines have traditionally been grown on gravel slopes, as well as the limestone valley floor where there has been recent planting. The predominant grape variety is at least 70% Auxerrois, blended with Merlot and Tannat.

At Castelfranc join the D911 heading E to Prayssac. Keep on the D911 to Puy l'Evêque, an important wine community and a good base for exploring neighbouring producers. Local producers include the 16th-century Ch de Cayrou and the Clos de Gamot, both owned by the Jouffreau family. The Domaine de Paillas, planted on the valley slopes is owned by the Lascombes family. The Domaine de la Pineraie blends Auxerrois and Merlot to produce a fruity wine with tannin for ageing. Clos Tringuedina is an estate of some 41ha owned by the Baldès family.

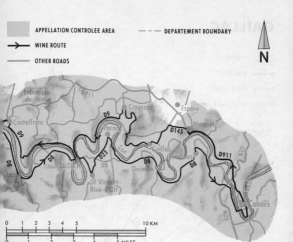

APPELLATION CONTROLEE AREA

WINE ROUTE

OTHER ROADS

DEPARTEMENT BOUNDARY

N

From Puy l'Evêque, follow the D911 to Duravel and then take the D58 through the hills to the medieval village of Montcabrier. Turn left onto the D673 running along the Thèze valley to St-Martin-le-Redon. Turn right into the village, then left eastwards and at the T-junction with the D158 turn right to Ch de Bonaguil. This partly ruined structure dates back to the 13th century and is one of the largest in France. Retrace your steps to the D673 and at the junction with the D911 turn left through Soturac to Touzac where you cross the river into the village. Take the D8 to Vire-sur-Lot. (The D911 continues w through Fumel and Monsempron-Libos to Villefranche-sur-Lot.) There are various wineries in Vire, including Domaine des Garriques where Roger Labruyère produces light style wines. You can also visit the cellars of the Domaine de Gaudou which is owned by Durou & Fils. Continue on the D8 back to Puy l'Evêque and then cross to the south bank of the Lot by turning right onto the D44 which becomes the D8 again as it loops around the river into the wine village of Grézels with its nearby château.

Drive N out of Grézels and turn left off the D8 at St-Benoit and follow the road as it hugs the loop in the river to Pescadoires. From here take the D237 through Lagardelle and then the D8 to Bélaye.

The road then joins the D45 and heads N parallel to the river and always matching its course. Through Anglars-Juillac, the road becomes the D8 again and enters Albas at the next tight loop in the river. At Albas is the Prieuré de Cénac property producing impressive wine bottled by Rigal & Fils. Stay on the D8 to Luzech, then cross the river and turn right to St-Vincent-Rive d'Ott.

Take the D23 and follow it to Parnac where the largest cooperative of the region is based. It is well worth a visit to see its state-of-the-art winery and temperature-controlled fermentation vats – a striking contrast to the small privately-owned estates. The Ch de St-Didier is also found in Parnac, owned by the négociants Rigal & Fils. Turn left heading S off the D23 to Les Fosses and continue travelling parallel to the river until you turn left onto the D8. Stay on the D8 through Douelle and Pradines and return to Cahors.

GAILLAC

VINEYARDS

→ WINE ROUTE

UTHER ROADS

- - - DEPARTEMENT BOUNDARY

0 1 2 3 4 5 10 KM

0 1 2 3 4 5 MILES

N

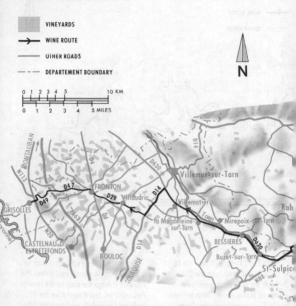

Gaillac is one of the largest and most productive wine districts of southwest France. Partly as a result of the complex range of wines available from each producer, exports are slow. Locally, however, the wines are drunk with great enthusiasm and the better restaurants, in particular, often carry an exciting selection.

THE WINE ROUTE

The Wine Route starts in the small town of Gaillac on the banks of the Tarn dating back to the 10th century. The wines of Gaillac range from reds, produced from a variety of grapes including Gamay, Négrette, Syrah, Cabernet Sauvignon, Merlot, Cabernet Franc; to whites made from Mauzac. Blanc, Sauvignon, Sémillon, Loin de l'Oeil and others; to sparkling wines.

In Gaillac itself is one of the two estates owned by Robert Plageoles – Domaine Très-Cantoux – producing some of the best Gaillac available.

From Gaillac take the D922 (north) and then turn off on the D964 to

Castelnau-de-Montmirail out of the Tarn Valley. At the crossroads with the D115 turn left as the D964 heads E to Castelnau where you will find the Domaine de Roucou-Cantemerle.

Head N on the D4 away from Castelnau and after crossing the river Vère turn right on th D1. Continue on this road through Le Verdier and along the river to Cahuzac-sur-Vère, home for the producer Jean Cros.

By turning left and N at Cahuzac-sur-Vère you pick up the D922 again. Stay on this road, passing Donnazac on the right, crossing the D33 and as the road becomes the D122 follow it towards Cordes, joining the D600 from the right.

At Cordes the leading producer is

Ch de Frauseilles. Return along the D600 in the direction of Albi. Cross the river Vère, pass La Mennonié on your left, then take the right hand turn to Villeneuve-sur-Vère on the D25. A left turn on the D31 takes you to Castanet, home of Domaine de Labarthe, one of the better producers in the region. Retrace your steps back to the D600 and keep on this road all the way to the town of Albi which is just outside the wine area but well worth visiting. From Albi journey due w on the N88 to Marssac-sur-Tarn. Cross the Tarn on the N88 then immediately turn off right on the D30 to Labastide-de-Levis where the huge cooperative is situated. This is Gaillac's major producer with over 800 members.

Return to the N88 and follow the road through Gaillac once again and then through Lisle-sur-Tarn along the river valley to Rabastens-sur-Tarn with its medieval castle. Continue on the N88 heading sw to St-Sulpice but instead of entering the town, keep on the N88 until you come to the junction with the D630. Turn right towards

Bessières, following the river Tarn. Go through Bessières and, further along the D630, Villamatier. Turn left at Pechnauquié onto the D14 heading sw to Toulouse.

At the crossroads with the D14b turn right, through Les Millets into Villaudric. The wine here is called Côtes du Frontonnais; red and rosé wines are made from the local red grape, the Négrette.

In Villaudric itself is the Domaine de la Colombière, owned by Baron François de Dreisen. At the end of the village turn right on the D29 and follow the road to Fronton.

Producers based in Fronton include the Domaine de Bel Air and Domaine de Laurou, but the star is Ch Bellevue la Forêt. Take the D47 (becoming the D49) westwards out of Fronton, over the autoroute and across the N20 and the canal to Grisolles.

From the town of Grisolles take the N20 northwards to Montauban where you can pick up the D999 which will take you eastwards along the Tescou Valley back to Gaillac.

WINE INFORMATION

GAILLAC
Maison de la Vigne et du Vin
Abbaye St-Michel

THE PYRENEES

APPELLATION CONTROLEE AREA

→ WINE ROUTE

— OTHER ROADS

- - - DEPARTEMENT BOUNDARY

0 1 2 3 4 5   10 KM

0 1 2 3 4 5 MILES

Some of the least-known wine districts of France lie in the foothills of the western Pyrenees. The most northerly is the Côtes de St-Mont, which takes in part of Armagnac. Then come Madiran, Tursan, Béarn, Jurançon and deep into Basque country, Irouleguy. Most of the grape varieties are strictly local. The main black grape is the Tannat which, according to tradition, was brought here from Bordeaux by monks in the eleventh century; white wines are made from locally named grapes such as Gros Manseng, Petit Manseng and Courbu. Although several of the small districts have been on the verge of disappearing altogether as a source of wine, today the wines of the Pyrenees are steadily gaining recognition.

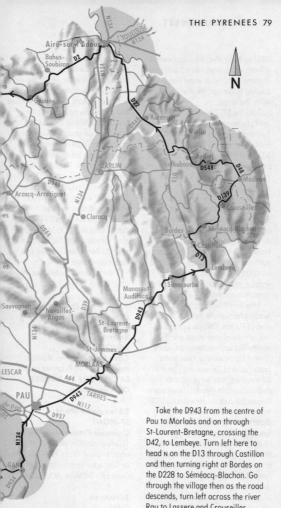

THE WINE
ROUTE

A land of hidden valleys and secret
vineyards, this area in the Bas
Pyrénées is one of great beauty and
tranquility revealing rediscovered
wines. The wine tour begins in the
lovely old spa town of Pau. To the
west of the château is the ancient
Parc National and to the east, the
Boulevard des Pyrénées with its
breathtaking views of the mountains.

Take the D943 from the centre of
Pau to Morlaàs and on through
St-Laurent-Bretagne, crossing the
D42, to Lembeye. Turn left here to
head N on the D13 through Castillon
and then turning right at Bordes on
the D228 to Séméacq-Blachon. Go
through the village then as the road
descends, turn left across the river
Rau to Lassere and Crouseilles.

This is the area of production for
Madiran, and Crouseilles is the base
of the largest cooperative for Madiran
and the biggest producer of the white
Pacherenc du Vic-Bilh. Madiran is
deep red and tannic and needs plenty
of ageing to soften the rough edges.
The white wine, Pacherenc du Vic-
Bilh, often has a slightly pungent style
whether dry or slightly sweet.

Follow the D139 (north) to Madiran
itself and the Ch de Perron, then head
N out of the town on the D48. Turn left
on the D548, and left again on the

D317 to Aydie. Pierre Laplace owns Ch d'Aydie which produces a traditional Madiran matured in wood and needing bottle age. He also makes white Pacherenc.

Take the D317 (west) out of Aydie until you reach the D292 at Jouandou. Turn right and head N on the D292 until you come to a junction with the D136. Turn left westwards across the river Larcis and at the T-junction turn right, heading N on the D13 which shortly becomes the D22.

Follow the road along the valley through Aurensan with the wine district of Côtes de St-Mont to the east, and then straight on N to Aire-sur-l'Adour. The Côtes de St-Mont is the most recent as well as the northernmost appellation. It reached its VDQS in 1981 and is a wine to watch – whites are refreshing and some reds are matured in wood.

Take the D2 heading SW out of Aire heading for Geaune through the VDQS area of Tursan. This area produces red, white and rosé wines and their quality has been increasing steadily. Almost all the wine is made at the cooperative at Geaune. Keep on the D2 travelling W to Samadet, over the river Gabas and through the village to Hagetmau. Join the southbound D933 to the Pyrénées-Atlantiques département and the AC area of Béarn. The road passes through Castaignos-Souslens and Sault-de-Navailles, across the hills and valleys of the Luy until you reach the market town of Orthez where the local delicacy, Bayonne ham, is cured.

Join the N117 westwards and once through Baigts-de-Béarn turn off left on the D933 over the river to Bérenx and the spa town of Salies-de-Béarn. To the southwest of this village, practically on the Spanish border (reached via the D933), is the isolated wine district of Irouleguy.

To continue the tour, take the D30 (southeast) from Salies through Orion and Orriule and Narp to a T-junction with the D936. Turn left and follow the road through Araujuzon, Araux and Villenave-de-Navarrenx, then at the crossroads turn left on the D2 into Navarrenx. Through the village on the

D111, travel E to Viellességure and Mourenx. Take the D9 (southeast) to Lahourcade to enter one of the most beautiful wine districts in the whole of France, Jurançon. This hilly, wooded and beautifully peaceful region produces delicious sweet wines made from overripe grapes and preferably affected by "pourriture noble" but less rich than Sauternes.

Following the D9 to Monein you find a variety of producers including Clos Uroulat making good quality dry and sweet wines. Turn E out of Monein and then meander southwards along the D34 through restful countryside to Lasseube. At the T-junction with the D24 turn left and E to Gan where you will find the *cave coopérative*.

Refreshed and rested take the N134 (north) back to Pau.

LOCAL PRODUCERS

Bearn
BELLOCQ
Cave Coopérative: Notable especially for its Cabernet rosé
LA CHAPELLE DE ROUSSE
Cru Lamouroux

Côtes de St-Mont
ST-MONT
Union de Producteurs Plaimont: This organization also bottles the white and red Vin de Pays des Côtes de Gascogne from master chef Michel Guérard's Domaine du Meunier.

Jurançon
GAN
Cave Coopérative
Château Jolies
LAHOURCADE
Alfred Barrère
MONEIN
Domaine Bru-Baché
Raymond Gaillot

Madiran
AYDIE
Vignobles Laplace
CROUSEILLES
Cave Coopérative: Notable for its Château de Gayon and Rôt du Roy in

particular; also the biggest producer of Pacherenc du Vic-Bilh.
MAUMUSSON
Domaine Barréjat
Château Montus

WINE INFORMATION

Jurançon
MONEIN
Maison du Vin

HOTELS AND RESTAURANTS

AIRE-SUR-L'ADOUR, 40800
Chez l'Ahumat (C), tel: 58 71 82 61
Restaurant with traditional regional cooking. Also a hotel. *Demi-pension* only in summer.
Le Commerce (B), tel: 58 71 60 06
Regional dishes served in restaurant around an old hearth. Noisy hotel rooms overlooking the street.
BOSDARROS, 64290
Auberge Labarthe (C), tel: 59 21 72 03
Traditional and popular restaurant.
EUGENIE-LES-BAINS, 40320
Relais des Champs (B), tel: 58 51 18 00
For anyone who wants to eat at *Michel Guérard's* but finds staying here too expensive (see below).
Michel Guérard/Les Prés et les Sources d'Eugénie (A), tel: 58 51 19 01
A place of pilgrimage for gastronomes. Impressive wine list. Also luxurious hotel rooms.
GAN, 64290
Le Tucq (C), tel: 59 21 61 26
Relaxed restaurant with hunting trophies on the walls.
GEAUNE, 40320
Hotel de France (C), tel: 58 44 51 18
Hotel restaurant where you can drink red Tursan.
JURANÇON, 64110
Hostellerie de Canastel (B), Avenue Rausky, tel: 59 06 13 40

Hotel with its own park on the road to Oloron-Ste-Marie. Swimming pool. Restaurant.
Chez Ruffet (B), 3 Avenue Charles-Touzet, tel: 59 06 25 13
Try the fresh salmon with a Jurançon wine at this restaurant.
ORTHEZ, 64300
Auberge St-Loup (B)
tel: 59 69 15 40
Good cooking.
PAU, 64000
Mapotel Continental (A)
2 Rue Marèchal-Foch, tel: 59 27 69 31
Large, distinguished hotel. *Le Conti* restaurant.
Montpensier (B), 36 Rue Montpensier, tel: 59 27 42 72
Renovated hotel in central location.
Hotel Paris (B), 80 Rue Emile-Ganot, tel: 59 27 34 39
Central but comparatively peaceful.
Chez Pierre (A), 16 Rue Louis-Barthou, tel: 59 27 76 86
Excellent and expensive restaurant.
Roncevaux (B), 25 Rue Louis-Barthou, tel: 59 27 08 44
Comfortable hotel behind Boulevard des Pyrénées.
PLAISANCE-DU-GERS, 32160
La Ripa-Alta (B), tel: 62 69 30 43
Friendly restaurant with hotel on the village square. Fine selection of armagnacs (some very old).
RISCLE, 32400
La Paix (C), tel: 62 69 70 14
Restaurant recommended for duck dishes and regional wines. Also fairly quiet hotel.
ST-ETIENNE-DE-BAIGORY, 64430
Hotel Arcé (A/B), tel: 59 37 40 14
One of most pleasant places to stay in the region. *Le Trinquet* restaurant.
ST-JEAN-PIED-DE-PORT, 64220
Les Pyrénées (A/B), tel: 59 37 01 01
The best restaurant of the district. Also a hotel.
SEGOS, 32400
Domaine de Bassibé (A)
tel: 62 09 46 71
Small, luxurious hotel and restaurant (B).

SW

CHAMPAGNE

Champagne has many attractions for visitors: cellars, vineyards, charming towns and villages and a varied landscape. Most of the major champagne-making *maisons* are grouped in Reims and Epernay, although there are other firms in Tours-sur-Marne, Châlons-sur-Marne and Ay. Every village in the vineyard district has small cellars belonging to farmers who both grow grapes and make champagne, although the normal pattern of the district is for

growers to sell their grapes to the *maison* or take them to cooperatives.

There are few wine regions more accommodating to visitors. Nearly all the major firms are open to visitors at specific times, usually 10am-12 noon and 2pm-4pm. Many offer guided tours of their cellars, literature, audio-visual displays and sometimes a glass of champagne. Those wishing to visit the smaller concerns, or to penetrate beyond the well-trodden visitor trail, would do well to arrange an introduction from their wine supplier.

THE WINE ROUTE

The *Route du Champagne* is quite well signposted. The following Route diverges from it occasionally, but it follows the general trend. Champagne's most important vineyards are strung out along the edge of the Montagne de Reims (a wooded plateau s of the city) along the Marne valley and along a further range of hills, the Côte des Blancs, s of Epernay. This Route begins in Reims, covers the Montagne vineyards, then passes through Epernay to cover the Côte des Blancs.

A visit to a champagne cellar can be made in Reims (see town plan for location of major producers) before starting the Route, or aim to be in Epernay in the afternoon to take advantage of the cellars there. The Route also passes through Ay, where several smaller firms can be visited.

Leave Reims on the A4 autoroute, which passes through the city, in the direction of Paris. Leave the A4 at the

Tinqueux junction, joining the N31 towards Soissons. In less than 2km turn left onto the D26, which forms part of an old motor-racing circuit. Observe the vineyards of the Montagne de Reims rising up on your left. Continue on into Gueux and follow the signs to Vrigny, still on the D26. The road crosses the autoroute, and you run through vineyards into Vrigny. Turn hard right, signposted to Coulommes, passing several small growers' cellars and, at the edge of the village there is the local cooperative. A good view of the countryside opens up. Pargny is the next village. Turn right at the give way sign, climbing up the hill on the main road (RD 380) into the woods. As you begin to descend, take the D6 left to Ville-Dommange. At the top of the hill is a detour off to the Chapelle St-Lie, a little hilltop church in a copse with a splendid view across the vineyards and the plain.

Ville-Dommange is a steep little town with plenty of growers who sell their own champagne. Follow the D6 down past the church, turning right onto the D26. The road skirts Sacy, passes through Ecueil, Chamery and into Nogent. Take care here to keep left on the D26: a sweeping right bend takes you onto the wrong road, the D22. Follow the road carefully through twisty little Sermiers, turning left onto the N51 and then immediately right, signposted to Villers-Allerand and Verzy, still on the D26. Pass through the wine villages of Villers-Allerand, Rilly-la-Montagne,

NE

Chigny-les-Roses and Ludes (with Canard-Duchêne's *caves* open for visits), following the signs for Verzy. Cross the D9 into the smart little town of Mailly, past the cooperative (visits). Continue on towards Verzenay, the rare old Heidsieck Monopole windmill, on its superbly-sighted knoll overlooking the plain, is clearly visible on the left. Pass through Verzenay, which is enclosed by very steep vine-clad slopes. Verzy is at the end of the north-facing slope of the Montagne de Reims, and nearby is the highest point where the Mont-Sinac observatory has been set up.

Continue on the D26, trending SE, to Villers-Marmery, where the ground is flatter. There is a gap in the vineyards between Villers-Marmery and Trépail. The land here is more open and in larger plots than in the north. The sea of vines face SE rather than NE. Pass a proud sign declaring that Ambonnay is "Grand Cru Classé 100%". Drive through the smart and prosperous village, turning right onto the D19 towards Bouzy. If you look to the right you will see the Montagne slope, with the woods crowning it and the white limestone soil showing in the vineyard tracks. In Bouzy there is a choice of Routes: right on a minor road to Louvois, or left on the D19 to Tours-sur-Marne. Either Route takes you to Ay.

To take the Louvois Route, follow a minor road through some non-vineyard countryside, turn right at a T-junction, crossing a low ridge into a valley which leads up into the Montagne. Louvois has a fine old château: turn left in front of it onto the D9 towards Tauxières-Mutry and Epernay. Corn and wheat grow in the valley and vines appear only on the top of the slope to the right. Pass through Fontaine-sur-Ay and Avenay with its Gothic-style cathedral and shops and back into continuous vineyards. Look to the left to see the Côte des Blancs across the Marne Valley, with the Montagne de Reims still on the right. Leave Avenay via a right turn onto the D201, past the station and across the railway, and on into Ay.

The alternative Route from Bouzy follows the D19 to Tours-sur-Marne. A sign on the left directs you to Laurent-Perrier, which is one of the most important in the region. Turn right at a little tree-lined triangle in the direction of Ay. Follow the Marne valley, with the canal close by, through Bisseuil, where local honey is for sale. The ground rises steeply on the right and a roadside quarry displays the Champagne limestone strata – and the very thin soil. Ahead is the noted Clos des Goisses, Philipponat's vineyard which is supposed to look in profile like a prone champagne bottle. Very steep slopes rise above the canal and road, with the little stone markers that show Philipponat's ownership. Pass the firm's premises, and those of Montebello in a tree-lined canal-side square.

Ay is a small, rather grey town crammed with illustrious Champagne houses such as Ayala and Bollinger and signs indicate where all the firms are situated. The Musée Champenoise shows how winegrowing and making have evolved. Vineyards rise above the town, well-sited with a perfect southern exposure. Leave on the D1 to Dizy, following the signs N51 and Reims, avoiding the main Epernay road which runs SW across the valley. At Dizy join the old main road, turning right and climbing up the long twisty vineyard slope to the Montagne. Pass through Champillon, with its splendid view, joining the new N51 towards Reims. Turn left to St-Imoges. In the village turn left (signposted Hautvillers) on the D71 through the forest. Turn left again at a T-junction onto the D386 towards Hautvillers. The road emerges from the forest, coming abruptly to the edge of the slope with fine views across to Epernay. Drop down into Hautvillers, a trim little hillside town with a famous Benedictine abbey where Dom Pérignon was cellarmaster. He is buried before the altar beside Dom Ruinart in the abbey church. It is worth taking a look around the town and there is a useful town plan outside the abbey. Note the wrought-

iron tradesmen's signs outside many buildings. The abbey, apart from the church, belongs to Moët & Chandon and contains a museum – visits only by appointment. The western edge of the town has a well-appointed picnic spot.

Follow the road down the steep hill to Cumières, where you can leave the Wine Route to follow the Marne westwards in the direction of Paris, passing beside the Marne valley vineyards and through Damery and on to Verneuil. To continue on the Route for the Champagne region, turn right into Cumières then immediately left across the bridge and along the D301 to Epernay. Cross the railway and turn left at traffic lights onto the main N3, then bear right at a roundabout.

Epernay is a bustling town, with many champagne companies, mostly grouped in the Avenue de Champagne (see town plan). Pass the market square, heading out to the south through one-way streets, reaching a roundabout where a sign points out the road to the Côte des Blancs. The new N51 bypass (not on older maps) curves around the east and south of Epernay, join it, and follow signs for Avize. Join the D10 past the edge of Cuis, passing the Butte de Saran hill on the left and the Montagne d'Avize, the northern end of the Côte, on the right. Go through steep vineyards to Cramant, and on towards Avize (following signs to Vertus) past the Lycée Viticole de la Champagne. Drive through Oger and Le Mesnil-sur-Oger, where Krug has its noted Clos de Mesnil vineyard. Outside the village, join the D9 to Vertus, across a flat vineyard plain with the Côte rising up on the right. Pass through Vertus, heading further s, still on the D9, towards Bergères-les-Vertus. An isolated hill, the Mont Aimé, rises up above Bergères to the south marking the end of the Côte des Blancs.

CHAMPAGNE HOUSES

AY
Ayala & Co: Serious, traditional small firm.

Bollinger: One of the great names of Champagne. Its own vineyards supply 70% of needs. Handsome, much-photographed 19th-century premises. RD is the vintage champagne.

Deutz & Geldermann: Dynamic small firm with some 40ha of vineyards.

Gosset: Proud of being the oldest firm in Champagne (founded 1584). Owns 10ha of land.

Ivernel: Stylish wines.

CHALONS-SUR-MARNE
Joseph Perrier: A firm with a growing name for quality. About a third of the grapes comes from its 20ha of vineyard.

CHOUILLY
R. & L. Legras: Carefully made wines almost exclusively from white grapes. 22ha of vineyards.

EPERNAY (see town plan)
Alfred Gratien: Small firm that uses traditional methods.

Moët & Chandon: With an annual production of 18 million bottles, about 485ha of vineyard and 28km of cellars this is by far the biggest firm in the Champagne region.

Perrier-Jouët : Champagnes have great vitality.

Pol Roger: Very conscientious family firm with classic champagnes. About 70ha of its own vineyards.

LE MESNIL-SUR-OGER
Salon: Only wines from white grapes and of superior vintages are marketed by this small prestigious firm. Owns just 1ha of vineyards.

OGER
F. Bonnet & Fils: Family firm with 22ha of vineyard in the Côte des Blancs (providing two-thirds of their needs).

MAREUIL-SUR-AY
Billecart-Salmon: Small house with a light, fresh style.

REIMS (see town plan)
Charles Heidsieck: Classic, long-lived, lively wines.

Heidsieck & Co Monopole: Firm belonging to Seagram with about 110ha of vineyards.

Henriot: White grapes dominate their champagnes, with fruit from the 110ha still owned by the Henriot family.

NE

Krug: Small firm (maximum sales of 500,000 bottles a year) aiming for total perfection. All the wine still ferments in small oak casks. Krug owns 15.5ha of vineyard.

Lanson Père & Fils: This firm is especially well known for its reliable, fresh NV Black Label. Owns 210ha of vineyards.

G. H. Mumm & Co: Large firm belonging to Seagrams. Their Crémant de Cramant is good. About one-fifth of production originates from its own 225ha of vineyards.

Bruno Paillard: Young firm, founded in 1981, that sells both carefully selected grapes and also makes top-class wines.

Piper-Heidsieck: A technically and commercially progressive firm, with interests in Touraine, California and elsewhere. The style of its wines is light and fresh.

Pommery & Greno: The buildings and cellars are among the most striking in Reims. Quality has recently much improved. Owns more than 320ha vineyards.

NE **Louis Roederer**: This family concern obtains about 80% of its grapes from its own 185ha of vineyards. It produces its wines with extraordinary care and a great feeling for tradition.

Ruinart Père & Fils: Modern buildings house the oldest champagne firm in Reims and stand over chalk cellars that have been declared a historic monument. Owns 15ha of vineyard.

Taittinger: The high Chardonnay content in Taittinger's wines shows in an elegance of style. About half of production is provided for by this family firm's 250ha.

Veuve Clicquot-Ponsardin: Classic, utterly reliable meticulously made wines. The house owns 280ha of vineyards and a wide spread of business interests. Also owns Canard-Duchêne and Henriot.

TOURS-SUR-MARNE

Laurent Perrier: Pure, expertly made wines have led to tremendous growth. This is now one of the most important houses. Grapes come from about 500ha.

WINE INFORMATION

EPERNAY
CIVC (Comité Interprofessionel du Vin de Champagne)
5 rue Henri-Martin

HOTELS AND RESTAURANTS

BEAUMONT-SUR-VESLE, 51400
La Maison du Champagne (B/C)
tel: 26 03 92 45
Small, simple, spotless hotel in a village southeast of Reims, with restaurant. The plumbing varies.
CHALONS-SUR-MARNE, 51000
Hotel d'Angleterre (B/C)
tel: 26 68 21 51
Very good restaurant near the cathedral; also a hotel.
CHAMPILLON-BELLEVUE, 51160
Royal Champagne (A)
tel: 26 52 87 11
Beautifully placed with a fine view of the Marne valley. Totally renovated rooms. The cooking can be very good.
CHERVILLE, 51150
Le Relais de Cherville (B)
tel: 26 69 52 76
Fine establishment halfway between Epernay and Châlons. Opened in 1980 by a member of the Trouillard family, of the champagne firm.
DORMANS, 51700
La Table Sourdet (B)
tel: 26 58 20 57
The Sourdet family enjoys a good local reputation as caterers and restaurateurs.
EPERNAY, 51200
Les Berceaux (B), 13 Rue des Berceaux, tel: 26 55 28 84
The amenities at this old hotel have been improved in recent years. The cooking is fairly traditional. Les Berceaux runs a bar in the same street selling wines by the glass.
Jean Burdin (C), 10 Place Mendès-France, tel: 26 51 66 69
Regional dishes in a fin de siècle setting.
Le Champagne (B), 30 Rue Eugène-Mercier, tel: 26 55 30 22
Hotel with functional comfort.
Le Chapon Fin (C), 2 Place

Mendès-France, tel: 26 55 40 03
Many growers eat here. Regional
dishes are good value.

L'EPINE 51460

**Aux Armes de Champagne
(A/B)**, tel: 26 66 96 79
Tastefully furnished rooms, good
cooking, and a view of the basilica.

FERE-EN-TARDENOIS, 02130

Hostellerie du Château (A)
tel: 23 68 10 43
Luxurious 16th-century château hotel
nearly 50km west of Reims. Glorious
position in a park. Good standard of
cooking.

LE MESNIL-SUR-OGER, 51190

Le Mesnil (B), tel: 26 57 95 57
Fish specialities and a wide choice of
wine in the heart of the Côte des
Blancs.

MONTCHENOT, 51500

Auberge du Grand Cerf (B)
tel: 26 97 60 07
Stylish inn on the Reims–Epernay
road where guests are well received.
Seasonally orientated fine cuisine and
extensive cellar. Garden and terrace.

REIMS, 51100

Le Chardonnay (B), 184 Avenue
d'Epernay, tel: 26 06 08 60
Elegant, well-maintained restaurant
(it was formerly Gérard Boyer's
Chaumière; he is now at Les
Crayères). The cooking is of a good
standard. Garden.

Les Crayères (A), 64 Boulevard
Henri-Vasnier, tel: 26 82 80 80
Eating here is an experience. Not only
is the cooking, under the direction of
Gérard Boyer, sublime, but the whole
ambience is magnificent: a very finely
appointed small château in a beautiful
park with a view over Reims. The
hotel rooms are tastefully done.

Le Florence (A/B), 43 Boulevard
Foch, tel: 26 47 12 70
Elegantly furnished old building; the
service has style, the food finesse.

Foch (B), 37 Boulevard Foch,

tel: 26 47 48 22
Very pleasant, reliable restaurant;
great care is taken with the cooking
and the reception is friendly.

Hotel de la Paix (B)
9 Rue Buirette, tel: 26 40 04 08
One of the better places in Reims
within walking distance of the
cathedral. Functional rooms and a
swimming pool.

Le Vigneron (B)
Place Paul-Jamot, tel: 26 47 00 71
With its old posters, vast selection of
regional wines and dishes, this place
is pure Champagne.

SILLERY, 51500

Le Relais de Sillery (B)
tel: 26 49 10 11
Congenial place to lunch, in a wine
commune.

TINQUEUX, 51430

L'Assiette Champenoise (A)
40 Avenue Paul-Vaillant-Couturier,
tel: 26 04 15 56
Restaurant formerly in Châlons-sur-
Vesle now in this sw suburb of Reims.
Great care is taken over the cuisine.
Also has rooms.

TOURS-SUR-MARNE, 51150   NE

La Touraine Champenoise (C)
tel: 26 58 91 93
Charming inn by a canal, with rooms
(B/C). Straightforward, simple meals.

VINAY 51200

La Briqueterie (A/B)
tel: 26 54 11 22
Just a few kms south of Epernay, this
is an ideal place to stay for the wine
region. Modern comfort, gardens and
peace and quiet. The cooking is
talented.

**MOURMELON-LE-GRAND,
51400**

Cheval Blanc Sept-Saulx (A/B)
tel: 26 03 90 27
Country inn by a stream just east of
the Châlons road. Comfortable rooms:
very good food.

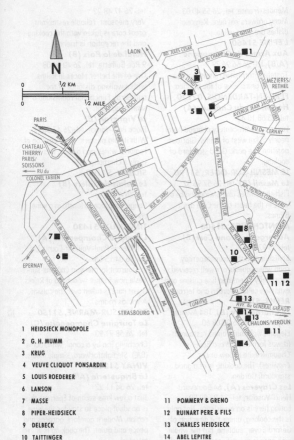

N

0   1/2 KM
0   1/2 MILE

LAON

PARIS

CHATEAU-
THIERRY/
PARIS/
SOISSONS
← RU du
COLONEL FABIEN

EPERNAY

STRASBOURG

RUE GOSSET
BD JULES CÉSAR
RUE du CHAMP de MARS
BD LUNDY
MÉZIÈRES/
RETHEL
AVENUE JEAN JAURÈS
RU De CERNAY
BD de la PAIX
RUE VOLTAIRE
BD St MARCEAUX
AVE HENRIES CLÉMENCEAU
RUE du PASTEUR
BD POMMERY
BD HENRI VASNIER
RUE COLBERT
TURMIRE
AVE du GÉNÉRAL GIRAUD
CHÂLONS/VERDUN
RUE St THIERRY
RUE ALBERT THOMAS
BD JOFFRE
BD FOCH
RUE JEANNE d'ARC
RUE LINGUET
BD PAUL DOUMER
CHAUSSÉE BOCQUAINE
RUE COLIN
RUE du JARD
RUE GAMBETTA
BD DIANCOURT

1   HEIDSIECK MONOPOLE
2   G. H. MUMM
3   KRUG
4   VEUVE CLIQUOT PONSARDIN
5   LOUIS ROEDERER
6   LANSON
7   MASSE
8   PIPER-HEIDSIECK
9   DELBECK
10 TAITTINGER
11 POMMERY & GRENO
12 RUINART PÈRE & FILS
13 CHARLES HEIDSIECK
14 ABEL LEPITRE

CHAMPAGNE TOWNS

REIMS

Cellars, churches and art are the triple attractions in Reims. The major champagne houses welcome visitors. The centre is dominated by Nôtre-Dame, one of the world's great cathedrals. It dates from the 13th and 14th centuries; the towers were completed in the 15th. All had to be restored, however, after the bombardment of World War I when the roof was entirely destroyed. The richly-decorated Gothic west front is of an exceptional quality and inside there is an impressive organ and brilliant stained-glass windows (some designed by Chagall). Nearly all the kings of France were crowned here. Beside the cathedral is the Palais de Tau containing a museum of sculpture (monumental works from the cathedral) and religious art. Also near the cathedral is one of France's richest art museums, the Musée St-Denis (tapestries, paintings by the

French masters, etc.). The 11th- and 12th-century basilica of St-Rémi looks austere from the outside, but grand within and is well worth a visit, as is the Musée St-Rémi beside it (ten tapestries of the life of St Rémi, archaeological finds). The history of Reims comes to life through engravings (including some Dürers), paintings, sculptures and furniture in the Musée Hôtel Le Vergeur (36 Place du Forum – where there are remains of the Roman forum). Mention should also be made of the chapel of Nôtre-Dame de la Paix, decorated by the painter Léonard Foujita (33 Rue Champ-de-Mars); the former Jesuit college (furniture, religious art, library, planetarium – 1 Place Museaux); the Porte Mars (Roman triumphal arch, just north of the centre); the Salle de la Reddition (where the German surrender was signed on 7 May 1945 – 12 Rue Franklin-Roosevelt); and the Musée de l'Automobile Française (84 Avenue Georges-Clemenceau).

EPERNAY

Underground Epernay, with its dozens of miles of wine cellars, is visited by many thousands of people every year. But above ground, too, this bustling town (population about 30,000 – less than one-sixth that of Reims) has a number of attractions. Foremost is the Musée Municipal, in the Avenue de Champagne, opposite Perrer-Jouët. It consists of three museums: the Musée de Vin de Champagne (implements, glasses, bottles, a diorama, etc.); the Musée des Beaux-Arts (fine arts); and the Musée de Préhistoire et d'Archléologie Régional. At the end of the same avenue the Champagne firm of Mercier has set up a museum for old wine presses – it has about 40 of them. Between the Avenue de Champagne and the river Marne are the cellars belonging to de Castellane, signposted by a quite remarkable water tower. This Tour de Castellane contains a wine museum with labels posters, etc., and can be visited.

1	MARNE & CHAMPAGNE	4	PERRIER-JOUËT	7	POL ROGER
2	ALFRED GRATIEN	5	BOIZEL	8	DE CASTELLANE
3	MOËT & CHANDON	6	DE VENOGE	9	MERCIER

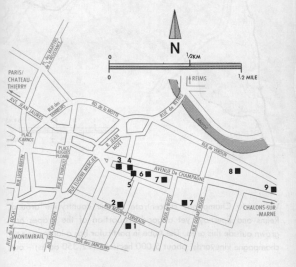

THE AUBE

APPELLATION CONTROLEE AREA

→ WINE ROUTE

— OTHER ROADS

---- COMMUNE BOUNDARY

Visitors to Champagne concentrate on the countryside around Reims and Epernay, yet a good proportion of the grapes are grown outside this area. The Aube in particular has a large area of champagne vineyards: about 5,000 hectares (12,350 acres) — out

of the total for Champagne of around 26,000 hectares (64,250 acres). The Aube vineyards lie southwest of Troyes, not far from the border with the Cote d'Or département, stretching between the towns of Bar-sur-Aube and Bar-sur-Seine. Although a large part of the grape harvest is processed by the Reims and Epernay houses, some of which own land here, there are also local cooperatives and individual growers who make and sell their own champagnes. With the recent growth in worldwide champagne sales the wines of the Aube have been in greater demand.

THE WINE ROUTE

There is a signposted *Route du Champagne* through the region – but the signposts are erratic and the route eccentric. The Wine Route described here joins the Aube and Seine, passes through the prettiest and most interesting places and provides a good insight into this reticent wine district. It can be used as a pleasant detour on the way s to Burgundy. Allow about half a day – more if possible.

Start from Bar-sur-Aube, a pleasant town on the N19, where there is a useful map in the main square showing the vineyards and the names and address of local growers, as well as shops, restaurants, cafés. This is the centre of the Aube

champagne business. Its most intriguing monument, a chapel on the bridge was sadly destroyed in the fighting of 1940. The chapel commemorated the incident in 1440 when the Bastard of Bourbon, who had rebelled against the Crown, was sewn up in a sack and thrown into the river on the orders of King Charles VII. The 12th- to 14th-century church of St-Pierre is surrounded by unusual wooden galleries. Just s of the town the Ste-Germaine hill offers a panoramic view and there is a chapel shaded by ancient trees. In summer wine can be tasted at a chalet on the N19 E of the town. Leave the town going sw across a bridge on the D4, which climbs steeply up the hill past vineyards onto an open, high plain.

Drive through Le Val Perdu, (ignore the *Route du Champagne* sign) and

continue on to Couvignon. Vineyards appear to the right and left, with the creamy limestone soil visible between the vines. Go straight on through Couvignon, bearing left a short while later onto the D44 which becomes the D4 towards Bligny, with vineyards spreading widely into the distance and a cooperative. Pass a picnic spot on the left and drive into the wine village of Bligny, continuing on the D4 through woods and past the Ch de Bossican then twisting up a wooded slope and down into Vitry.

Note the new vineyards being planted: it is expected that 2,000ha of new vineyards will be planted in the Aube before the end of the century. Continue through the wine village of Vitry along the D4 to Eguilly-sous-Bois. Leave the village going s on the D79 towards Essoyes, climbing up a hill with a series of S-bends and a fine view back over the vineyards. Turn sharp right at the first crossroads, passing a picturesque château and new vineyards on the road to Chacenay, a charming hill village. Leave on the D103 up the hill to the right of the church heading s ignposted Landreville) turning left at e first junction (signposted Loches) 1 ignoring the signposted route. ore also the D38 but turn right at : next junction to Essoyes on the 79. Crest the hill for a fine open view of wheat fields and sunflowers among the vineyards and woods.

After a left-hand turn you will see the roofs of Essoyes below. This is a pretty town, with a square beside a river and a *Maison de la Vigne et du Vin* in a converted and extended building. This is a wine museum and information centre (with a sculpture made from 300 bottles among the exhibits) and is open in the afternoons ?pm-6pm). The square has a town an with names of growers. You can o vist the graves of the painter re August Renoir, his wife and two children. Leave the town on :67 in the direction of Loches. .es has a *vente directe* champagne wer: Champagne d'Amyot. tinue on to Landreville, and turn .ght in the village by the butcher, up

a narrow street, right again and then left, joining the D104, which climbs over the hills to Ville-sur-Arce past lots of new vineyards.

Ville is a neat village with a lovely old church. In the town, turn left to visit the large local cooperative in its handsome 19th-century premises. To buy wine, look out for the sign in the main street, where Champagne Rémy Massin can also be visited. Cross the stream at the west end of the village, turning left on the D4 towards Merrey-sur-Arce. Fork left again to Merrey, then bear right in the village watching out for a sign marked *"vers route nationale"*. Turn left on the N71, turning right almost straight away to Polisot, with vineyards away on the right. Turn right at the church, and cross the Seine past the Hostellerie de la Seine. Continue up the main street, bear left and then left again for Polisy on the D36. This little town has a château by the river with a 16th-century enamelled tile floor. Turn right in Polisy to the three hamlets of Les Riceys on the D452.

First comes Ricey-Bas, with its champagne firms, medieval streets and Gothic and Renaissance church. An impressive avenue of plane trees, designed by Le Nôtre, leads up to the castle, the oldest parts of which date from 1088. Go over the bridge and turn right through Ricey-Haut, which runs into Ricey Haut-Rive. As in the other two Riceys, the church has been declared a historic monument. The three villages of Les Riceys make up the appellation noted for the rarest Aube wine, Rosé des Riceys. This dark, dry, still rosé with a distinctive aroma is made from Pinot Noir grapes and an average annual production of only 10,000-12,000 bottles. Leave Ricey-Bas by turning right in front of the church heading towards Gyé-sur-Seine. Climb through woods and over the hill to Gyé in the Seine valley, worth visiting for its 14th-century castle, a tree of liberty of 1792 and a partly 12th-century church.

You can either finish the Route by turning s on the N71, or return N up the same road to Bar-sur-Seine. This

little town between the cliffs and the river has half-timbered houses, the remains of a castle and the biggest wine cooperative of the district. There are several hotels and restaurants (see over), as well as the local headquarters of the CIVC, the champagne regulatory body.

If you are returning N, continue along the N71 to Troyes, the former capital of Champagne lies on the river Seine and the Haute-Seine canal. The old centre is resplendent with the cathedral of St-Pierre-et-St-Paul (Gothic, with a single tower which you can ascend); the extraordinarily beautiful basilica of St-Urbain (a Gothic masterpiece, with a statue of the Madonna with Grapes to the right of the choir); the 12th-century church of St-Martin, the town's oldest and many half-timbered houses. There are also various museums to visit, among them the Musée des Beaux-Arts (to the left of the cathedral, in a former monastery: fine arts, prehistory, natural history and a huge library); the Musée d'Art Moderne (to the right of the cathedral, with Braque, Derain, Dufy, La Fresnaye in the collection); the Hotel-Dieu-le-Comte with its dispensary; and the Musée Historique de Troyes et Champagne with its painting and sulpture. The Foire de Champagne takes place in Troyes in the second week of June.

LOCAL PRODUCERS

BAR-SUR-SEINE
Union Auboise des Producteurs de Vin de Champagne: Energetic group of cooperatives processing the larger part of the grape harvest from more than 700 growers. Léonce d'Albe, Abel Jeannin, Maurice Leroy and Paul de Richebourg are its brands.
RICEY-BAS, LES RICEYS
Horiot Père & Fils: Champagne and Rosé des Riceys.
RICEY-HAUT, LES RICEYS
Alexandre Bonnet: Modern equipment, a sizeable vineyard – 25ha (62 acres) – and an emphasis on quality put this estate among the

leaders in Aube. As well as various champagnes, Rosé des Riceys is also produced.
Morel Père & Fils: Exclusively Rosé des Riceys.

HOTELS AND RESTAURANTS

BAR-SUR AUBE, 10200
Le Commerce (B)
tel: 25 27 08 76
Good hotel in the heart of this little town. Good rooms and conservative cooking in restaurant (C).
BAR-SUR-SEINE, 10110
Barsequanais (C)
6 Avenue Général-Leclerc,
tel: 25 29 82 75
Simple, quietly situated hotel with restaurant.
POLISOT, 10110
Hôtellerie de la Seine (C)
tel: 25 38 54 41
Restaurant serving regional food and recommended by wine growers. Also a hotel (B).
TROYES, 10000
Grand Hotel (B)
4 Avenue Maréchal-Joffre,
tel: 25 79 90 90
A hundred rooms with modern comfort and four restaurants opposite the railway station.
La Valentino (B)
Cour de la Rencontre,
tel: 25 73 14 14
Enjoyable food in the centre of town with an emphasis on fish and interesting wines.

ALSACE

The Alsace vineyards are conveniently arranged for the visitor, strung out in a thin line along the foothills of the Vosges, sheltering in the lee of the hills and facing east across the open plain of the Rhine valley. A wine tour of the region should include Strasbourg, one of the major cities of France and also one of its most historic and cultured. The old city centre clustered around the 12th- and 15th-century cathedral, is worth a visit, as is the Petite France quarter with its old buildings and canals. The beautiful Orangerie park was designed by Le Nôtre in 1692.

Alsace wine is helpfully (and for France, unusually) labelled by grape variety. The second most important piece of information on a label is the name of the grower or merchant who bottles the wine and gives it identity. Until recently, geographical origin came a poor third in the hierarchy. This is changing as individual vineyards are identified as superior to the norm and officially granted the status Grand Cru. Thus the name of a site is more often seen on a label, and to identify these sites adds interest to a vineyard tour.

THE WINE ROUTE

Alsace is well organised for wine tourism. There is an official *Route du Vin* which dates from 1953 and is well signposted. Its basic length is about 120km, but it can be as long as 180km if you take all the optional diversions. Due to the extent of the vineyards only the heart of the area has been mapped on the following pages.

Start from Strasbourg, taking the N4 westwards towards the Vosges. The Route starts at Marlenheim. Pass through the village, turning off the N4 through Wangen onto the D142 to Westhoffen. The Route zigzags southwards through a string of

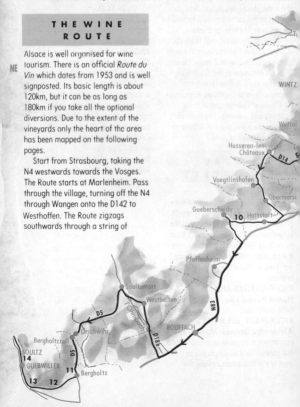

VINEYARDS

→ **WINE ROUTE**

—— **OTHER ROADS**

----- **COMMUNE BOUNDARY**

N

St-Hippolyte

STRASBOURG

Rorschwihr

4 RIBEAUVILLE   2

3   D1b   1

Bergheim

Riquewihr

D416

KAYSERSBERG

5

Kientzheim Mittelwihr

Bennwihr

Sigolsheim

Weiss

chwihr

morschwihr

N415

Ingersheim

cht

N83

Colmar

NE

0   1   2   3   4 KM

0   1   2 MILES

villages, following a collection of
minor roads. Village names are more
helpful here than road numbers: the
sequence is Traenheim, Bergbieten,
Dangolsheim, Soultz-les-Bains,
Avolsheim and Molsheim. The latter is
a town with a fine late medieval
guildhouse (the Metzig of 1525) and a
large 17th-century church.

Leave Molsheim on the D422,
turning off right on the D35 through
Rosheim and Boersch to Ottrott, then
take the D426 to Obernai, an
attractive old town with a signposted
wine walk through the nearby
vineyards. Continue s through
Bernardswiller and Heiligenstein to
Barr, a wine town with a maze of
narrow streets and an attractive
17th-century town hall. Leave Barr on
the D425, continuing on up a side-

valley to Andlau, returning down the
south side of the valley on the D253.
Join the D35 to pass through the
hamlets of Itterswiller, Nothalten,
Blienschwiller and Dambach-la-Ville.
The latter is the largest and most
important wine commune of the Bas-
Rhin département, with a lovely
historic centre with half-timbered
houses and a wine walk encircling the
town.

The *Route du Vin* follows the D35
southwards through Scherwiller,
Châtenois and Kintzheim to St-
Hippolyte. Join the D1b through
Rorschwihr and on past the
Kanzlerberg Grand Cru vineyard **1** (on
your right). The slope behind it (to the
west) is the Altenberg **2**. Drive on
along the D1b to Ribeauvillé, noting
the steep Geisberg **3** and Kirchberg **4**
Grands Crus vineyards. Ribeauvillé
boasts three castles and France's
oldest wine cooperative (1895).

Riquewihr, the next village, is the
tourist heart of Alsace and an
important wine commune. The entire
village has been declared a historic
monument and is especially popular
with visitors at weekends. It is one big
museum with marvellous old
buildings, 90% of them dating from before
1640. Shops, tasting rooms, wine
firms and restaurants all contribute
to the atmosphere. Riquewihr also
has a museum of history (in the
Dolder, a half-timbered tower of

1291); and the museum in the Tour des Voleurs (prison and torture chamber). It is the headquarters of noted wine firms (see Local Producers) such as Hugel, Dopff & Irion and Dopff "au Moulin".

Leave Riquewihr by the road you entered on, turning right immediately outside the town to pass the Sporen vineyard, through Mittelwihr and Bennwihr and around the foot of a curving hill of vineyards to Sigolsheim, Kientzheim and Kaysersberg. Note the steep, south-facing Schlossberg Grand Cru **5**. Stop in Kaysersberg to admire the superb old houses and perhaps to climb the steep path to the castle ruins for the fine view.

Leave Kaysersberg on the N415, turning off into Ingersheim, then up a minor road to Niedermorschwihr, with its Sommerberg Grand Cru **6** on the right. Drive s over the hill to Turckheim, passing the Brand Grand Cru **7** on the left just above the village. Cross the valley to pass through Wintzenheim, with the Hengst Grand Cru **8** on the right. Then divert up a spur road to Wettolsheim, returning to the main N83 for a short spell before turning right again to Eguisheim, a pretty wine village grouped around a (restored) château. Leave on the D14, up the hill and through the Eichberg Grand Cru **9** vineyard to Husseren-les-Châteaux. A minor road (the D1) takes you to Obermorschwihr and down to Hattstatt. Visit Gueberschwihr up the hill, with the Hatschbourg vineyard **10** to the right. Return to the N83 which you follow s past Pfaffenheim until you fork right to Rouffach. The town has several grand buildings grouped around the large Place de la République.

Although the Route skirts Colmar, it is worth making a detour to visit this sizeable ancient town with its many places of interest. Among them are the Maison Pfister (1537, with a remarkable wooden gallery); the Maison des Têtes (1608); the Ancienne Douane (1480); and the cathedral of St-Martin (13th to 14th century). One of the most visited

museums in France, the Musée Unterlinden is found here with a magnificent collection devoted to medieval art and wine.

From Rouffach take the N83, soon turning right onto a minor road which skirts the vineyards before reaching Westhalten and Soultzmatt. On the outskirts of this village turn left to Orschwihr and Bergholtz and on past the Spiegel **11**, Saering **12** and Kesler **13** Grands Crus into Guebwiller. This town is dominated by the Schlumberger estate which has 135ha of vineyards on the surrounding steep hillsides. The Kitterlé Grand Cru **14** above the town has an unusual southwest exposure.

From Guebwiller follow the D430 to Soultz and there turn off onto the D5 through Wuenheim, Wattwiller and Uffholtz to Cernay. Turn w onto the D35 to Thann, the end of the Route.

LOCAL PRODUCERS

AMMERSCHWIHR
Jérôme Geschickt & Fils: Gewürztraminer Kaefferkopf, etc.
Kuehn: Quality firm with old, vaulted cellars, a modest estate of its own and very attractive wines (including the Riesling Kaefferkopf). The Ingersheim cooperative has a majority shareholding.
André & Pierre Mercklé: Riesling and Gewurztraminer Kaetterkopt, also wood-aged Pinot Noir.
Sick-Dreyer: Family estate producing excellent wines, including Riesling, Gewürztraminer Kaefferkopf and Tokay.
ANDLAU
André Gresser: Estate run by the energetic Rémy Gresser, with notable wines including various Grands Crus.
Marc Kreydenweiss/Domaine Fernand Gresser: Exceptionally expert and committed winemaker whose labels artistically convey the style of each vintage. His wife runs a wine shop and négociant concern under the name Cathérine Lacoste.
BERGHEIM:
Marcel Deiss: Property run on modern lines (Gewürztraminer and

Riesling Altenberg).

BERGHOLTZ

Jean-Pierre Dirler: Very natural wines of high quality: Sylvaner Vieilles Vignes, Rieslings from the Kessler and the Spiegel.

DAHLENHEIM

Jean-Pierre Bechtold

DAMBACH-LA-VILLE

Louis Hauller: Klevner and Gewürztraminer of class.

EGUISHEIM

Léon Beyer: Committed family firm with an excellent name. Big supplier to high-class restaurants. Usually firm wines for drinking with meals. Among them powerful Gewürztraminers and Tokays.

Bruno Sorg: Rieslings Pfersigberg and Florimont and Gewürztraminer.

EPFIG

Domaine Ostertag: Delicious Sylvaner, Riesling Munchberg and Tokay.

GUEBWILLER

Domaines Viticoles

Schlumberger: With 135ha the largest estate in Alsace. Most of the vines gown on terraces up the steep hillsides. They give rich, rounded, powerful wines. The best comes from the Grands Crus Kitterlé, Kessler and Saering.

HELIGENSTEIN

Jean Heywang: Klevner de Heiligenstein, Gewürztraminer Kirchberg.

HUNAWIHR

Fréderic Mallo & Fils

HUSSEREN-LES-CHATEAUX

Kuentz-Bas: One of the very best firms in the region, with splendid balanced wines. The Rieslings in particular are brilliant. This family concern sells the vintage from its own vineyards as "Cuvée personnelle".

KAYSERSBERG

Domaine Dietrich

Faller Frères/Domaine

Weinbach: From not quite 25ha Mme. Colette Faller produces a range of exceptional (and expensive) wines.

KIENTZHEIM

Blanck/Domaine des Comtes de Lupfen: The Blanck family takes great care to match grape variety and soil type. The wines are then vinified

with the greatest possible care. Sound, very pure and utterly reliable wines are the result. Buying for its négociant firm of Blanck Frères is also very expert.

MITTELBERGHEIM

A. Seltz & Fils: The "Réserve" and "Réserve Particulière" from this house are excellent. Sylvaner Zotzenberg is a speciality.

MITTELWIHR

Patrick Schaller: Property with very successful Crémant d'Alsace, Muscat and Riesling.

NIEDERMORSCHWIHR

Albert Boxler & Fils: The best estate hereabouts.

Marcel Mullenbach: Muscat, Riesling, Tokay, Gewürztraminer.

RIBEAUVILLE

André Kientzler: Family holding where with great integrity and expertise a range of excellent wines is made.

Jean Sipp: Large estate of 20ha. Its wines are of very good quality across the whole range.

Louis Sipp: Négociant of average standard.

F.E. Trimbach: This house has acquired fame in Europe, and even more particularly in America, with its fragrant and characteristic wines. Some come from its own land (e.g. the Riesling Clos Ste-Hune and the Gewürztraminer Cuvée des Seigneurs de Ribeaupierre).

RIQUEWIHR

Hugel & Fils: Family firm famous for its ubiquitous exports. Among the leaders in Alsace. The Hugels have been involved in wine since 1639. The house style is one of full, supple, rounded wines, less dry than those from many other firms. A two-year stock is held. The simplest qualities comprise branded wines; at the top come wines from late-picked grapes (with the designations Vendange Tardive and Sélection des Grains Nobles).

RODERN

Charles Koehly & Fils: Christian Koehly makes fine, stylish wines from, e.g. the Grand Cru Gloeckelberg.

RORSCHWIHR

Rolly-Gassmann: Aromatic,

NE

sometimes almost luxurious wines (Auxerrois, Tokay, Gewürztraminer).
SOULTZMATT
Paul Kubler
TURCKHEIM
Cave Coopérative: The wines from this cooperative can match those from the best estates. The wood-aged Pinot Noir Cuvée à l'Ancienne is extraordinary and white wines are produced from the Grands Crus Brand, Hengst and Sommerberg and elsewhere.
Armand Hurst
Charles Schleret: Year after year this grower manages to surprise with his excellent wines.
WINTZENHEIM
Josmeyer & Fils: Under the direction of Jean Meyer the wines from this firm have continued to improve. Delicious Pinot Blanc, Pinot Auxerrois, Riesling Hengst, Gewürztraminer Hengst.
Domaine Zind-Humbrecht: Léonard Humbrecht believes firmly in the individuality of soil and microclimate, and bases his choice of grape variety on them. He was also the first in Alsace to adopt low-temperature fermentation. His efforts to replant the Rangen vineyard in Thann are worthy of praise. The Zind-Humbrecht wines have a good deal of personality and often require time.

WINE INFORMATION

COLMAR
Maison du Vin d'Alsace
12 Avenue de la Foire aux Vins

HOTELS AND RESTAURANTS

AMMERSCHWIHR, 68770
l'Abre Vert (B), tel: 89 47 12 23
Village hotel with country cooking.
Demi-pension in season.
Aux Armes de France (A/B)
tel: 89 47 10 12
This restaurant enjoys great fame. A splendid wine list, classic cuisine with modern elements. Rooms.
BERGHEIM, 68750

Winstub du Sommelier (B)
tel: 89 73 69 99
Carefully prepared regional dishes, expertly chosen wines.
COLMAR, 68000
Au Fer Rouge (B), tel: 89 41 37 24
A happy contrast: very modern cooking in a fine old building.
St-Martin (B)
38 Grand Rue, tel: 89 24 11 51
Decent hotel with 23 rooms in the centre of town.
Schillinger (B)
16 Rue Stanislas, tel: 89 41 43 17
Excellent stylish place. Ask to be shown the wine cellar.
Terminus-Bristol (A/B)
7 Place de la Gare, tel: 89 41 10 10
The best hotel in town and the restaurant *Le Rendez-vous de la Chasse* (B) is also excellent.
EGUISHEIM, 68420
Le Caveau d'Eguisheim
tel: 89 41 08 89
Strictly regional cuisine.
GUEBERSCHWIHR, 68420
Relais du Vignoble (B)
tel: 89 49 22 22
Comparatively new hotel, quietly placed about 10km s of Colmar. The owner makes wine. Restaurant (C)
GUEMAR, 68970
La Clairèrie (A), tel: 89 71 80 80
Country house surrounded by trees, halfway between Guémar and Illhaeusern. The place for visitors to *Auberge de l'Ill* to stay overnight.
ILLHAEUSERN, 68150
Auberge de l'Ill (A)
tel: 89 71 83 23
Run by the Haeberlin family, this restaurant's cooking, wine list and interior can only be described in superlatives.
ITTERSWILLER, 67140
Arnold (A/B), tel: 88 85 50 58
Pleasant hotel with a modern annexe. Also convivial, genuine Alsatian restaurant (B).
KAYSERSBERG, 68240
A l'Arbre Vert (C), tel: 89 47 11 51
Always busy restaurant with a relaxed atmosphere. Also a hotel across the square (B).
KIENTZHEIM, 68240
l'Abbaye d'Alspach (B)
tel: 89 47 16 00

Fairly small but neat rooms in an old building. Simple restaurant (C).
KINTZHEIM, 67600
Auberge St-Martin (B)
tel: 88 82 04 78
The speciality is *tarte flambée*.
MARLENHEIM, 67520
Hostellerie du Cerf (A)
tel: 88 87 73 73
Family restaurant that grows some of its own produce. Good hotel rooms (A) around the charming inner courtyard.
RIBEAUVILLE, 68150
Zum Pfifferhüs (C)
tel: 89 73 62 28
Authentic *winstub* with an excellent reputation.
Le Clos St-Vincent (B)
tel: 89 73 67 65
Hotel restaurant in glorious situation high above the town among the vineyards.
Hostellerie des Seigneurs de Ribeaupierre (A/B)
tel: 89 73 70 31
Handsomely furnished small hotel in a 17th-century building.
Hotel la Tour (C), tel: 89 73 72 73
Functional hotel owned by a wine-growing family. Restaurant.
Hotel des Vosges (A/B)
tel: 89 73 61 39
Stylish cooking in the restaurant. Ample wine list.
Auberge du Schoenenbourg (B)
tel: 89 47 92 29
Just outside the town walls and serving honest and inventive dishes.
RIQUEWIHR, 68340
Le Riquewihr (B), tel: 89 47 83 13
Hotel set among the vineyards. Rustic-style furnishings.
ROUFFACH, 68250
Château d'Isenbourg (A)
tel: 89 49 63 53
Luxurious rooms in this château hotel high above the town.
STRASBOURG, 67000
l'Ami Schutz (C), 1 Ponts-Couverts, tel: 88 32 76 98

Regional cuisine and ambience in the middle of the Petite France quarter.
Buerehiesel (A), 4 Parc de l'Orangerie, tel: 88 61 62 24
Old farmhouse in a beautiful city park. Cooking with finesse.
Le Crocodile (A/B), 10 Rue de l'Outre, tel: 88 32 13 02
The city's best restaurant: dishes that are culinary masterpieces.
Hotel Hannong (C), 15 Rue du 22-Novembre, tel: 88 32 16 22
Central, businesslike and around the corner (9 Rue Hannong) the hotel runs *Le Wyn' Bar*
Maison Kammerzell (B), 16 Place de la Cathédrale, tel: 88 32 42 14
Splendid building, an historic monument. Cooking both traditional and contemporary. There is also a *winstub* and an oyster bar in winter.
Monopole-Métropole (A/B), 16 Rue Kuhn, tel: 88 32 11 94
Congenial, friendly place to stay with an Alsace atmosphere.
Hotel des Rohan (A/B), 17 Rue Maroquin, tel: 88 32 85 11
Near the cathedral. Very small but comfortable rooms.
Chez Yvonne/S'Burjerstuewel (B), 10 Rue du Sanglier, tel: 88 32 84 15
Famous *winstub* where regional dishes are served with a smile. Dinner only.
TURCKHEIM, 68230
Hotel des Vosges (C)
tel: 89 27 02 37
Good regional cuisine. Rooms.
WETTOLSHEIM, 68920
Auberge du Père Floranc (B)
tel: 89 80 79 14
Austere restaurant on the outside but you can eat well here.
WINTZENHEIM, 68000
Au Bon Coin (C), tel: 89 27 48 04
Honest simplicity.
ZELLENBERG, 68340
Au Riesling (B), tel: 89 47 85 85
Modern hotel on the Wine Route. Restaurant also recommended.

NE

CHABLIS

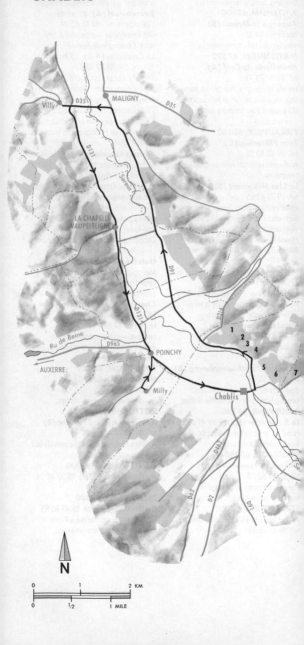

Chablis is the most northerly and isolated of the five wine districts of Burgundy, and is in fact closer to the champagne vineyards of the Aube than to the Côte d'Or.

Winegrowing in Chablis has traditionally been a risky business because of frost, but modern techniques have meant that more land has been planted with vines and that the average yield per hectare has increased. There are four categories of Chablis: at the top is Chablis Grand Cru, from one of the seven vineyards on slopes directly north and east of the village, on the opposite bank of the little river Serein. Premier Cru wines are usually slightly less rounded in character and come from some 580 hectares (1,430 acres) divided among 30 vineyards. However, most of the land produces straightforward Chablis which can vary greatly in quality, whereas the simplest wine of the district from outlying vineyards is called Petit Chablis.

VINEYARDS

→ WINE ROUTE

— OTHER ROADS

- - - COMMUNE BOUNDARY

THE WINE ROUTE

Chablis does not have a signposted Wine Route as such, but this short journey provides a good introduction to the district. The wine area is centered on the town of Chablis and the vineyards are on the slopes of the hills which rise up from the valley of the river Serein.

Start in the town of Chablis, which is easily reached on the D965 from the A6 autoroute junction some 12km to the west.

From the town centre, cross the only bridge in an easterly direction. Turn left on the D91, heading N along the east bank of the river Serein. The Grands Crus, the best vineyards of the district, rise up on the right as you leave the last of the buildings behind. These seven vineyards have between them only 100ha. Their position on a relatively steep slope facing s is unrivalled in Chablis, and their wines are intense, solid and demanding bottle age. From north to south the *crus* are: Bougros **1**; Les Preuses **2**; Vaudésir **3**; Grenouilles **4**; Valmur **5**; Les Clos **6** and Blanchots **7**. The road runs across a flat plain for a little while, coming closer to the Grand Cru slope. Where the road bends left, by Ch des Grenouilles, you pass immediately beside the Vaudésir

vineyard on your right.

Continue along the D91, past the junction with the D216 which marks the end of the Grands Crus territory. The open land for the next 2km is devoid of vines: in this cool northern area the vineyards are only sited on slopes, away from the moist, cold river-valley flat-lands. The best sites are slopes which face s or sw and this is the exposure of the Grands Crus. The long stretch of vineyard that next appears on the right-hand side is the Premier Cru of Fourchaume. Further on, note the vineyards higher up the slope, which do not have Premier Cru status and produce mere appellation Chablis. In the village of Maligny the old château, which dates from the 12th and 18th centuries, is being restored by a leading wine grower, Jean Durup. The château, with its vast ancient kitchens, interesting collections and riverside park can be visited.

Leave Maligny on the D35 to the west crossing the river and pausing in Villy, a winegrowing hamlet whose church has a fine Romanesque porch. Return to the junction with the D131 and drive s to La Chapelle-Vaupelteigne, a classic wine village with a few dozen growers. The church here dates from the 12th and 13th centuries. The vineyards above the village are on east-facing slopes and do not benefit from the shelter and good exposure that those on the other side of the valley enjoy. Consequently the wine is only Appellation Contrôlée Chablis.

Driving on s along the D131 note the valley to the west, where south-facing vineyards have Premier Cru status. The road to the autoroute and Auxerre runs along the southern edge of the valley. In the next village, Poinchy, take the side road to Milly. In the medieval chapel here you can see a fine sculpted figure of a kneeling monk. The local château is also medieval. Milly lies at the foot of the southeast-facing Premier Cru vineyard Côte de Léchet. Walk up through the vineyard for a splendid view over Chablis. As you pause in the vineyard, here or elsewhere, note the

Chablis soil: limestone-rich Kimmeridgean clay. The Wine Route ends by returning to Poinchy and there turning right on the D965 for Chablis.

Chablis itself suffered at the time of the invasion of 1940, leaving only a few old streets with their wine-grower's houses intact. The Rue des Moulins has houses with cellars in some cases dating from the 13th century. Several merchants and large growers have their headquarters in Chablis and many can be visited (see Local Producers).

The other vineyards of the département of Yonne are less well-known and smaller than Chablis. However, their wines are of interest and the villages attractive. Red wines are made in Irancy and Coulanges-la-Vineuse, two charming small places reached from Chablis as follows. Take the D91 southwards, turning right in some 8km onto the D956, then after 13km turn left onto the D38. First you reach Irancy, then, after crossing the Yonne valley, Coulanges.

Just N of Irancy is St-Bris-le-Vineux, where an isolated vineyard of Sauvignon Blanc produces interesting white wine which has something in common with both Chablis and Sancerrre. The neighbouring hamlet of Chitry, sited on the D62 between St-Bris and Chablis, makes similar wine.

LOCAL PRODUCERS

CHABLIS
Cave Coopérative La Chablisienne
René & Vincent Dauvissat
Jean-Paul Droin
Domaine Laroche: Premises worth a visit.
Domaine de la Maladière (William Fèvre)
Domaine des Malantes (formerly Domaine Rottiers-Clotilde)
Louis Michel & Fils
Domaine Pinson
François & Jean-Marie Raveneau

A. Régnard & Fils (merchant)
Simonnet-Febvre (merchants)
Domaine de Vauroux
Domaine Robert Vocoret & Ses
Fils
BEINES
Alain Geoffroy
LA CHAPELLE-VAUPELTEIGNE
GAEC de Chantemerle
FLEYS
André Philippon
FONTENAY
GAEC du Colombier
LIGNORELLES
Roland Lavantureux
MALIGNY
Domaine de l'Eglantière (Jean
Durup)
MILLY
Domaine des Courtis
Domaine Jean Defaix
POINCHY
Gérard Tremblay (Domaine
des Iles)
PREHY
Domaine des Maronniers
Domaine Ste-Claire

WINE INFORMATION

CHABLIS
La Maison du Vigne et du Vin

HOTELS AND RESTAURANTS

CHABLIS, 89800
Hostellerie des Clos (B)
tel: 86 42 10 63
Comfortable and modern hotel with
restaurant. Proprietor, Michel

Vignaud serves creative food of high
quality. Restaurant (A).
l'Etoile (B), tel: 86 42 10 50
A country hotel lacking character and
offering limited comfort. Cooking is
correct. Interesting wine list.
Au Vrai Chablis (C)
tel: 86 42 11 13
Simple and usually busy restaurant on
the market square.
LIGNY-LE-CHATEL, 89144
Auberge du Bief (B)
tel: 86 47 43 42
About 10km from Chablis. Good
cooking and a friendly atmosphere.
Very popular with the locals.
Le Relais St-Vincent (B)
tel: 86 47 53 38
About 10km from Chablis. Charming
small hotel in 17th-century residence.
ST-BRIS-LE-VINEUX, 89350
Le St-Bris (C), tel: 86 53 84 56
You can enjoy a good-value menu and
local wines either inside or out (on the
terrace) at this restaurant about 18km
from Chablis.
TONNERRE, 89700
l'Abbaye St-Michel (A)
tel: 86 55 05 99
Very luxurious hotel and restaurant
with a medieval interior and a view
over a river valley and meticulous
cuisine.
Hotel du Centre (C)
tel: 86 55 10 56
Almost opposite the Ancien Hôpital.
VAUX, 89290
La Petite Auberge (B)
tel: 86 53 80 08
Talented Parisien chef at this rustic
inn beside the Yonne. About 25km
from Chablis.

THE COTE D'OR

The heart of Burgundy is the Côte d'Or, a long, irregular hillside that starts just south of Dijon and ends 50 kilometres (31 miles) to the southwest of Santenay. The wine villages and their vineyards lie along the N74 that links Dijon with Chagny. There are very few large consolidated vineyards belonging to a single owner in Burgundy and the growers here mostly cultivate a number of small plots scattered over various ancient fields. The result is that most winegrowers make small amounts of a range of diverse wines and shippers play an important part in buying and marketing wines. The enormous variation in the wine produced by a single vineyard means that in the Côte d'Or it is at least as important to know the reputation of a winemaker as well as the classification of the vineyard.

The Côte d'Or itself is divided into two. The southern part is called the Côte de Beaune and the northern the Côte de Nuits. All the great white wines of the Côte d'Or are produced in the Côte de Beaune, whereas the emphasis is on red wines in the Côte de Nuits.

WINE AUCTIONS

The world's greatest charity auction is held annually in Beaune, at which wines from the vineyards of the Hospices de Beaune come under the hammer. Over the centuries the charitable hospital has been donated plots in fine Côte d'Or vineyards. With the world's press looking on, burgundies, still young and in the cask, are sold at extremely high prices, the proceeds going to run the large modern hospital that lurks behind the medieval building. The auction takes place on the third Sunday in November and is the climax of three days of festival, Les Trois Glorieuses. Wine tastings and banquets are organized on the preceding Saturday and Beaune is decorated with flowers. On the following Monday Meursault celebrates its Paulée, in the Ch de Meursault. This is a big lunch party to which every grower takes bottles from his own cellar. Nuits-St-Georges also has an auction, at the Hospices de Nuits, held on Palm Sunday. On this day and on the Saturday before, hundreds of Côte d'Or wines can be tasted in the local *salle des fêtes*.

HOTELS AND RESTAURANTS

ALOXE-CORTON, 21420
Hotel Clarion (A)
tel: 80 26 46 70
Small hotel with a good reputation. Rooms are furnished in styles from the 1930s to 1950s. Chassagne marble in the bathrooms and lounge.
AUXEY-DURESSES, 21190
La Cremaillière (B)
tel: 80 21 22 60
Rather formal restaurant but cooking is good.
BOUILLAND, 21420
Hostellerie du Vieux Moulin (A/B), tel: 80 21 51 16
Hotel restaurant with some charm. Attractive lower-priced set menus. Large and rather expensive wine list.
CHOREY-LES-BEAUNE, 21200
Le Bareuzai (B), Route de Dijon, tel: 80 22 02 90
Notable restaurant with acceptable prices.
Ermitage de Corton (A), Route de Dijon, tel: 80 22 05 28
Excellent restaurant in a luxurious hotel north of Beaune on the N74.
FIXIN, 21200
Chez Jeannette (C)
tel: 80 52 45 49

Rustic decor and traditional cuisine, plus a simple hotel.

FLAGEY-ECHEZEAUX, 21640
Balvay (C), tel: 80 62 88 10
Very popular with local winegrowers because of its well prepared regional dishes.

GEVREY-CHAMBERTIN, 21220
Hotel Les Grands Crus (B)
tel: 80 34 34 15
Comfortable hotel built in 1976 in a quiet position near the local château. Stylish rooms and a garden.

Les Millésimes (B)
tel: 80 51 84 24
Family restaurant with a friendly welcome. The dining room is a vaulted cellar. Long wine list.

Rôtisserie du Chambertin (A)
tel: 80 34 33 20
Restaurant in a luxuriously converted 18th-century cellar.

LEVERNOIS, 21200
Hostellerie du Châteloy (A)
tel: 80 24 75 58
Relatively new (1988), stylish hotel with a splendid park, excellent restaurant and impressive cellar.

Hotel du Parc (B), tel: 80 22 22 51
A few kms from Beaune, east of the autoroute. Rooms at the front are quiet.

MARSANNAY-LA-COTE, 21160
Les Gourmets (B)
tel: 80 52 16 32
Reliable cooking at this atmospheric restaurant. Good value set menus during the week.

MAREY-LES-FUSSEY, 21700
Maison des Hautes-Côtes (C)
tel: 80 62 91 29
Restaurant southwest of Nuits on the D115. Wines from the Hautes-Côtes are served with regional dishes.

MEURSAULT, 21190
Hotel du Chevreuil (B)
tel: 80 21 23 25
Hotel with average but enjoyable cooking.

Le Relais de la Diligence (C)
tel: 80 21 21 32
Good traditional cooking at this

restaurant that is not in the village itself but some distance east of the route nationale.

NUITS-ST-GEORGES, 21700
Hostellerie La Gentilhommière (B), tel: 80 61 12 06
A spacious old building in a peaceful setting west of Nuits, on the road to Meuilley. Good food is served in a traditionally furnished kitchen.

PULIGNY-MONTRACHET, 21190
Le Montrachet (B)
tel: 80 21 30 06
This restaurant is worth a detour. Excellent cooking and choice selection of local and regional wines.

ST-GERVAIS-EN-VALLIERE, 71350
Le Moulin d'Hauterive (B)
tel: 85 91 55 56
The cooking is recommended at this small hotel (A) southeast of Beaune (outside the wine district). *Demi-pension* obligatory in season.

SAVIGNY-LES-BEAUNE, 21420
l'Ouvrée (B), tel: 80 21 51 52
A pleasant place to sleep and eat. *Demi-pension* only in season.

TERNANT, 21200
La Ferme de Rolle (C)
Hameau de Rolle, tel: 80 61 40 10
Restaurant in an old farmhouse on the D35 beyond Villars-Fontaine. Regional cuisine and interesting cheeseboard.

VOLNAY, 21190
Auberge des Vignes (C)
tel: 80 22 24 48
The chef produces good-value set menus at this rustic restaurant. Estate names appear on the wine list.

VOSNE-ROMANEE, 21700
Le Toute Petite Auberge (C)
tel: 80 61 02 03
Small restaurant on the N74 with a loyal clientele.

VOUGEOT, 21640
Les Gastronomes (B)
tel: 80 62 85 10
Regional cooking and fine wine list.

SANTENAY

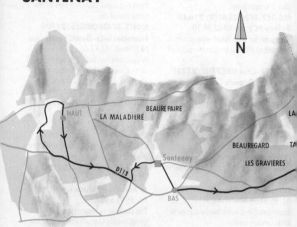

Santenay is the southernmost village of the Côte d'Or and is the first stage of the Côte de Beaune wine tour given on the following pages. Compared with most of the wine-producing communes of the Côte d'Or which are only simple, rustic villages, Santenay might almost be described as fashionable. The village is known not only for its wine but also for its waters: medicinal springs were discovered here in Roman times and they are still being exploited. Under an idiosyncratic French law, casinos are only allowed in spas and the casino here employs 40 people, which is by far the largest single business concern in Santenay.

THE WINE ROUTE

Santenay's vineyards face s rather more than those of the rest of the Côte d'Or, giving good exposure, but the underlying geology here is very complex. Soils vary considerably from vineyard to vineyard so that different styles of wines emerge. It is claimed that the best vineyards in Santenay are located to the east of the church tower – in other words, those situated between Santenay and Chassagne-Montrachet. It is here that most of the Premiers Crus are found. Good Santenay has a fine, deep colour, a lively bouquet and a strong taste. It is certainly not a light wine to be drunk

young, but the good vintages will develop very well if left to age. In the western part of the area a slightly lighter, flatter wine is usually produced.

Santenay lies w of Chagny, which is on the N74 highway that runs down from Dijon and Beaune. To reach Santenay from Chagny take the D974 through Remigny, which has vineyards entitled to use the Santenay appellation. Pass through the village on the D113, drive past the casino (on the left) then take a right turn to Santenay Haut, the upper half of the village. The solitary Premier Cru at the western end of the commune, Les Fourneaux, is a field away on the left. In Santenay Haut turn right, following

VINEYARDS

→ WINE ROUTE

—— OTHER ROADS

– – – DEPARTEMENT BOUNDARY

–·–·– COMMUNE BOUNDARY

CHASSAGNE-
MONTRACHET

LES CLOS

D113a

REMIGNY

0   ½   1 KM

0   ½ MILE

the road around a right turn to descend to the D113. Turn left along the road to return to Santenay Bas, the larger portion of the village. This is where the wine is made and home for the most of the commune labourers and their families. There are two châteaux belonging to growers here. Philippe le Hardi (the Bold) stayed in the château which bears his name and has been restored by its owner M. Pidault. The second château is Ch du Passe-Temps. The upper and lower sections of the village are divided by a km band of vineyards with the Premiers Crus of La Maladière and Beaurepaire on the slope to the left.

Turn left off the D113 to enter the top end of Santenay Bas, turning right to pass down the main street and rejoin the road, where you turn left onto the D113a to Chassagne. The road runs below a succession of Premiers Crus: Passetemps, Les Gravières (with Beauregard above it) then Clos de Tavannes (with La Comme above it). Les Gravières with its heavy, stony soil is the best-known, while Clos de Tavannes has a name for solid, reserved wines. La Comme, further up the slope, has lighter soil and corresponding wine. At a sharp left-hand bend in the road the appellation boundary is reached and the next right-hand bend takes

you into Chassagne-Montrachet. The D113a continues through a clutch of Chassagne Premiers Crus, now on both sides of the road. Les Grand and Les Petits Clos are on the uphill, left side, followed by Les Fairendes and en Cailleret. Note on the left the increasingly looming presence of the wooded Grand Montagne. This land formation, with the flat-topped wooded hill crowning a slope of vines, will become increasingly familiar as you drive along the Côte d'Or.

The D113a runs into Chassagne-Montrachet and the Burgundy Wine Route travelling north through the Côte d'Or continues on the following pages.

LOCAL PRODUCERS

SANTENAY

Adrien Belland

Domaine Joseph Belland

Château de la Charrière

Michel Clair

Domaine Fleurot-Larose: Based at the Château du Passe-Temps with its impressive cellars. Correct wines.

Jessiaume Père & Fils

Domaine Lequin-Roussot

Prosper Maufoux: An important wine firm.

Jean Moreau

Mestre Père & Fils: Has good Premiers Crus from Santenay.

Château Philippe-le-Hardi

Domaine Prieur-Brunet

FROM CHASSAGNE TO VOLNAY

The route nationale N6, which until the advent of the autoroute was the greatest highway in France, curves through a gap in the Côte d'Or hills between the two villages which take the suffix Montrachet. Chassagne, to the south of the highway, and Puligny, to the north, share the 8 hectares (20 acres) Montrachet Grand Cru vineyard. This walled vineyard is the source of what is beyond debate the finest white burgundy, a majestic wine with a splendid concentration in both its rich perfume and its noble, complex taste. The Chassagne-Montrachet district produces considerable more red than white wine, however the red wines do not in general reach the exalted level of the whites.

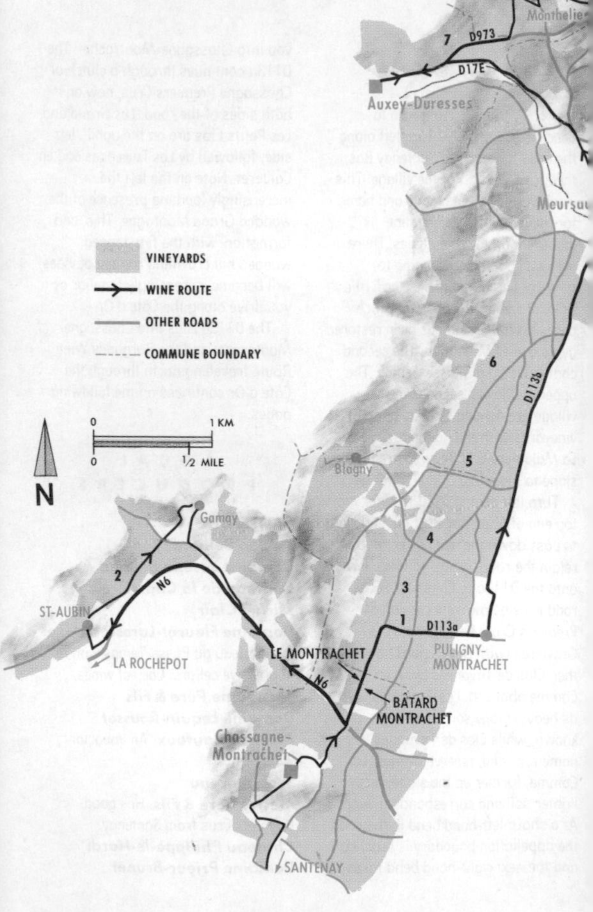

VINEYARDS

→ **WINE ROUTE**

OTHER ROADS

----- **COMMUNE BOUNDARY**

0 _____ 1 KM

0 _____ 1/2 MILE

N

Monthelie

D973

D17E

Auxey-Duresses

Meursault

D113b

Blagny

Gamay

6

5

4

3

2

N6

1

D113a

ST-AUBIN

LA ROCHEPOT

LE MONTRACHET

PULIGNY-MONTRACHET

N6

BÂTARD MONTRACHET

Chassagne-Montrachet

SANTENAY

into Puligny, an unremarkable and even rather dull village.

If you wish you can make a diversion up the N6 into the hills behind Chassagne and Puligny to the village of St-Aubin and its associated hamlet of Gamay, set in a side valley which here pierces the Côte d'Or. Production here has greatly increased and the vineyard area expanded as demand for white burgundy has grown in the 1980s. The wines are not the finest, but can be good value. The best-known vineyard is the Premier Cru Les Frionnes **2**, which produces both red and white wines. Return along a minor road through Gamay, the village that gave the Beaujolais grape its name.

Leave Puligny on the D113a towards Meursault. The straight road passes through the commune's vineyards, with the Clavaillon **3** and Les Perrières **4** Premiers Crus further up the slope on the left. At the boundary with Meursault, the Charmes Premiers Crus **5** come right down to the edge of the road. Meursault has no Grands Crus but does have some very renowned Premiers Crus. The best-known of these are: Charmes, Genevrières **6** and Perrières. They are situated here at the southern end of the large commune, on the boundary with Puligny-Montrachet.

Continue on into the large, straggling village of Meursault, noting the large number of signs advertising the premises of various growers and merchants. This is one of the most energetic of the Côte d'Or wine communities and it is relatively easy to buy direct from the growers. Levels of commercialism vary. At some cellars it is hard to taste without making a commitment to buy. Whereas in the cellars of the Ch de Meursault there is permanent wine-tasting arranged by the owners, Patriarche Père & Fils. Most Meursault is white and what little red wine is made is often sold under the Volnay name.

Leave Meursault on the D17E towards Auxey-Duresses, a village in a subsidiary valley with a row of

THE WINE ROUTE

The second stage of the Côte d'Or wine tour begins in the modest village of Chassagne-Montrachet set on a slope below a solid block of Premiers Crus vineyards. Above these is the steep-edged cliff of La Grande Montagne. Red wines are more in evidence than whites in Chassagne, although the whites have more distinction.

Leave Chassagne on the D113a, crossing the N6 and following signs for Puligny. Almost immediately the Grand Cru Le Montrachet vineyard appears up the slope to the left. To the right is the almost equally famous Bâtard-Montrachet Grand Cru. About halfway along the wall surrounding Montrachet you cross the boundary into Puligny. At the sharp right corner, the Montrachet vineyards come to an end, to be succeeded on the left by the noted Premier Cru Les Pucelles **1**. Follow the road downhill

Premiers Crus, the best-known of which is Les Duresses **7**. The red wines are mainly sold as Côte de Beaune-Villages and far more is produced than of the better quality white wine. The red wines come from the west- and southwest-facing vineyards adjoining Volnay, while the whites predominantly come from the other side of the valley, closer to Meursault. Further on still, behind the Côte d'Or and reached by a narrow winding road from Auxey-Duresses, is the hamlet of St-Romain, where attractive red and white burgundies are made.

From Auxey-Duresses take the D17e back down the valley, branching left on the D973 and then left again on a minor road to Monthelie, a little red-wine village built on a hill. Monthelie borders on Auxey-Duresses, Meursault and Volnay and the wines produced here most resemble those from Volnay. The best vineyards are the Premiers Crus Les Champs Fulliot **8** and Sur La Velle **9**, both of which border on Volnay. At the other end of the commune, Monthelie can claim part of the Premier Cru Les Duresses, which it shares with Auxey. White Monthelie is rare.

Leave the village on a minor road heading E, rejoining the D973 and following the signs for Volnay and Pommard. The boundary of Volnay is soon reached and the road runs along the middle of a slope with the best Premiers Crus on either side. The Clos des Chênes **10** is on the left, Cailleret **11** on the right. Volnay wines have a long history and were favoured centuries ago by French royalty. At their best they are elegant, soft and perfectly balanced. Turn left by a cemetery, passing the château (once royal property) to reach the heart of the village. There are several growers based here (see over) and a restored 14th-century church.

COTE DE BEAUNE PRODUCERS

Producers are listed under the village in which they are based. Most own land in more than one commune.

ALOXE-CORTON
Domaine Daniel Senard
Domaine Michel Voarick
AUXEY-DURESSES
Henri Latour
Leroy: Fine expensive burgundies mainly of mature vintages.
Michel Prunier
BEAUNE
Domaine Besançenot-Mathouillet
Albert Bichot: Very large wine-exporting firm with numerous brand names. The best burgundies are those from the Domaine du Clos Frantin (Vosne-Romanée) and the Domaine Long-Depaquit (Chablis).
Bouchard Père & Fils: Very conscientious firm with more than 80ha of its own vineyards. Harmonious wines full of character. Headquarters in the Ch de Beaune in the town ramparts – a fascinating visit.
Domaine Cauvard Père & Fils
Joseph Drouhin: Stylish, subtle burgundies with backbone. The firm's own estate covers some 60ha, about 36ha in Chablis.
Domaine des Hospices de Beaune: The wines from this charitable estate are auctioned on the third Sunday in November.
Louis Latour: Excellent firm with about 43ha of vineyard.
Patriarche Père & Fils: Firm that puts the emphasis on volume – but also with some particularly fine wines, such as that from the Ch de Meursault. Their splendid cellars stay hospitably open.
Domaine des Pierres Blanches
Domaine des Terregelesses
CHASSAGNE-MONTRACHET
Domaine Bachelet-Ramonet Père & Fils
Blain-Gagnard
Georges Déléger
Jean-Noël Gagnard
Gagnard-Delagrange
Bernard Morey
Jean-Marc Morey
Marc Morey
Michel Niellon
Domaine Ramonet: Magnificent white Grands Crus and Premiers Crus, as well as some delightful reds.

CHOREY-LES-BEAUNE
Tollot-Beaut & Fils: Harmonious wines with finesse from Corton and neighbouring vineyards.
LADOIX-SERRIGNY
Prince Florent de Mérode
MEURSAULT
Robert Ampeau & Fils: About 15 different whites plus red wines of exquisite quality.
Raymond Ballot-Millot Père & Fils: Includes Veuve Ch Dancer-Lochardet and Ballot & Dancer.
Pierre Boillot
A. Buisson-Battault
Jean-François Coche-Dury
Domaine des Comtes Lafon
Henri Germain
Maison Jean Germain: Wine merchants, specializing in white wine.
François Jobard
Domaine Latour-Giraud
Château de Meursault: The showpiece of the village, worth a visit for its cellars as well as its wines.
Michelot-Buisson: Four other Michelot names are also used.
Raymond Millot & Fils
Patrick Millot-Battault
Domaine René Monnier
Domaine Jean Monnier & Fils
Pierre Morey
Pitoiset-Urena
Domaine Jacques Prieur
Domaine Rougeot
Domaine Guy Roulot
MONTHELIE
Xavier Bouzerand
Eric de Suremain: Of the Château de Monthelie.
PERNAND-VERGELESSES
Domaine Bonneau du Martray: A top producer of Corton and Corton-Charlemagne.
Domaine P. Dubreuil-Fontaine Père & Fils: Famous property with fragrant wines.
Domaine Rapet Père & Fils
POMMARD
Comte Armand

Domaine Billard-Gonnet
Domaine de Madame Bernard de Courcel
Domaine Michel Gaunoux
Domaine Lejeune
Domaine Parent
Château de Pommard: Very good and very expensive wines.
Pothier-Rieusset
PULIGNY-MONTRACHET
Louis Carillon & Fils
Domaine Jean Chartron
Domaine Henri Clerc & Fils
Domaine Leflaive: Reckoned by many the best white-wine estate of the Côte d'Or: stylish, sensual wines of the very highest standard.
Olivier Leflaive Frères: A négociant firm started in 1985.
Domaine Etienne Sauzet
ST-AUBIN
Domaine Roux Père & Fils
ST-ROMAIN
Domaine René Thévenin-Monthelie & Fils: Likeable, pure white and red wines.
SAVIGNY-LES-BEAUNE
Simon Bize & Fils: Pleasant wines with good bouquet.
Capron-Manieux
Domaine Chandon de Briailles: The little 18th-century château with its garden and statuary is a historic monument. Charming, quite concentrated wines.
Domaine Antonin Guyon: Wine estate of nearly 50ha that produces subtle, carefully-nurtured burgundies.
VOLNAY
Domaine Marquis d'Angerville: Almost satiny Volnays of the highest quality.
Domaine Henri Boillot: Substantial red and white wines. Almost 20 different bottlings.
Domaine Michel Lafarge
Domaine de la Pousse d'Or: A beautifully-situated manor house and garden. Premiers Crus of the top level with grace, here and in Santenay.

E

BEAUNE

Beaune is the wine capital of Burgundy, and in many ways the wine centre of France itself. Nowhere else has such a concentration of cellars and a gathering of historical and cultural wealth. A day can easily be spent wandering the narrow streets of the town centre – cars are of little use inside the ring road that circles the old town wall. Beaune is at the heart of a broad tract of vineyards that starts in the south at Pommard, sweeps across the hill above the town and continues up to the pronounced hill of Corton, whose vineyards are the northernmost of the Côte de Nuits.

THE WINE ROUTE

The Route begins in Pommard (continuing on from the Wine Route for Chassagne to Volnay on page 108). The northern half of the commune has no Grands Crus, but there are many Premiers Crus. The best vineyard is Les Rugiens, situated on the slope behind the village, where the reddish soil contains iron. The Ch de Pommard with its walled 20ha vineyard proves that a Pommard of village level can be impressive. The

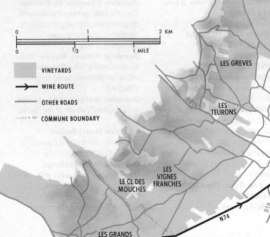

0   1   2 KM
0   ½   1 MILE

◼ VINEYARDS
→ WINE ROUTE
— OTHER ROADS
--- COMMUNE BOUNDARY

Savigny-les-Beau

LES GREVES

LES TEURONS

LE CL DES MOUCHES

LES VIGNES FRANCHES

BE

LES GRANDS EPENOTS

POMMARD

MEURSAULT

N74

D973

N

PERNAND-VERGELESSES

1

2

NUITS-ST-GEORGES

D18

D1154

Ladoix

DES HAUTES VERGELESSES

LES BASSES VERGELESSES

D1154

ALOXE CORTON

N74

le Rhoin Rau

N74

Bouchard Père & Fils by itself vinifies about half of all the wine produced by the commune. In addition to this very big firm, Beaune numbers dozens of négociants-éleveurs of varying degrees of importance (see town plan).

The slope above Beaune has several famous Premiers Crus such as Le Clos des Mouches and Les Vignes Franches, close to the Pommard border. On the Montagne de Beaune, a modest ridge NW of the town, you will find Les Grèves directly above the city and Les Teurons, virtually in the suburbs low down on the slope.

After pausing in Beaune, leave the city on the N74 towards Dijon, but turn left while still in the suburbs onto the D18 (becoming the D2) which leads to Savigny-lès-Beaune. The road passes through intermittent housing and factory development until it reaches the bridge over the A6: The autoroute closely follows the line of the appellation boundary and as you cross the bridge you enter Savigny-lès-Beaune. Here the vineyards again sweep down to the road: on the left are the Premiers Crus Les Peuillets and, further up the hill, Les Marconnets. Fork left on the D2 and follow the valley up to Savigny-lès-Beaune. The land to the right, which is entitled to the Savigny village appellation, is virtually flat and one of the few non-sloping vineyards in the Côte de Beaune-Village appellation. Savigny is chiefly a red-wine village with land on south-, east- and north-

château cellars can be visited and wine can also be bought here (prices are exorbitant). On the left of the D973, the road to Beaune, is Les Grands Epenots, one of several vineyards where the Hospices de Beaune own land. Where the D973 meets the N74 marks the boundary between Pommard and Beaune. Continue along the N74 into the city – an alternative is to turn left off the D973 and bypass Beaune on the minor roads to the west, joining the D18 near the A6 autoroute.

Wine production in Beaune is largely dominated by the shippers:

1 CHANSON PERE & FILS
2 BOUCHARD AINE & FILS
3 PATRIARCHE PERE & FILS
4 CAVES DE LA REINE
   PEDAUQUE
5 REMOISSENET PERE & FILS
6 BOUCHARD PERE & FILS
7 LOUIS LATOUR
8 LEON VIOLLAND
9 LOUIS JADOT
10 CALVET
11 LES CORDELIERS
12 JOSEPH DROUHIN
13 JAFFELIN

facing slopes. The soil here varies considerably and the wines do too, ranging from the firm and long-lived to the light and supple.

Cross the small stream and turn left into Savigny. Bear right by the château (which is also a museum), then right again to leave the village by the D2a. Continue down the valley with the stream to your right, forking left onto a minor road in the direction of Pernand-Vergelesses. A band of south-facing Premier Cru vineyards lines the road to the left. At a T-junction turn left onto the D18 and in a short while you pass the boundary between Santenay and Pernand-Vergelesses. The steeply-sloping vineyard on the left is the Premier Cru Hautes Vergelesses, with its twin Basses Vergelesses to the right of the road. Note the forest-

capped hill of Corton on the right, across a small valley. Continue on the D18 into the little village of Pernand-Vergelesses with its steep and winding streets. Drive through the village and leave by the road you entered by, turning left just outside the village onto the D115d.

The vineyards to the left, on the Corton slopes, are the Grand Cru Corton-Charlemagne **1**, source of a superb white burgundy. This portion of the Corton hill comes within the commune of Pernand-Vergelesses, but the road shortly crosses the boundary into Aloxe-Corton. This is the only commune in the Côte de Beaune where the Grand Cru vineyards outnumber Premier Cru and other vineyards combined. The village has a share in the Corton-Charlemagne Grand Cru as well as being the source of red

Corton. The rules are of great complexity as the Corton Grand Cru embraces a dozen different adjacent vineyards, the top one of which is called Le Corton **2**. The visitor can see for himself that some parts of the hill have reddish marl soil: here red wines do best. Other parts are whitish from the underlying limestone and here Chardonnay is planted for white wine.

Drive into the village of Aloxe-Corton, which has some wine-merchants' premises including Ch Corton Grancey. This château is owned by the firm of Louis Latour, the biggest landowner in the commune with 9ha of Corton-Charlemagne and 17ha of Corton. Continue through the village and out into the vineyards: here the land is only of Premier Cru or village status, the land being flatter and the soil less good. At the junction with the N74 turn left towards Nuits-St-Georges. The hamlet of Ladoix-Serrigny, on the route nationale, has a share in the Corton Grand Cru. The village name is sparingly used on labels, most local growers preferring to use the Côte de Beaune-Villages appellation.

Continue north along the N74 to reach the start of the Nuits-St-Georges Route.

HOTELS AND RESTAURANTS

BEAUNE, 21200
Alain Billard/Dame Tartine (B)
3 Rue Nicolas Rolin,
tel: 80 22 64 20
Small restaurant where cooking is creative but portions can be small.
Belle Epoque (A), 15 Faubourg Bretonnière, tel: 80 24 66 15
Comfortable rooms and apartments.
Hotel Bellevue (C), 5 Route de Seurre, tel: 80 22 26 85
Simple hotel with restaurant.

Au Bon Accueil (C), La Montagne, tel: 80 22 08 80
This is where the French eat on the Montagne de Beaune. Strictly regional cuisine at low prices.
Hostellerie de Bretonnière (B)
43 Faubourg Bretonnière,
tel: 80 22 15 77
A decent place to stay with a simple garden. Built around inner car park.
Central Hotel (B), 2 Rue Victor-Millot, tel: 80 24 77 24
Both dining rooms are always busy at this hotel restaurant.
La Closerie (B), 61 Route de Pommard, tel: 80 22 15 07
Functional comfort. Much used by wine merchants and their customers.
Hostellerie de l'Ecusson (B), Place Malmédy, tel: 80 22 83 08
Restaurant offering good value for money set menus. Lengthy wine list.
Hotel Henry II (A/B), 12-14 Faubourg de Nicolas, tel: 80 22 83 84
Comparatively new, but in a historic building. Attractive rooms.
Jacques Lainé (B), 10-12 Boulevard Foch, tel: 80 24 76 10
Restaurant in old dignified town house where great care is taken with the cuisine. Terrace.
Grand Café de Lyon (C), 36 Place Carnot, tel: 80 22 23 33
The place to meet in Beaune for a glass and a chat.
Rôtisserie de la Paix (B), 47 Faubourg Madeleine, tel: 80 22 33 33
Good-value set menus and very talented cooking at this restaurant tucked away in an alley.
Hotel de la Poste (A), Boulevard Clemenceau, tel: 80 22 08 11
Choose a room at the rear. You can eat very well in the elegant restaurant. Large wine list.
Le Relais de Saulx (B), 6 Rue Louis-Véry, tel: 80 22 01 35
Small restaurant that is renowned locally. Booking is essential.

NUITS-ST-GEORGES

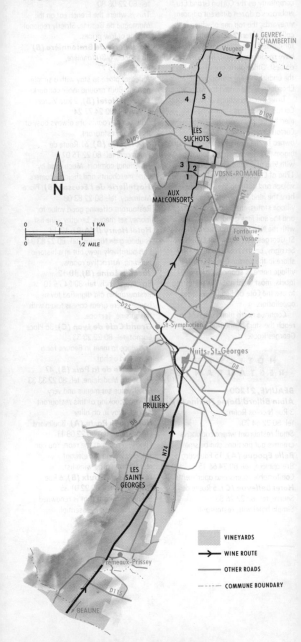

The northern part of the Côte d'Or, the Côte de Nuits, extends from several miles south of Nuits-St-Georges, beyond Corgolin to south of Dijon. The little town of Nuits-St-Georges is a major centre of the Burgundian wine business and a number of important négociants have their headquarters here. The wines of the Côte de Nuits are predominantly full-bodied and long-lasting red wines, almost all Pinot Noir. The most renowned of the wine villages in this part of the Burgundy countryside is Vosne-Romanée, with no fewer than five Grands Crus.

THE WINE ROUTE

The N74 from Beaune passes through Ladoix-Serrigny on the slopes of the Corton hill (see Beaune Wine Route on page 112). Then comes a relatively low-key passage in the Côte d'Or. The three villages between Ladoix and Nuits: Buisson (to the left of the road); Corgoloin (on the plain to the right) and Comblanchien all make wine, but their names are little known. In fact the giant quarries above Comblanchien (you can watch the marble-like stone being sawn from the hillside) are more important to the area than is viticulture. The Corgoloin vineyards straddle the border between the Côte de Beaune and the Côte de Nuits: a roadside sign in the walled Clos des Langres vineyard beside the N74 marks the boundary.

Prémeaux-Prissey, the next wine village N from Comblanchien, has vineyards which are entitled to the Nuits-St-Georges appellation. The vineyards on the steep slopes to the left of the road all have Premier Cru status and use Nuits-St-Georges rather than Prémeaux-Prissey on their labels. Just past the village, the appellation boundary is crossed. The first large vineyard in Nuits-St-Georges proper is Les St-Georges, the Premier Cru from which the commune takes the second part of its name.

Continue along the N74 towards the town of Nuits-St-Georges. The vineyards on your immediate left are "village" wines, those above them Premiers Crus, while to the right of the road the low-lying land is mere AC Bourgogne – a good illustration of the

hierarchy of Burgundy appellations. The Premier Cru Les Pruliers, one of the best-reputed in the commune, lies just above the outskirts of the town.

Nuits-St-Georges is an ancient town whose history has left it with sadly few monuments. In appearance, Nuits is more utilitarian than Beaune and there are hardly any beautiful buildings with a continuous stream of heavy traffic trundling noisily through the centre. However, it is a major centre of the Burgundian wine business and the base for many important wine firms. Visitors to the town can happily spend some time visiting the various cellars, and inspecting the Roman remains in the town museum.

Leave Nuits by the road to the northwest through the suburb of St-Symphorien. Turn right here past the church and drive between two cemeteries. Turn left along the D25 for a short distance, then bear right up a minor road, leaving some new houses on your left. Turn left at the crossroads to join the road which runs along the vineyard slope. All the vines to the left are Premier Cru, whereas to the right of the road is appellation Nuits-St-Georges land. The road climbs gently, then dips, then climbs again, and at this point you enter the commune of Vosne-Romanée. This undistinguished-looking village produces a number of Burgundy's most outstanding wines, within its boundaries there are five Grands Crus.

The first vineyard to your left as you come into the commune is the Premier Cru Aux Malconsorts. The road bends right, then left, and the

little vineyard to the left is the Grand Cru La Tâche **1**. Turn left at a T-junction and the strip of vineyard running up the hill on your left is La Grande Rue, a Premier Cru about to be promoted to the Grand Cru status enjoyed by its neighbours. To the right is Romanée-St-Vivant **2**, another Grand Cru. Turn right, and immediately on your left is the most famous Grand Cru, La Romanée-Conti **3**. This vineyard, which is distinguished by its gravelly red soil and a simple stone cross, is the exclusive property of the Domaine de la Romanée-Conti. The same estate also own all of the Grand Cru La Tâche, together with plots in Le Richebourg and La Romanée-St-Vivant. With less than 1ha situated above La Romanée-Conti, La Romanée Grand Cru is the smallest appellation in France. Next along the slope is the fifth Grand Cru, Le Richebourg. Turn right at the next junction, which is at the end of La Romanée-Conti. Drive down through the middle of Romanée-St-Vivant into Vosne-Romanée, a village with little but the fame of its vineyards to detain you. Turn left by the church, curving back up the hill (ignoring two roads branching to the right) driving beside the Grands Crus (to your left) and with the big Premier Cru, Les Suchots to the right of the road. Turn right through Les Suchots along the side of the hill.

The boundary with the commune and appellation of Flagey-Echézeaux marks the return of Grand Cru land. The village is well away on the flat land east of the route nationale, but its appellation extends in a narrow band up the slope, taking in the Grands Crus of Echézeaux **4** and Grand-Echézeaux **5**. These are the only wines to use the Flagey-Echézeaux name as the Premiers Crus and village wines use the Vosne-Romanée AOC.

Down the hill to the right you will see the commanding wall which surrounds the Clos de Vougeot vineyard **6**. The Ch de Vougeot, headquarters of the Confrérie des Chevaliers du Tastevin, was built in the 16th century by the monks who

originally farmed the 50ha Clos. Today, the château is a museum, with exhibits including enormous wooden wine presses. The land inside the Vougeot walls is now owned by 70 different growers who have on average less than a hectare each. The diversity of wines produced here make it essential that you select wine according to the reputation of the producer (as you probably should do with any burgundy). Just before you pass the château, the boundary of Vougeot is reached. Turn right just past the château and follow the road downhill beside the Clos and into the village of Vougeot. Turn left at the bottom of the hill, and continue into the next village of Chambolle-Musigny where you can pick up the second stage of the Côte de Nuits Wine Route.

COTES DE NUITS PRODUCERS

Producers are listed under the village in which they are based. Most own land in more than one commune.

NUITS-ST-GEORGES
Marcel Bocquenet
Jean Claude Boisset: One of the largest wine firms of Burgundy, partly due to its takeover of such houses as Lionel J. Bruck, Pierre Ponnelle, Thomas-Bassot and Charles Viénot; various brand names.
F. Chauvenet: Energetic firm with moderate wines and a 50% interest in Louis Max.
Jean Chauvenet: Faultless estate wines.
Robert Chevillon: One of the best domaines in Nuits-St-Georges, consistently good.
Dufouleur Père & Fils: Wines distributed by this firm include those of Domaine Guy Dufouleur and various Domaine Liger-Belair wines.
Joseph Faiveley: Has more than 100ha of its own vineyards and its generous, firmly structured wines are some of Burgundy's best; those from the Côte de Nuits and Mercurey in particular invite attention.
Geisweiler & Fils: Has 70ha in the Hautes-Côtes. British owned.
Domaine Henri Gouges: Fruity

red wines with finesse from Nuits, as well as a rare white, La Perrière.

Hospices de Nuits: Wines from this charity, a smaller version of the Beaune hospice, are auctioned two weeks before Easter.

Labouré-Roi: Fairly small firm with carefully-made red and white wines.

Alain Michelot: Specialist in Premiers Crus from Nuits.

Moillard: The average quality from this large firm has improved appreciably.

Henri Remoriquet

PREMEAUX-PRISSEY

Robert Dubois & Fils

Domaine Machard de Gramont: A considerable estate producing more than 20 different wines, mainly red.

Domaine Rion & Fils: Fruity, fragrant wines.

VOSNE-ROMANÉE

Robert Arnoux: The Grands Crus and Premiers Crus in particular are alluring.

Jacques Cacheux-Blée & Fils

Domaine René Engel

Forey Père & Fils

Domaine François Gerbet

Jean Grivot: Balanced wines with personality; the Clos de Vougeot and Echézeaux are sublime.

Jean Gros: In all categories, from Hautes-Côtes to Grand Cru, the wines here have allure.

Henri Jayer: Talented winemaker who matures most of his wines in new casks.

Jacqueline Jayer

Domaine Lamarche: La Grande Rue is the great speciality here.

Domaine Méo-Camuzet

Mongeard-Mugneret: Aristocratic burgundies rich in fruit.

Georges Mugneret: Also operates as A. Mugneret-Gibourg.

Gérard & René Mugneret: Sound red wines including Les Suchots.

Domaine Charles Noëllet: In 1988 taken over by Lalou Bize-Leroy of Domaine de la Romanée-Conti.

A. Pernin-Rossin

Domaine de la Romanée-Conti: The most famous of Burgundy's wine estates; almost 90% of the 30ha is made up of Grands Crus: La Romanée-Conti, La Tâche, Richebourg, Romanée St-Vivant, Grands Echézeaux, Echézeaux, Montrachet and Bâtard-Montrachet (an invitation to visit is very difficult to arrange although occasional groups are admitted).

VOUGEOT

Domaine Bertagna: Since being taken over by a German grower the quality has greatly improved.

Georges Clerget

Michel Clerget

Alain Hudelot-Noëllat: Mouth-filling and at the same time fine wines.

Domaine Jean Grivot: For nearly 2ha in the Clos (a relatively large holding) and makes fine, characterful wines.

Domaine Jean Gros: Vosne-Romanée grower with a small plot in the Clos.

Domaine Mongeard-Mugneret: One of half a dozen or so local concerns carrying the name Mugneret (see Vosne-Romanée). This one has some fine Vougeot land.

Domaine des Varoilles: See Gevrey-Chambertin. Vougeot which need time in bottle.

FROM CHAMBOLLE TO DIJON

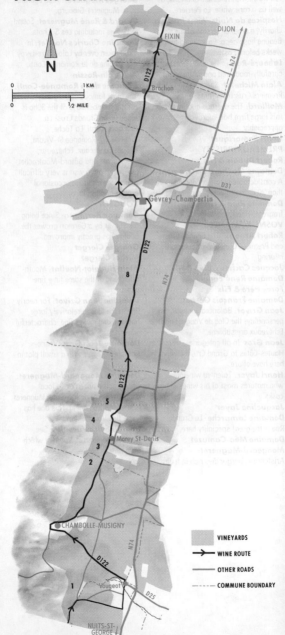

N

0 _____ 1 KM
0 _____ ½ MILE

DIJON

FIXIN

Brochon

Gevrey-Chambertin

8

7

6

5

4

Morey St-Denis

3

2

CHAMBOLLE-MUSIGNY

1

Vougeot

NUITS-ST-
GEORGE

	VINEYARDS
→	WINE ROUTE
—	OTHER ROADS
---	COMMUNE BOUNDARY

The northern half of the Côte de Nuits has a reputation for making the richest, firmest red burgundies, wines which need time in bottle to come to their best. Soil and slope here combine to produce a solid block of Grand Cru land running without a break from Chambolle-Musigny to Gevrey-Chambertin. The Côte ends in the north in the suburbs of Dijon, which as the ancient capital of Burgundy makes a fitting climax to a wine tour. The Wine Route runs along the middle of the vineyard slope, through several famous villages and beside even more notable vineyards.

THE WINE ROUTE

This Wine Route is a continuation of the Nuits St-George tour (see page 116) and begins in the next village, Chambolle-Musigny.

Leave Vougeot in the direction of Dijon, but turn left while still in the village, just after crossing the stream. Here too is the boundary between the Vougeot appellation and that of Chambolle-Musigny. The change of commune coincides with a change in the soil: clay gives way to limestone conferring a lighter note on the wines. Chambolle-Musigny is a peaceful, and hospitable village as underlined by an inscription that appears in several places: "Le bon vin et l'amour font passer d'heureux jours" (Good wine and love make for happiness).

Although the soil of the Côtes de Nuits consists mainly of clay, that of Chambolle is principally limestone. This very particular soil composition lowers the yield per hectare and gives the wine a distinct personality. Chambolle-Musigny has two Grands Crus, one at each end of the commune. Les Musigny **1**, just across the road from the top end of the Clos de Vougeot, makes a red wine of great finesse. Les Bonnes Mares **2** (a small part of which belongs to the neighbouring commune of Morey-St-Denis), N of the village, makes a more rounded wine which matures more slowly.

Follow the D122 up the hill from Vougeot to Chambolle-Musigny, passing the Charmes Premier Cru on the right, one of a band of Premiers Crus between Musigny and Bonnes Mares. The village, tucked into a wooded combe, is prettier and more attractive than its neighbours and worth a quiet stroll. Although there are no noteworthy monuments, two curiosities of interest to visitors are the very old linden tree, next to the church, and a small cave said to be the entrance to an underground passage leading to Morey-St-Denis (no one has actually dared to explore it). Chambolle is probably one of the very few villages in France without either a *tabac* or a proper restaurant. The 500 or so inhabitants are winegrowers and the commune has close ties with Schwabenheim in Germany and Sonoma in California.

Drive past the church and turn right at the top of the village, then right again to continue along the D122. The road runs below the Grand Cru Bonnes Mares before crossing into Morey St-Denis, with its continuous row of Grands Crus. The Grands Crus are: Clos de Tart **3**; immediately on your left and the exclusive property of the firm of Mommessin; Clos des Lambrays (promoted to Grand Cru in 1981) **4**; Clos St-Denis **5**; Clos de la Roche **6** from where the firmest wines come. The land below the village, which has Premier Cru status nearly as far down as the N74, produces some excellent wines. These wines are not well known and this is partly due to the small production, but wines of all categories can taste marvellous.

Stay on the D122 through Morey-St-Denis. Just past the village is the Clos St-Denis, from which the village takes its name. The soil here, and in the neighbouring Clos de la Roche, is

rich in lime, overlying the marlstone subsoil. Both contribute to the longevity and personality of the wines. Cross the appellation boundary into the large commune of Gevrey-Chambertin. From here until virtually the edge of the village you drive between Grand Crus to the left and right. Gevrey-Chambertin is principally famed for its Grand Cru Chambertin whose name has been synonymous with that of the village since 1847. The famous Chambertin **7** lies to the left of the road and the vineyard is advertised by brightly-coloured hoardings by the side of the road. The next vineyard is the Clos de Bèze **8**, which was actually planted before Chambertin, by the monks of the abbey of Bèze. The story of the Clos de Bèze can be traced back to the Dark Ages: the monks acquired the land in the year 630. Chambertin was also monastic land, and its wine enjoyed a high reputation which reached imperial heights when Napoleon let it be known that he drank nothing else. Sadly the Emperor was no connoisseur: he watered his Chambertin and drank it chilled.

Several other vineyards on the south side of Gevrey-Chambertin have a sort of subsidiary Grand Cru status: they are allowed to add Chambertin to their names. Thus Latricières, the second vineyard on your left, is allowed to label its wine Latricières-Chambertin.

Drive into the centre of the large and straggling village of Gevrey-Chambertin, then turn left and continue up the valley, bearing right in the outskirts to curve around and rejoin the D122. The hill to your left has Gevrey-Chambertin's Premiers Crus, of which Clos St-Jacques (straight ahead, immediately above the village) has the best reputation. This curving band of vineyards is extremely well placed, with a southerly slant to its exposure. The wine is almost up to Grand Cru standard.

The D122 now leads through a wide belt of village AOC vineyards into Brochon, whose southern vineyards are entitled to use the Gevrey-Chambertin name but the northern half has to be content with the Côte de Nuits-Villages appellation. This last section of the Côte used to be called the Côte de Dijon, but urban sprawl has reduced the vineyards to a shadow of their 18th-century reputation.

Next on the D122 comes Fixin, a charming village with a fine church. Its Premier Crus are up on the hill to the left: Clos du Chapitre and Clos de la Perrière, to the southwest of the village (on your left as you enter the village) are regarded as being the best. The D122 continues through Couchey, a name never seen on labels, to Marsannay-la-Côte. Both communes can make the Marsannay Pinot Noir rosé, and recently Marsannay has acquired appellation status for its red, white and rosé wines. Marsannay-la-Côte is the most northerly winegrowing commune in the Côte de Nuits, indeed in the entire Côte d'Or.

The suburbs of Dijon have now replaced the vineyards which used to extend to the outskirts of the old city. Today there are only a few growers in the Dijon area (e.g. the municipality itself) who make a small amount of wine. Dijon itself is the ancient capital of Burgundy and has many treasures worth a detour, not least the great octagonal kitchen which the Duke Phillip the Bold made the centrepiece of his palace in the high Middle Ages. This remarkable room can still be seen in the Musée des Beaux Arts which shelters a wonderful collection of Burgundian art.

The city marks the end of the Côte d'Or Wine Route.

COTES DE NUITS PRODUCERS

Producers are listed under the village in which they are based. Most own land in more than one commune.
CHAMBOLLE-MUSIGNY
Gaston Barthod-Noëllat
Domaine Berthau
Daniel Moine-Hudelot: Grands and Premiers Crus full of character.
Domaine Jacques-Frédéric

Mugnier: Important Le Musigny owner.

Domaine G. Roumier: Splendid property with memorable wines.

Hervé Roumier

Servelle-Tachot

Domaine Comte Georges de Vogüé: This estate has the largest holding in Musigny. The Domaine owns land in Connes-Mares, Les Amoureuses and Chambolle-Musigny. The Musigny Cuvée Vieilles Vignes represents the very peak of finesse.

FIXIN

Vincent & Denis Berthaut

Jacques Durand-Roblot

Philippe Joliet: Sole owner of the Clos de la Perrière.

Domaine Pierre Gelin: Sinewy Grands and Premiers Crus from Fixin and Gevrey-Chambertin.

GEVREY-CHAMBERTIN

Domaine Bachelet

Philippe Batacchi

Lucien Boillot & Fils

Pierre Bourée Fils: Small wine firm with durable burgundies.

Alain Burguet: Sound, balanced village wine.

Camus Père & Fils: An impressive range of Grands Crus.

Domaine Pierre Damoy: Biggest owner in Chambertin Clos de Bèze.

Domaine Drouhin-Laroze: Fragrant and vital wines.

Geantet-Pansiot

Laurent Goillot-Bernollin

Frédéric Humbert

Philippe Leclerc

Domaine René Leclerc

Henri Magnien: Small estate that never has enough wine to meet demand.

Domaine Maume

Naigeon-Chauveau: Reliable firm.

Domaine Pernot-Fourrier

Domaine Les Perrières

Domaine Henri Rebourseau

Philippe Rossignol

Joseph Roty: An extraordinarily painstaking wine grower.

Domaine Armand Rousseau Père & Fils: A great reputation – but has been variable in quality.

Domaine Tortochot

Louis Trapet Père & Fils

G. Vachet-Rousseau

Domaine des Varoilles: A rich palette of red wines, including the Clos des Varoilles, a local Premier Cru.

André Ziltener Père & Fils: Swiss wine firm.

MARSANNAY-LA-COTE

André Bart

René Bouvier: One of the few growers with land in Chenôve.

Domaine Philippe Charlopin-Parizot

Bruno Clair

Domaine Clair-Daü: An excellent estate that has belonged to the firm of Louis Jadot since 1986.

Cave Coopérative

Domaine Hugenot Père & Fils

MOREY-ST-DENIS

Domaine Pierre Amiot & Fils: Firm, elegant wines with softness and depth.

Domaine Arlaud Père & Fils: Classic red burgundies, among them four Grands Crus.

Bryczek Père & Fils: Expressive concentrated wines.

Domaine Dujac: Morey-St-Denis at its best from Grand Cru to village wine; the estate also has land in other villages.

Domaine Robert Groffier

Domaine des Lambrays: Owner of all except a quarter of a hectare of Clos des Lambrays (a Grand Cru since 1981).

Georges Lignier & Fils: A large, high-quality domaine.

Hubert Lignier

Michel Magnien: Charming, unfiltered wines.

Henri Pierre-Minot

Domaine Ponsot: Intense red wines and a rare white Morey-St-Denis.

Jean Raphet & Fils

Domaine Louis Rémy

Domaine B. Serveau & Fils

Clos de Tart: This whole Grand Cru is the property of the firm of Mommessin, based in the Mâconnais.

J. Taupenot-Merme: Distinguished red wines from an estate with modern equipment.

J. Truchot-Martin

E

THE CHALONNAIS

The Chalonnais is a southward continuation of the Côte d'Or, but the slope is less regular and the vineyards are more broken up. The district takes its name from the town of Chalon-sur-Saône to the east, which in antiquity was one of the great wine ports of the Empire. Today, however, the region is dominated by Mercurey, the biggest and best known of the wine parishes.

Some of the best-value burgundies can be found here, with reds made from Pinot Noir and whites from Chardonnay, the classic Côte d'Or varieties. Five communes here have their own appellations: Bouzeron, Rully, Mercurey, Givry and Montagny. In addition much wine is made under the regional appellations as straightforward red and white burgundy. The Chalonnais also produces a considerable amount of sparkling wine.

THE WINE ROUTE

The Wine Route begins in Chagny, a small town on the plain close to the southernmost Côte d'Or vineyards of Santenay. Leave Chagny on a minor road, the D219, to Bouzeron. This commune has its own appellation for Bourgogne Aligoté, the white-wine grape little regarded elsewhere in Burgundy but which here reaches such a high standard that since 1979 its sale with the name of the village added has been permitted.

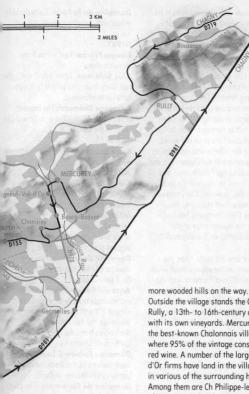

From Bouzeron follow the signs for Rully, crossing a wooded ridge to drop down into this expanding wine village that produces both red and white wines. Red Rully is often a fairly, light modest wine, whereas white Rully nearly always merits attention. The high acidity in Rully whites makes them ideal for sparkling wines and several sparkling wine firms have their premises in the village including the leading and influential firm of André Delorme. The relatively new Crémant de Bourgogne AOC has led to an expansion in the amount of sparkling wine made in the Chalonnais: the best is very good.

Leave Rully on the road to the south, signposted Mercurey, crossing

more wooded hills on the way. Outside the village stands the Ch de Rully, a 13th- to 16th-century castle with its own vineyards. Mercurey is the best-known Chalonnais village where 95% of the vintage consists of red wine. A number of the larger Côte d'Or firms have land in the village and in various of the surrounding hamlets. Among them are Ch Philippe-le-Hardi of Santenay with 75ha; Faiveley of Nuits-St-Georges with nearly 60ha; Bouchard Aîné of Beaune with more than 20ha; and Ch Genot-Boulanger of Meursault with almost 13ha.

Leave Mercurey on the D978 to the east, turning right to Chamirey and then onto the D155 through St-Martin-sous-Montaigu and St-Jean-de-Vaux to St-Denis-de-Vaux. From here head s to Jambles, then on around the slopes of Mont Avril to Cercot. Follow the side of the mountain through Mont Bogre, then turn right to cross the N80 to St-Désert and join the D69 to Bissey-sous-Crouchard. From here the D125 continues on to Buxy, a village with some 15th-century houses, a Romanesque church and some surviving town walls. This is another

well-known wine commune, as is its neighbour Montagny to the west, which gives its name to the wine of all this southern end of the Côte. Montagny, which is reached via the D977, is a white-wine commune. A curious rule allows all Montagny of 11.5% or stronger to be sold as Montagny Premier Cru.

Return to Buxy and take the D981 northwards, crossing the N80 then turning left to Poncey and on to Givry. The emphasis here is on red wines, and once the village was regarded as the wine centre of the Chalonnais, not least because the French court and nobility drank so much of the local wine. Today, however, Givry makes a lot less wine than Mercurey. From Givry the D981 continues heading N, skirting the eastern edge of the vineyard district on the way back to Chagny.

If your onward route takes you s, leave Givry on the eastern road which joins the N80 and connects with the A6 autoroute junction and Châlon-sur-Saône. Châlon is an interesting old town which began its wine career as a Roman river port: tens of thousands of amphorae have been found in the river during dredging works. From the Tour du Doyenne, on an island in the river Saône, you have a good view over the town centre.

LOCAL PRODUCERS

BOUZERON
Chanzy Fréres/Domaine de l'Hermitage: Wines that have often won awards, among them Aligoté from Bouzeron and white and red wines from Rully and Mercurey.
A. & P. de Villaine: Aromatic, softly fruity wines from a grower who is joint owner of the Domaine de la Romanée-Conti.

BUXY
Cave Coopérative: Well-equipped concern that has as its specialities Montagny Premier Cru, Bourgogne Aligoté and a Bourgogne Pinot Noir matured in small casks.

CHAGNY

Domaine de la Folie: Considerable estate with excellent white and red wines.

GIVRY
Lumpp Frères: Fine wines from expert makers.
Clos Salomon. After a bad spell, the red Givry from this property is again fully up to standard.
Domaine Thénard: The biggest property in Givry, also with Grand Cru plots in the Côte d'Or.

JAMBLES
René Bourgeon: Givry and regional wines.

JULLY-LES-BUXY
Pierre Bernollin: Splendid Montagny and Crémant de Bourgogne.

MERCUREY
Michel Juillot: Beautiful red and white Mercureys from one of the biggest private estates here.
Domaine de la Monette: Firmly structured red Mercurey; the owner is Paul Jean Granger.
Antonin Rodet: Dynamic négociant, increasingly quality-orientated, with almost 25ha of land; among the best wines are the red and white Mercureys from the firm's own Château de Chamirey.
Domaine Fabien & Louis Saier: Joint owners of the Domaine des Lambrays in Morey-St-Denis.
Domaine de Suremain: Complex, noble red Mercureys.

MONTAGNY
Château de la Saule: Montagny wines of the highest standard.

RULLY
Jean-Claude Brelière: Juicy white Rully Les Margotey and a steadily improving red.
Domaine de la Renarde: Superior sparkling wines that are excellent alternatives to champagne; the firm's own Domaine de la Renarde – almost 60ha – produces fairly light wines of which the white Rullys and the Aligoté from Bouzeron are the best.
Château de Rully: Farmed by Antonin Rodet.

ST-VALLERIN
Jean Vachet: Distinguished, quite generous Montagnys and good red burgundies.

WINE INFORMATION

CHALON-SUR-SAONE
Maison des Vins de la Côte
Chalonnaise
Promenade Ste-Marie

HOTELS AND RESTAURANTS

CHAGNY, 71150
Hostellerie du Château de Bellecroix (A)
tel: 85 87 13 86
Quietly situated hotel south of the town, just beside the N6. The rooms are comfortable and the cooking very good in the restaurant (B).
Lameloise (A), Place d'Armes, tel: 85 87 08 85
Excellent, famous and expensive restaurant where regional ingredients are prepared with great finesse. Splendid wine list. Also a hotel with stylish rooms.
Hotel de Paris (C)
6 Route de Beaune,
tel: 85 87 08 38
Quite decent cooking. Rooms also.
CHASSEY-LE-CAMP, 71150
Auberge du Camp Romain (B)
tel: 85 87 09 91
Hotel in a tranquil and beautiful setting with a fine view. Rooms simple but snug. Restaurant closed in winter.

DRACY-LE-FORT, 71640
Le Dracy (B), tel: 85 87 81 81
Functional, modern place to stay the night about halfway between Givry and Chalon-sur-Saône, with restaurant.
FONTAINES, 71150
Auberge des Fontaines (C)
tel: 85 43 07 35
Hotel and restaurant with local dishes and wines.
GIVRY, 71640
La Halle (C), tel: 85 44 32 45
Mainly Burgundian fare. Also a hotel.
MERCUREY, 71640
Les Tempiers de Mercure (B)
tel: 85 45 23 63
Restaurant in classical style over a wine-tasting room.
Hostellerie du Val d'Or (B)
tel: 85 47 13 70
Carefully run village inn with cuisine showing increasing finesse and an excellent wine list. Frogs' legs and duck are among the specialities. Also a hotel.
MESSEY-SUR-GROSNE, 71940
Auberge du Moulin de la Chapelle (B)
tel: 85 44 00 58
Large, worthwhile restaurant by a river. Also a simple hotel.
RULLY, 71150
Le Commerce (C), tel: 85 87 20 09
Traditional dishes and also a hotel.

THE MACONNAIS

VINEYARDS

→ WINE ROUTE

OTHER ROADS

—·— DEPARTEMENT BOUNDARY

—··— COMMUNE BOUNDARY

N

After the ordered logic of the Côte d'Or, with vineyard following vineyard along the slope, the jumbled countryside of the Mâconnais comes as a contrast. Here, woods and hills divide patches of vines and other crops. There is no clear pattern to the topography. The appellations at least are simpler than in the Côte d'Or: Mâcon is the basic appellation for the whole area, with Villages and Supérieur grades for a restricted zone and an extra degree of alcohol respectively. This wide zone produces much white (Chardonnay) and red (mostly Gamay) wine of quality from fair to very good. The best bottles come from the southern corner around Pouilly, where Pouilly-Fuissé, Pouilly-Vinzelles and St-Véran make more concentrated, sometimes very good, Chardonnays.

THE WINE ROUTE

The Wine Route given here carves a rough figure of eight across the heart of the Mâconnais, visiting first the northern part of the region then returning to Pouilly and its neighbours. It does not always coincide with the official *Route des Vins Mâconnais-Beaujolais*, which is 450km long and covers more than 60 villages. Information about the official Wine Route is supplied in the Cellier-Expo at Crèches-sur-Saône, a village just s of Mâcon on the N6.

Our Route begins on the N79 roughly halfway between Cluny and Mâcon. Both towns are worthy of a visit for their old houses, monuments and museums or for a meal at one of the restaurants recommended over. Cluny is famous for its abbey which until the building of St Peter's in Rome was Europe's largest. The industrial and commercial town of Mâcon was the birthplace of the writer, poet and politician, Alphonse Prat de Lamartine and there is a museum dedicated to him and a Circuit Lamartine that can be followed around the town.

From La Roche Vineuse (N79), take the D85 N through Verzé and Igé (which has a wine museum and tasting-room in a Romanesque chapel). Continue on the D85 over a low hill to Azé which has prehistoric caves and a museum that is open in the season. Join the D82 through Bassy and the old village of St-Gengoux to Bissy, where the D82

bends right to Lugny, one of the best known Villages communes. Turn left onto the D56, soon turning left again to pass through Collongette to Cruzille, which has a large museum devoted to some 30 agricultural and rural crafts. Leave the village on the road up the hill to the west, keeping right to join the D356 which takes you to Fissy. Turn left here, rejoining the D56 and following this road through undulating country to Chardonnay, the village that gave its name to the grape now grown worldwide. Next head E to Uchizy, turning right in this straggling village (with frescoes in the beautiful 12th-century church) to join the D210 to Thurisey and then onto the D106 to Viré which has a wine museum.

The D15 takes you to Le Buc and here turn left onto the D403b to Clessé, where the parish church is older still than that at Uchizy. From Clessé take a minor road w to St-Maurice, and then cross the stream and following another little road s through the Bois de la Roche, to Satonnay and on, joining the D434 at a T-junction, to Verzé. Next take a minor road w up a little valley, forking left to pass through Les Martins and left again to meet the D220 at a T-junction, where you turn left. At Berzé-la-Ville pass through the village (noting the Ch des Moines which has 12th-century wall paintings in its Romanesque chapel) to turn right along the N79 for the short distance before branching off left, passing under the TGV rail tracks, to Sologny.

Leave the village and pass through Milly-Lamartine on the D185, dropping down on the same road through Pierreclos, then crossing the valley and continuing on the D177 to Vergisson. Now you are in the Pouilly-Fuissé appellation area. The Roche de Vergisson (on the left) and the Roche de Solutré (ahead) rise sharply out of the lower wooded hills. Below the Solutré cliff the fossilized bones of thousands of horses have been found: they were driven over the edge by prehistoric hunters. There is also a small museum of prehistory in the village.

From Vergisson, leave the village on the westward (uphill) road, curving around the side of the hill to meet the D54 and on into Solutré, then along a minor road to Pouilly. Here turn right along the D172 through Fuissé, climbing sharply to turn left on the D31 through Leynes. Continue SE on the D31, turning left at La Roche to pass through Chaintré (15th-century château), Vinzelles and Loché. From Loché the D89 leads back through St-Léger and Prissé to the N79 and back via the D85 to Verzé.

LOCAL PRODUCERS

BRAY
Henri Lafarge: Sound, fairly generous red and white wines.
CHAINTRE
Cave Coopérative: The biggest producer of Pouilly-Fuissé.
Roger Duboeuf & Fils: White wines, including Pouilly-Fuissé and white Beaujolais with a lot of charm.
CHARNAY-LES-MACON
Trénel Fils: Firm, substantial wines from the Beaujolais and Mâconnais; also excellent fruit liqueurs. A family business.
DAVAYE
Henri-Lucius Gregoire: Successful St-Vérans and an enjoyable Crémant de Bourgogne.
FUISSE
Château de Beauregard: Jacques Burrier ferments and ages his Pouilly-Fuissés and St-Véran in casks.
Louis Curveux: Small-scale,

quality-conscious winegrower.
Château Fuissé: The unofficial "first growth" of Pouilly Fuissé. Large property with excellent white and red wines, including the glorious Pouilly-Fuissé Vieilles Vignes.
Gilles Noblet: Very good, subtly nuanced Pouilly-Fuissé.
LEVIGNY
Domaine Maciat-Poncet: Juicy, white wines made in the modern way. The village is near Charnay-lés-Mâcon.
LUGNY
Cave Coopérative: One of the region's best. Exemplary producer of excellent still and sparkling wines.
VINZELLES
Cave Coopérative: An active and well-regarded concern which produces almost 90% of all Pouilly-Vinzelles (and Pouilly-Loché).
VIRE
Domaine André Bonhomme: Pure, firm Mâcon-Viré.
Cave Coopérative: Soundly run cooperative.
Domaine de Roally: Limited production, high quality.

WINE INFORMATION

MACON
Maison Mâconnaise des Vins
Avenue de Lattre-de-Tassigny
Supplies information, sells wine and also has a simple restaurant.

HOTELS AND RESTAURANTS

BUSSIERES, 71960
Relais Lamartine (B)
tel: 85 36 64 71
Regional dishes, including roast chicken. Some rooms.
CLUNY, 71250
Hotel Le Moderne (B), le Pont de l'Etang, tel: 89 59 05 65
Food of quality that is also good value. Also a hotel. *Demi-pension* obligatory in summer.
LA CROIX-BLANCHE, 71960
Relais du Mâconnais (B)
tel: 85 36 60 72
Near Sologny. The cooking is creative

and light. Also a hotel.

FLEURVILLE, 71260

Château de Fleurville (B)
tel: 85 33 12 17
About 15km north of Mâcon. A pleasant place to stay – an old building surrounded by a park with a restaurant.

Le Fleurvil (C)
tel: 85 33 10 65
Traditional, straightforward cuisine. Also a cheap hotel.

IGE, 71960

Château d'Igé (A), tel 85 33 33 99
Small 13th-century castle hotel with excellent rooms and a medieval ambience. The cuisine tends to be classical. Restaurant (B).

LEYNES, 71570

Relais du Beaujolais-Mâconnais (C), tel: 85 35 11 29
Simple regional dishes. The restaurant faces the charming square at Leynes, one of the villages of St-Véran.

LUGNY, 71620

Caveau St-Pierre (C)
tel: 85 33 20 27
Wine-tasting room with a simple restaurant, open from March to the end of October. Panorama.

MACON, 71000

Mapotel Bellevue (B), 416 Quai Lamartine, tel: 85 38 05 07
Comfortable hotel with a good restaurant.

Auberge Bressane (B), 114 Rue du 28-Juin, tel: 85 38 07 42
A very famous place. Specialities include snails and eels.

Altea (B), 26 Rue de Coubertin, tel: 85 38 28 06
Modern comfort. There are always fresh-from-the-market dishes on the restaurant menu.

Hotel de Genève (B), 1 Rue Bigonnet, tel: 85 38 18 10
Not far from the station, a functional sort of hotel with a restaurant.

Maison Mâconnaise des Vins (C)
Avenue de Lattre-de-Tassigny, tel: 85 38 36 70
A simple, spacious restaurant. (See Wine Information.)

Au Rocher de Cancale (C)
393 Quai Jean-Jaurès, tel: 85 38 07 50
Good-value, carefully prepared set meals with usually at least one fish dish.

Terminus (B), 91 Rue Victor-Hugo, tel: 85 39 17 11
Quite tastefullly decorated rooms with soundproofed windows. With restaurant.

SOLUTRE, 71960

Relais de Solutré (B)
tel: 85 35 80 81
Quiet hotel near vineyards. Restaurant (C).

E

BEAUJOLAIS

VINEYARDS
WINE ROUTE
OTHER ROADS
DEPARTEMENT BOUNDARY
COMMUNE BOUNDARY

0 1 2 3 KM
0 2 MILES

JULIENAS
1

ST-A

Prazilly
Arlois Ro
St Ambu
Juliénas
La Mau
Emeringes

CHENAS
D68
les Deschamps
Chénas
D68
les Tho

2
MOULIN-A-VEN

FLEURIE
ROMANECH
THORIN

FLEURIE
D119
D68
la Pierre
Ch de

CHIROUBLES
CHIROUBLES
D68
la Plotre
Lancie
Rau de l'Ardie

VILLIE-MORGON

MORGON
D68
D18
Coccelles
en Beaujo
Bas Morgon

Pizay
l'Ardere R.
D18

BROUILLY
BEAUJEU
Cercie
D37

COTE DE
BROUILLY
St-Lager
Belleville

D43
D68E
VILLEFRANCHE-
SUR-SAONE
le Payebade
Bussières

3
Odenas
Charentay
D43
D43

N

More than half the Burgundian vineyards are in Beaujolais, which makes this district by far the largest of the region. It is also one of the most beautiful with the wooded, gently mountainous countryside making ideal territory for a wine tour. Add an approachable, enjoyable wine and a multitude of places to taste and buy and you have perfection, spoilt only occasionally by the influx of people from Lyon and Paris bent on the same pursuit. Avoid weekends and high summer, though, and you can have Beaujolais to yourself.

THE WINE ROUTE

The Wine Route below covers only the northern part of Beaujolais, the area where the best wines are made. These are the Crus – Morgon, Fleurie and so on (see map). Ordinary Beaujolais comes from a wide area, mostly to the south, while 38 communes, mostly in the northern half of the district are allowed to make Beaujolais Villages.

The Route begins s of Mâcon, close to the southern junction between the N6 and the A6 autoroute. Take the D31 from Crêches-sur-Saône, a village on the N6, driving w to Le Bourg Neuf. Turn left onto the D186, turning left again to join the D486 which takes you into the St-Amour Cru (part of which lies within the Mâconnais). Like all the Crus the wine has to contain at least 10.5% alcohol – 11% if the name of the vineyard appears on the label.

Continue on the D486, crossing into the Juliénas Cru and then reaching Juliénas itself. Juliénas has a fine château: the Ch de Juliénas 1 is in parts 14th-century and its cellars still house wine. Leave the village on the western road, joining the D26 which you follow until a small bridge. Turn sharp left here onto the D68, which runs through the Chénas Cru as far as the village of Chénas which marks the boundary of the Moulin-à-Vent Cru. Stay on the D68, passing the Ch de Poncié 2 and the boundary of the Fleurie Cru. The D68 marks the Route on through Fleurie.

Travel southwards on the D68

until a crossroads with the D119, where you turn right. This road leads w into the Chiroubles Cru. Climb over a small ridge, then keep right, following a small valley up to Le Pont then turning left back to Chiroubles village. Leave Chiroubles on the D86 which takes you to Villié-Morgon, the centre of the Morgon Cru. Rejoin the D68 and follow it s through the hamlet of Les Bruyères where Brouilly begins. Cross the Ardière valley (still on the D68) and note Mont Brouilly rising up ahead. The Côte de Brouilly Cru covers the slopes of the hill, while Brouilly takes in the flatter land to the north, east and south. On the edge of the village of Cercié turn right on the D37. Follow the road for 2km then turn left on the D43, passing through Le Poyebode to Odenas. The Ch de la Chaize 3, just w of here, is a historic monument with a fine old cuvier and immense cellars which can be visited. Turn sharp left on the D68e which runs e of Mont Brouilly and through St-Lager to Cercié.

Turn right at Cercié following the D37 to Belleville where you can join the N6 to travel N to Mâcon or s to Villefranche. The latter is the headquarters of the Union Interprofessionelle des Vins du Beaujolais (210 Boulevard Vermorel). Just N of Belleville, on the N6, there is the Maison des Beaujolais, which has a restaurant and an information bureau.

E

LOCAL PRODUCERS

The Crus

CERCIE (Appellation Brouilly and Côte de Brouilly)

Jean Lathuilière: Much-commended Brouilly Pisse Vieille.

Domaine Ruet: Substantial, fruity and bottled early.

LA CHAPELLE-DE-GUINCHAY (Partly in the Chénas appellation)

Château Bonnet: Pierre Perrachon's best wine is the Chénas.

Hubert Lapierre: Wines that win awards with nearly every vintage.

CHENAS (Appellation Chénas)

Domaine Champagnon

CHIROUBLES (Appellation Chiroubles)

Domaine Cheysson-les-Fargues: Typically elegant Chiroubles.

Alain Passot

Francis Tomatis & Fils: Supplies top French restaurants.

FLEURIE (Appellation Fleurie)

Domaine Bernard: Excellent Fleurie.

Michel Chignard

Domaine de la Grand Cour

JULIENAS (Appellation Juliénas)

Château de Juliénas: The biggest local producer.

Raymond & Michel Tête: The best of Juliénas; good even in lesser years.

ODENAS (Appellation Brouilly and Côte de Brouilly)

Bernard Champier: Strong, juicy Côte de Brouilly

Claudius Guérin: Top-class Côte de Brouilly.

Château Thivin: Wines from both Crus.

ROMANECHE-THORINS (Appellation Moulin-à-Vent)

Domaine de la Bruyère: Concentrated strong Moulin-à-Vent.

Georges Duboeuf: Successful company that despite its scale has managed to maintain a high average quality; many wines are marketed under their estate names.

Château des Jacques: Pure, fine wines, including a white Beaujolais (Grand Clos de Loyse).

Château du Moulin-à-Vent: Large estate where the wines are aged in small casks.

ST-AMOUR (Appellation St-Amour)

Domaine des Ducs: Absolutely sound, delicious wines.

Domaine de la Cave Lamartine: Charming St-Amours.

Georges Trichard: A property of repute.

ST-ETIENNE-LA-VARENNE (Appellation Brouilly):

G.F.A. de Combiaty: Small estate; Dominique Piron is the owner.

ST-LAGER (Appellation Brouilly and Côte de Brouilly)

l'Ecluse/Lucien & Robert Verger: Exquisite Côte de Brouilly.

VILLIE-MORGON (Appellation Morgon)

Domaine de la Chanaise: Aromatic wines, supple and not too heavy.

Georges Passot: The owner lives here but makes an excellent Chiroubles (and a Fleurie).

Domaine Savoye: Meaty Morgon Côte du Py, often with an aroma suggesting cherries.

WINE TASTINGS

Like every wine district, the Beaujolais has many cellars where visitors are welcome. What is exceptional is the large number of *caveaux de dégustation*, usually run by the wine-growers of the commune. The main villages are as follows:

BEAUJEU: Le Temple de Bacchus, variable opening times.

CHATILLON-D'AZERGUES: Le Pavillon des Pierres Dorées, open weekends.

CHENAS: Caveau du Cru Chénas, run by the cooperative. Daily mid-July to mid-October, weekends only at other times.

CHIROUBLES: The Terrasse de Chiroubles stands high above the village. Only open afternoons in the season.

COGNY: Le Caveau des Voûtes, variable opening times.

FLEURIE: Le Caveau de Dégustation

des Viticulteurs, open daily.
GLEIZE: Le Caveau de Gleizé, in the cooperative, open afternoons at weekends and public holidays.
JULIENAS: Le Cellier de la Vieille Eglise, open daily. The cooperative has a wine-tasting room in the 17th-century Ch du Bois de la Salle.
JULLIE: Caveau de Jullié, open Sundays.
LEYNES: Le Relais Beaujolais-Mâconnais, mainly a simple restaurant. Closed Wednesdays.
POMMIERS: La Terrasse des Beaujolais, at the Notre-Dame-de-Buissante chapel. Also a restaurant. Closed Wednesdays in winter.
REGNIE-DURETTE: Le Caveau des Deux-Clochers, weekend afternoons from Easter to mid-September.
ROMANECHE-THORINS: Le Caveau de l'Union des Viticulteurs du Moulin-à-Vent, by the N6, also serves simple dishes. Second tasting room, Le Caveau du Moulin-à-Vent, by the famous windmill; closed Tuesdays.
ST-AMOUR: Le Caveau du Cru St-Amour, variable opening times.
ST-JEAN-D'ARDIERES: La Maison des Beaujolais, on the N6, represents the whole district. Also a restaurant. Closed Wednesday evenings and Thursdays.
ST-JEAN-DES-VIGNES: Le Refuge des Pierres Dorées, open Sundays and public holidays.
ST-LAGER: Le Cuvage des Brouilly, open daily except Tuesday morning.
ST-VERAND: Le Caveau de l'Union des Viticulteurs de St-Vérand, variable opening times.
SALLES-ARBUISSONAS: La Tassée du Chapitre is open weekends and public holidays, May to October.
VAUX-EN-BEAUJOLAIS: Le Caveau de Clochemerle, variable opening times.
VILLIE-MORGON: Le Caveau des Morgon, variable opening times.

WINE INFORMATION

VILLEFRANCHE-SUR-SAONE
Union Interprofessionelle des Vins du Beaujolais
210 Boulevard Vermorel

HOTELS AND RESTAURANTS

BELLEVILLE, 69220
Le Beaujolais (C), 40 Rue Maréchal-Foch, tel: 74 66 05 31
Hotel restaurant serving carefully prepared regional dishes.
CERCIE, 69220
Le Relais Beaujolais (C)
tel: 74 66 19 51
Traditional restaurant with fine selection of Brouilly wines.
CHENAS, 69840
Daniel Robin (B), tel: 86 36 72 67
Recommended for lunch. Good quality regional cooking.
FLEURIE, 69820
Auberge Le Cep (A)
tel: 74 04 10 77
Inventive cooking. Expensive.
Restaurant des Sports (C)
tel: 74 04 12 69
Speciality is coq au vin, which is prepared in each Beaujolais village with the local wine.
JULIENAS, 69840
Le Coq au Vin (C), tel: 74 04 41 98
Restaurant (also a hotel) named after its speciality.
Chez la Rose/La Petite Auberge (C), tel: 74 04 41 20
Regional cuisine, also rooms.
ODENAS, 69460
Christian Mabeau (C)
tel: 74 03 41 79
Small, good-value restaurant.
PIZAY, 69430
Château de Pizay (A)
tel: 74 66 51 41
Splendid château-hotel complex between Pizay and Villié-Morgon.
ROMANECHE-THORINS, 71570
La Maison Blanche (C)
tel: 85 35 50 53
Restaurant that is short on atmosphere but cooking is good.
Les Maritonnes (B)
tel: 85 35 51 70
Good hotel with garden and renowned restaurant. Swimming pool.
ST-JEAN-D'ARDIERES, 69220
La Maison des Beaujolais (C)
tel: 74 66 16 46
Very good value regional set menus. Also wine information centre.

JURA

The wine district of Jura is centred on the small town of Arbois which lies halfway between Beaune and Geneva. The wide range of wines made by the majority of the producers is a characteristic of the district. The overall appellation is Côtes du Jura which covers a long strip of country from north of Arbois to south of Cousance. In addition there are regional specialities such as *vin jaune* which is similar to fino sherry, as well as limited production of *vin de paille* which is made from grapes that have been laid out to dry.

THE WINE ROUTE

The circuit of Jura vineyards begins in Arbois, a hard-working provincial town, plagued by heavy traffic. It was

the home of Louis Pasteur (1822-95) and his house is now a museum. The Musée de la Vigne et du Vin in the basement of the town hall is also of interest.

From Arbois take the main N83

Besançon road northwards, passing the vineyard which used to belong to Pasteur, La Vigne de Pasteur **1**. Take the first turning right to Montigny-les-Arsures then continue s to Vauxelle. This countryside is the heart of the Arbois appellation, the biggest of the Jura wine zones. About half of all the region's vineyards are around Arbois and most of them are on the gentle sloping hillsides of limestone and gravel soil.

The largest estate and biggest producer of the region is the Henri Maire domaine with some 300ha. No one has done more to promote Jura as a wine district. Leave Vauxelle on the D107e back towards Arbois, but almost immediately turn left on the D54, a minor road which snakes through the vineyards and woods before joining the D107. Turn right at this junction back to Arbois.

Leave Arbois on the N83, heading s towards Poligny through general farming country. More vineyards occur N of the town. In the old town centre, the cooperative occupies a fine Gothic church, the vats fitting in neatly between the columns. Bypass Poligny, keeping on the N83 through the Forêt de Vaivres. 18km from Poligny turn right on the D120 to Arlay, noting the Ch d'Arlay **2** on the left. Built in the 17th century in classical style, the château was originally a monastery, now a museum and also one of the best wine estates of the Jura. The red Côtes du Jura resembles an elegant light burgundy; the rosé is called Corail and the white is about 90% Chardonnay.

Turn left in the village to Ruffey-sur-Seille, where you turn left onto the D38 which takes you into the l'Etoile appellation, known for its fresh still and sparkling white wines. The Ch d'Etoile is the biggest producer in the district and makes good quality wines; the white is about 98% Chardonnay. Drive through the village of l'Etoile to rejoin the N83 just N of Lons-le-Saunier. Continue into the town, which has an atmospheric old centre.

After visiting Lons-le-Saunier,

return on the N83 heading N, taking a right turn at the large junction at the end of the town's bypass. From this junction take the D70, soon turning off to the left through Le Pin, with its fine feudal castle offering a splendid panoramic view of the countryside. Continue N to Montain, turning right there to rejoin the D70, and turning left at the junction to pass through Le Vernois to Voiteur. Here take the D5 into Château-Chalon, which has its own appellation for *vin jaune*, the sherry-like (but unfortified) wine which only comes from this corner of the Jura. Leave the village on the D5, which crosses hilly, forested country.

Pass through Granges de Ladoye and then turn left onto the D96 which takes you through Plasne to Miéry, where you join the D259 to Poligny. From here the N5 goes NW to Dôle and Dijon, or SE to Switzerland.

WINE INFORMATION

LONS-LE-SAUNIER
Société de Viticulture
BP 396, Avenue du 44 RI

HOTELS AND RESTAURANTS

ARBOIS, 39600
Hotel de Paris (B), 9 Rue de l'Hôtel-de-Ville, tel: 84 66 05 67
A provincial hotel offering good food and regional wines.
La finette (C), 22 Avenue Pasteur, tel: 84 66 06 78
Country-style cooking.
LONS-LE-SAUNIER, 39570
Hotel du Cheval Rouge (B)
47 Rue Lecourbe, tel: 84 47 20 44
Hotel with reliable restaurant that has been run by the same family for four generations.

SAVOIE

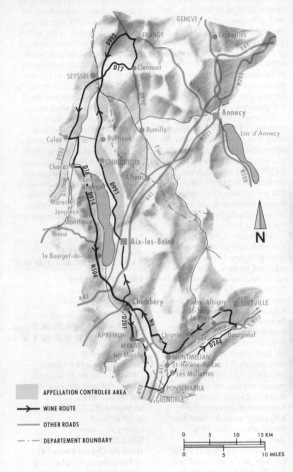

Savoie is mountain country, and the vineyards here are scattered and small. They are worth seeking out for their superb settings and their delicate, interesting wines. Despite the small size of the vineyards there is a confusingly large number of different named wines. There are two main groups: Vin de Savoie and Roussette de Savoie, both of which can come from a specific Cru. There are 15 Crus for Savoie and four for Rousette. The laws also distinguish district wines.

THE WINE ROUTE

The Wine Route begins in the north at Frangy on the N508 Bellegarde-Annecy road, runs s to Chambéry, then explores the vineyards of the Isère valley before returning to Chambéry and running through Aix-les-Bains and back to Frangy. Naturally the Route can be divided into two by travellers wishing to include a tour of the Savoie vineyards as part of a journey going to the south or north.

Frangy is the centre of a wine district of 11 communes to the north of Seyssel which produces the noted Seyssel whites from the Roussette grape. The black Mondeuse, a grape rich in tannin and colour, also makes excellent red Savoie wines.

Shortly after leaving Frangy travelling w, turn left on the D992 which takes you down a gentle winegrowing valley to Seyssel on the upper Rhône. The appellation named after the town makes still Roussette de Savoie as well as sparkling white wines. Cross the river, continuing s on the D992 to the junction with the D904 on the outskirts of Culoz. Turn left here, cross the bridge, then almost immediately turn right onto the D921. At Chanaz turn sharp left onto the D18, passing through vineyards and skirting a steep wooded slope. Continue along the shore of the Lac du Bourget, leaving the D18 just past Conjux to climb steeply on the D914, which runs along the mountainside with superb views across the lake. The D914 joins the N504 just N of Le Bourget-du-Lac: follow the N504 and the N201 into Chambéry (town plan in Michelin). Although parts of the town were destroyed during the war, many old buildings remain, including the Ch des Ducs de Savoie.

Leave the town on the D201, which runs parallel to, and sw of, the A41 autoroute. This road takes you through the vineyards of Apremont and Abymes, both of which are Crus of Vin de Savoie. At Les Marches join the N90, turning right and driving s to the bridge at Pontcharra. Turn

left to cross the bridge over the Isère, turn left again in the town and follow the D923 for 4km to Les Mollettes. Turn right here, following a minor road to St-Hélène-du-Lac. This area falls within the Cru of Montmélian (Vin de Savoie). Turn right in St-Hélène to La Chavanne. Here, turn right again, joining the D204 which runs up a small valley parallel to the Isère.

At Bourgneuf turn left, turning left again onto the N6. Cross the river then go straight across at the end of the bridge onto the D32 (the N6 goes left). At Le Bourget turn left onto the road to St-Pierre-d'Albigny. Continue through the village and on along the north side of the Isère valley, passing through St-Jean-de-la-Porte and Cruet to Arbin and into Montmélian. The latter and Arbin are Vin de Savoie communes: Arbin also makes notable Mondeuse reds. Turn right in Montmélian onto the N6 (direction Chambéry) for a short distance, then turn right again to Chignin, a wine village where red and white wines are made. Rejoin the N6 at St-Jeoire-Prieuré and drive N to Chambéry.

From Chambéry take the D991 travelling N along the eastern shore of the Lac du Bourget to Aix-les-Bains. Continue on the same road along the lake shore. Vineyards are sparse here: it is too steep. They reappear N of the lake around Chindrieux and Ruffieux. Follow the D991 up the valley to Seyssel, turning right here to climb the valley side through vineyards on the D17, which passes through Droisy and Clermont to join the D910. Turn left back to Frangy.

HOTELS AND RESTAURANTS

CHAMBERY, 73000
Roubatcheff (B), 6 Rue du Théâtre, tel: 79 33 24 91
One of the best restaurants in town with good selection of local wines.
CHIGNIN, 73800
Le Chignerain (C), tel: 79 28 10 01
Village restaurant in one of the best wine communes.

THE MASSIF CENTRAL

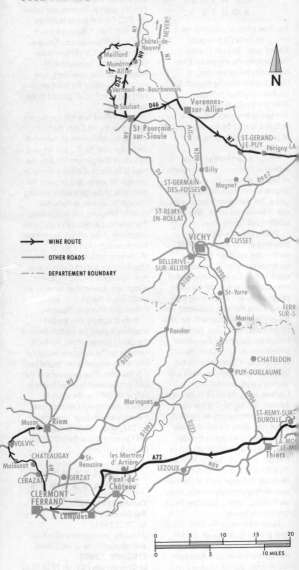

Map legend:

→ WINE ROUTE

— OTHER ROADS

–·–·– DEPARTEMENT BOUNDARY

Places on map:

Châtel-de-Neuvre

Meillard

Monétay-sur-Allier

Verneuil-en-Bourbonnais

Saulcet

St Pourçain-sur-Sioule

Varennes-sur-Allier

ST-GÉRAND-LE-PUY

Périgny LA

Billy

Magnet

ST-GERMAIN-DES-FOSSES

ST-REMY-EN-ROLLAT

VICHY

CUSSET

BELLERIVE-SUR-ALLIER

St-Yorre

FERR SUR-S

Randan

Mariol

CHATELDON

PUY-GUILLAUME

Maringues

ST-REMY-SUR-DUROLLE

LA-MO LE-MO Thiers

Mozac

Riom

VOLVIC

CHATEAUGAY

St-Beauzire

les Martres d'Artière

LEZOUX

Malauzat

CEBAZAT

GERZAT

Pont-du-Château

CLERMONT-FERRAND

Lempdes

A72

N89

0 5 10 15 20

0 5 10 MILES

As only a limited quantity of the wines from the Massif Central and the adjoining districts is sold outside the region, the way to taste the wines is by travelling around the area. The granite plateaux, extinct volcanoes and hot springs of the Massif makes it particularly attractive to visitors. However, the extent of the district makes the vineyards difficult to find as there are no large estates and the vines are surrounded by other crops. The most northerly wine district is St-Pourçain, which takes its names from the little town of St-Pourçain-sur-Sioule.

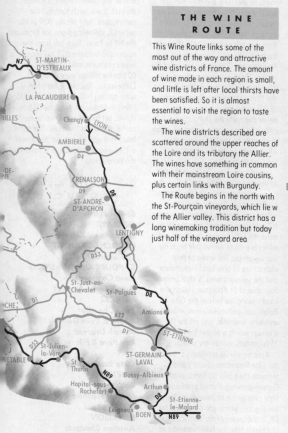

THE WINE ROUTE

This Wine Route links some of the most out of the way and attractive wine districts of France. The amount of wine made in each region is small, and little is left after local thirsts have been satisfied. So it is almost essential to visit the region to taste the wines.

The wine districts described are scattered around the upper reaches of the Loire and its tributary the Allier. The wines have something in common with their mainstream Loire cousins, plus certain links with Burgundy.

The Route begins in the north with the St-Pourçain vineyards, which lie w of the Allier valley. This district has a long winemaking tradition but today just half of the vineyard area produces a VDQS and the rest of the wine has only a local following. The nearest large town is Moulins, which is on the N7 Paris-Lyon highway. From Moulins take the N9 (south),

turning right at Châtel-de-Neuvre onto the D33. You now enter the St-Pourçain vineyards, which are a mere shadow of their pre-Phylloxera extent. Reds are made from Gamay and Pinot Noir and whites usually from the local Tresallier in combination with Sauvignon and Chardonnay. The white wines are usually the more interesting.

Turn left from the D33 on the D217 towards Meillard, but then turn left again through the hamlet of Alinard to join the D34. Turn right to head s through Verneuil-en-Bourbonnais and then turn left onto the D415 through the wine village of Saulcet to St-Pourçain-sur-Sioule, the capital of the region. There is a wine museum (Musée de la Vigne et du Vin) close to the 12th-century church in the centre of this small town. Now you can either complete the St-Pourçain circuit by returning n up the N9, or go eastwards on the D46 across the Allier towards the next district, the Côte Roannaise.

Heading e on the D46, join the N7 at Varennes-sur-Allier and follow the route nationale through Lapalisse to La Pacaudière. Shortly after this village you come to Changy. Leave the N7 here, turning right onto the D8 to enter the Côte Roannaise, where red wines are made exclusively from the Gamay grape. The wines of this district are of only local importance and the vineyard area is little greater than that of St-Pourçain. Follow the road s along the hills of the Côte Roannaise and visiting wine villages en route. Ambierle, just off the D8, is a village worth a detour for its 15th-century monastery church.

Keep on the D8 travelling s, out of the Côte Roannaise country and towards the Côtes du Forez, another Gamay-growing district producing a light alternative to Beaujolais. Boën-sur-Lignon, which you reach via the D8, is the centre of the district. From St-Etienne take the N89 heading e to visit St-Etienne-le-Molard, another wine village. The remarkable château here, La Bastie d'Urfé, has a fairytale shell grotto. From St-Etienne you can either continue on the D189

eastwards to join the A72 autoroute, or retrace your steps to Boën to continue the Wine Route.

From Boën take the N89 (heading nw towards Clermont-Ferrand) and you enter the hilly landscape of the foothills of the Massif Central. Join the A72 autoroute at Le Monnerie, or continue along the route nationale to the industrial town of Clermont-Ferrand, the capital of the Auvergne and of the Côtes d'Auvergne wine district. If you wish to avoid the centre, turn right off the N89 in the suburbs, following signs for Riom on the N9 to Paris. Turn left from the main road onto the D21 to Cébazat, a wine commune, and continue on the D21 to the hilltop wine village of Châteaugay. The castle here has a wine-tasting hall. Next take the D15 (east) to Malauzat, then the D15 to Volvic, set below its ruined feudal castle, the Ch de Tournoël. The D986 leads to Riom, an ancient town with a 15th-century church, and the end of the Wine Route.

VILLEMONTAIS
GIE des Producteurs Vins du
Roannais
Auguste Néron

Côtes du Forez
BOEN-SUR-LIGNON
Georges Bouchand
Cave Coopérative

Côtes d' Auvergne
AUBIERE
Jean-Baptiste Bayle
Jean-Marie Bourcheix
BOUDES
Albert Charmensat
Claude Savat
CHATEAUGAY
Pierre Lapouge
Michel & Roland Rougeyron
CORENT
Paul Champroux
Louis Chapelle
Michel Montorier
Bertrand Nicoulaud
LE CREST
Michel Blanc
ORCET
Raymond Roumeuf
VEYRE-MONTON
Cave Coopérative
Pierre Chevalier

HOTELS AND RESTAURANTS

St-Pourçain
CHATEL-DE-NEUVE, 03500
Hotel du Commerce (C)
tel: 70 42 07 77
Good cooking and a simple hotel.
ST-POURCAIN-SUR-SIOULE
Le Cellier (C), 69 Boulevard Ledru-
Rollin, tel: 70 45 43 48
Restaurant with a tasting and sales
room for local wines and cheeses.
Le Chêne Vert (B), 35 Boulevard
Ledru-Rollin, tel: 70 45 40 65
Busy hotel, worth recommending for
good value restaurant.
Les Deux Ponts (B), 4 Le Tivoli,
tel: 70 45 41 14
Large hotel on island in the river
Sioule. Restaurant.
Hotel-Restaurant du Commerce
(C), tel: 70 47 12 95
Excellent-value menus go well with

the local wines. Some simple rooms.
SAULCET, 03500
Chez Lucien (C), tel: 70 45 44 61
Good stop for an inexpensive lunch.

Côte Roannaise
RENAISON, 42370
Central (C), tel: 77 64 25 39
Simple hotel with restaurant in this
wine village.
Jacques-Coeur (B)
tel: 77 64 25 34
Restaurant and hotel with garden.
ROANNE, 42300
Terminus (B), Place de la Gare,
tel: 77 71 79 69
Functional hotel for overnight stay.
Troisgros (A), Place de la Gare,
tel: 77 71 66 97
First-class restaurant (and also a
hotel) with worldwide reputation, run
by father and son team. Extensive
wine list with emphasis on burgundy.
ST-ANDRE-D'APCHON, 42370
Le Lion d'Or (B), tel: 77 6 81 53
Restaurant serving well-prepared
food and local wines. Also a hotel.

Côtes d'Auvergne
ISSOIRE, 63500
Le Pariou (C), 18 Avenue Kennedy,
tel: 73 89 22 11
Pleasant hotel where you can enjoy
the wines of the region. Terrace.
LUZET, 63530
La Rose des Vents (B)
tel: 73 33 50 77
Holiday hotel quietly situated near
Volvic. Swimmming pool. Restaurant.
RIOM, 63200
Les Petits Ventres (B), 6 Rue
Anne-Dubourg, tel: 73 38 21 65
A restaurant of quality.
ROYAT, 63130
La Belle Meunière (B), 25 Avenue
de la Vallée, tel: 73 35 80 17
Traditional cuisine at this restaurant
in spa town. Also a hotel.
Le Pont des Soupirs (B)
tel: 73 35 82 66
Substantial but not typically regional
cooking.
Royat (B), Boulevard Dr Roumeuf,
tel: 73 35 82 72
Small modern restaurant. Also a
hotel.

THE NORTHERN AND CENTRAL RHONE

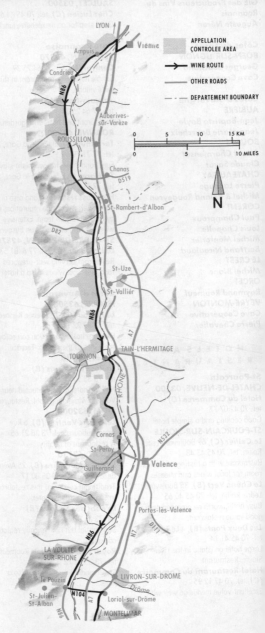

APPELLATION
CONTROLEE AREA

→ WINE ROUTE

OTHER ROADS

DEPARTEMENT BOUNDARY

LYON

Vienne

Ampuis

Condrieu

N86

Auberives-
sur-Vorèze

ROUSSILLON

Chanas

D519

St-Rambert-d'Albon

D82

N7

St-Uze

St-Vallier

N86

TOURNON

TAIN-L'HERMITAGE

A7

RHONE

Cornas

St-Péray

N532

Guilherand

Valence

Portès-lès-Valence

N7

D111

N86

LA VOULTE-
SUR-RHONE

LIVRON-SUR-DROME

le Pouzin

Drôme

St-Julien-
St-Alban

N104

A7

Loriol-sur-Drôme

MONTELIMAR

N86

0   5   10   15 KM

0   5   10 MILES

N

The Rhône, in its narrow valley between the mountains of the Massif Central and the foothills of the Alps, is one of the great natural arteries to and from northern Europe and the Mediterranean. Today, thousands of tourists and other travellers pass through the valley every year on the Autoroute du Soleil, the A7.

The Rhône vineyards extend from near Vienne to just below Avignon, some 200 kilometres (125 miles) to the south. In the north the valley is relatively narrow and the vines are often grown on small terraces on the steep slopes, whereas further south the valley becomes steadily wider. Just as the Loire valley produces mainly white wine, so red is the speciality of the Rhône.

THE WINE ROUTE

This is a long and straightforward Wine Route from Vienne in the north to Montélimar in the south, following the course of the river Rhône and the unsettling wind, the mistral, through very spectacular hilly countryside and visiting some of the world's finest vineyards.

Take the N86 out of Vienne and head s. Although not a wine town, Vienne is worth visiting for its monuments and museums which are relics of its Roman past. The town was once strategically important as a crossing of the Rhône. Almost immediately after leaving Vienne you enter the Côte Rôtie district (meaning "roasted slope") with its very steep southeast-facing slopes. At the heart of the Côte Rôtie are two slopes: the Côte Brune (to the north) where the soil is brown from the iron content and the Côte Blonde with more chalky soil. Some growers vinify and bottle wines from the two slopes separately but generally they are blended and the single grape variety is Syrah. A good Côte Rôtie combines strength and finesse and needs long maturing. The sheer slopes rise steeply behind the village of Ampuis on the right of the road. It seems impossible that any cultivation is possible in such conditions and because all cultivation is by hand, the cost of production is high.

Many of the wines of the Côte Rôtie are under the control of the Guigal family and include: La Mouline, La Landonne and Châtillone – a Vidal-Fleury wine (now owned by Guigal).

Keep on the N86 travelling s from Ampuis and several kms downstream on the same south-facing right bank of the river is Condrieu. The terraced vineyards here are planted with Viognier, a white grape variety almost exclusive to the Rhône and this small area. Just s of the village of Vérin lies the district's best-known vineyard at Ch Grillet. It covers only 3ha and is, after La Romanée in Burgundy, the smallest appellation in France. The vineyard faces SE in a natural amphitheatre that traps the warmth of the sun to provide a superb microclimate for one of France's most expensive and rare white wines.

From Condrieu you continue heading s along the west bank of the Rhône and you come to the very extensive vineyards of St-Joseph which stretch for some 55km. The district takes in more than 20 communes and covers every sort of soil and slope. Consequently the wines lack consistency. Here the vineyards vie for space with expensive holiday villas, although the best locations are centred around the town of Tournon on terraces overlooking the Rhône. Among the best producers in the area are Gérard Chave, Chapoutier and Paul Jaboulet Aîné.

By crossing the river at Tournon the Route takes you into the little town of Tain l'Hermitage on a bend in the river, caused by a dramatic granite outcrop – the Hermitage. Historians believe that vines planted on these slopes are some of the oldest

vineyards known in France. The name
Hermitage derives from the small
13th-century chapel now owned by
the Hermitage growers and
négociants Paul Jaboulet Aîné, who
have named their top wine "La
Chapelle".

The Hermitage hill faces s (at an
angle that maximizes the warmth
from the sun) with an impressive view
across the river. The climate is warm
and sheltered becoming increasingly
Mediterranean as you journey to
Montélimar. Even in wet years
Hermitage usually produces wines
that achieve an impressive quality.
Four-fifths of the vineyards are
planted with Syrah, the rest with two
white grapes; Roussanne and
Marsanne. These not only produce
impressive white Hermitage, but can
also be used up to a maximum 15% in
the red Hermitage which is one of the
world's strongest wines.

The wines of Crozes-Hermitage
are very much a lesser breed. The
extensive vineyards consist of 11
communes which lie in a broad band
around Tain-l'Hermitage and extend s
halfway to Valence on the east bank
of the river. It's best to enjoy the
wines when young and full of fruit.

Cross the river Rhône again and
rejoin the N86 on its route to the
south. Passing through the vineyards
of St-Joseph (about 6km NW of
Valence) you come to the small
appellation of Cornas. This is one of
the most underrated districts of the
Rhône valley. Its best wines are
grown on the steep hillside sites
above the town, sheltered from the
mistral, rather than the flatter
vineyards near the river.

The village of Cornas dates back to
Charlemagne and is home for
producers such as Auguste Clape,
whose cellars are right on the street;
together with those of Noël Verset. In
the south the vineyards of Cornas
border on those of St-Péray where
sparkling white wine, from Marsanne
and Roussane grapes, is produced.
Near to the wine village of St-Péray is
the ruined Ch de Crusse from which
you can enjoy the breathtaking view
of the valley past Valence and if you

turn off the main road, the scenery to
the west is also very spectacular.

Continuing the Wine Route on the
N86 the scenery is particularly
interesting: the Rhône basin (and
further still, the Alps) to the east; and
twisting, precipitous roads and wild
countryside to the west. Drive through
La Voulte-sur-Rhône to Le Pouzin
where you can cross the river on the
N104 to Loriol-sur-Drôme. Continue
on this road towards Crest through
the Drôme valley. Past small
picturesque villages to the east of
Crest where the valley narrows and
you come to the small town of Die and
the appellation of Clairette de Die.
Winemaking here is centred on
making a traditional *méthode
champenoise* sparkling wine from
Muscat grapes.

To continue your journey heading s
along the Rhône (and to join up with
the southern Rhône Wine Route),
retrace your steps to Loriol-sur-
Drôme to pick up the N7 for
Montélimar.

WINE INFORMATION

AVIGNON
La Maison du Tourisme et du Vin
41 Cours Jean-Jaurès.
(This is the only official centre for
wine information in the extensive
Rhône valley. Local Syndicats
d'Initiative can also be helpful).

HOTELS AND RESTAURANTS

CHARMES-SUR-RHONE, 07800
La Vieille Auberge (B)
tel: 75 60 80 10
Sound, traditional cooking in this
village restaurant on the west bank of
the river.
CHAVANAY, 42410
Alain Charles (B), tel: 74 87 23 02
Restaurant serving regional dishes in
village in Condrieu district.
CHONAS-L'AMBALLAN, 38121
Domaine de Clairefontaine (B)
tel: 74 58 81 52
Hotel with spacious rooms and
surrounded by park. Restaurant.

Le Marais de St-Jean (A)
tel: 74 58 83 28
Small hotel and restaurant (B) in a
restored old building.
CONDRIEU, 62420
Beau Rivage (A/B)
tel: 74 59 52 24
Classic cuisine of a high standard at
this hotel restuarant. Perfect place to
drink Condrieu.
CORNAS, 01730
Restaurant Ollier (C)
tel: 75 40 32 17
Country inn in a wine village.
CREST, 26400
La Porte de Montségur (B)
tel: 75 25 41 48
Fine cooking at this restaurant on
north bank of Drôme. Terrace.
DIE, 26150
Hotel St-Dominigue (C)
tel: 75 22 03 08
Unpretentious holiday hotel with
restaurant serving regional dishes.
La Petite Auberge (C), 13 Avenue
Sadi-Carnot, tel: 75 22 05 91
Good value restaurant. Also a hotel.
GRANE, 26400
Giffon (B), tel: 75 62 60 64
Hospitable restaurant on the road to
Die.
MERCUROL, 26600
l'Abricotine (B), tel: 75 07 44 60
Small quiet villa-hotel. Restaurant.
PONT-DE-L'ISERE, 26600
Chabran (A), tel: 74 84 60 09
Excellent restaurant with outstanding
wine list. Also a hotel.
**LES ROCHES-DE-CONDRIEU,
38370**
Hotel Bellevue (B)
tel: 74 56 41 42
Splendid view of Condrieu and the
Rhône. Conservative cuisine.
ST-PIERRE-DE-BOEUF, 42410
La Diligence (B/C)
tel: 74 87 12 19
Reliable restaurant wtih resonable
prices and extensive wine list.

ST-ROMAIN-DE-LERPS, 07130
Château du Besset (A)
tel: 75 58 52 22
Splendid hotel surrounded by vast
park. Good standard of cuisine.
ST-VALLIER, 26240
Hotel Les Voyageurs (C)
tel: 75 23 04 42
Traditional cooking is the attraction
of this modest hotel.
Lecomte (B), tel: 75 23 01 12
Attractive set menus and local wines.
Also a hotel.
SERRIERES, 07340
Schaeffer (C), tel: 75 34 00 07
Friendly hotel and pleasant
restaurant.
TAIN L'HERMITAGE, 26600
Hotel du Commerce (B)
1 Avenue Docteur Paul Durand,
tel: 75 08 65 00
Comfortable hotel with *Pintadeau de
la Drôme* restaurant.
Hotel des Deux Côteaux (B), 18
Rue Joseph Péala, tel: 75 08 33 01
Well-run riverside hotel.
Restaurant Reynaud (B)
82 Avenue Président-Roosevelt,
tel: 75 07 22 10
Best place to eat in the district with a
terrace overlooking the river. Good
wine list.
TOURNON, 07300
Hotel du Château (B)
tel: 75 08 60 22
Large rooms and adequate
restaurant.
Le Manoir (C), tel: 75 08 20 31
Small, quiet hotel on the road to
Lamastre. Swimming pool.
VALENCE, 26000
Pic (A), 285 Avenue Victor Hugo,
tel: 75 44 15 32
One of the most welcoming three-star
restaurants in France. Excellent
cuisine and selection of Rhône wines.
Few luxury rooms available.

SE

THE SOUTHERN RHONE

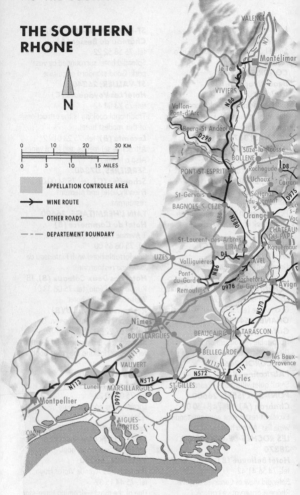

The southern part of the Rhône valley produces by far the most wine. The vast Côtes du Rhône appellation, which embraces more than 100 communes in six different départements, consists of more than 40,000 hectares (99,000 acres) of vineyards. Recently production has increased and the average quality of wine has improved due to better winemaking techniques. The great bulk of the wines are red and the average Côtes du Rhône is likely to come from a cooperative, to cost little and be a pleasant everyday wine. There are 65 villages which are permitted to carry the appellation Côtes du Rhône Villages; 17 of these can be sold as Côtes du Rhône with the village name added.

plums, as well as vegetables such as asparagus, tomatoes, onions and olives. The Rhône valley is a horn of plenty spilling out into the Mediterranean.

Follow the N86 along the right bank of the Rhône through Viviers to Bourg-St-Andéol. To the north and west is the Ardèche and across the river to the east is the Coteaux du Tricastin stretching between Donzère in the north (s of Viviers) and Bollène, just off the A7, the Autoroute du Soleil. Avoid the autoroute, especially in August, when it becomes severely jammed with traffic heading for the southern coast.

Stay on the N86 to Pont-St-Esprit where you can make a scenic detour just after crossing the river Ardèche, by turning off the main road onto the D901 which takes you into the hills. Turn off to the right for St-Martin-d'Ardèche and then take the D290 through the Gorges de l'Ardèche with magnificent views and very winding roads to Vallon-Pont-d'Arc.

Retrace your steps to Pont-St-Esprit and continue travelling s on the N86 away from the Rhône. A small turning on the right (the D980) takes you to St-Gervais where the church stands on the site of a former temple of Jupiter in Roman times. Return to the main road and drive into Bagnols-sur-Cèze where you turn off left onto the N580 towards Avignon. Between the road and the Rhône to the east lies Chusclan and off to the right of the road past an old Roman camp (known as the "Camp de César") is Laudun. To the east across the Rhône is the town of Orange and to the southeast, Châteauneuf-du-Pape.

Follow the N580 and after the D980 left fork, take the right turn on the D101 to St-Laurent-des-Arbres where the 13th-century fortified church is well worth a visit. Drive through St-Laurent on the D26 for about 3km to Lirac, whose wines (with those from the neighbouring villages) once supplied the old port of Roquemaure across the river from Châteauneuf-du-Pape. Roquemaure in the 16th century was a very busy port and once the capital of the Côtes du

SE

THE WINE ROUTE

This Wine Route extends from Montélimar in the north to Montpellier in the south and provides a gloriously spectacular journey through the rugged landscape of the southern Rhône. This area is popular with tourists for its great natural beauty, sunny Mediterranean climate and full-bodied wine, and also the ancient remains of its Roman and medieval past.

From Montélimar take the N86 (south) running parallel to the Rhône - don't forget to collect some nougat, made from locally-grown almonds, whilst in the district. The further south you travel the more the valley floor opens out, with broad plateaux between the low hills to allow general agriculture. Crops grown include fruits such as peaches, apricots and

Rhône. Red Lirac from certain estates can be surprisingly good and is at present greatly undervalued. The soil is gravel littered with stones, the climate favourable and the potential enormous, particulary for the red wines which have an individual fruity, flowery character, lighter in style than nearby Châteauneuf. The Ch de Clary near Tavel, situated in a forest where a Roman site was found, produces very good full-bodied wine.

At Lirac turn left to Tavel lying on a hot dry plateau whose vineyards are similar to these of Châteauneuf-du-Pape, characterized by rounded stones and chalky soil. The rosé wines of the area, drunk young, are considered some of the world's best, and are made from a selection of nine grape varieties, among them Grenache, Cinsaut, Syrah and Clairette. The majority of the vineyards lie to the east towards Orange and Roquemaure. Off the D976 towards Roquemaure is the beautiful 17th-century Ch d'Aquéria, surrounded by over a hundred acres of vines. By ageing the Tavel in big casks for a few months they aim to stiffen it a little to survive longer in bottle. Off the D26 in the direction of Nîmes is Ch de Trinquevedel, dating back to the French Revolution and producing an exceptional full-bodied rosé.

An obligatory diversion of a non-vinous variety is to the Pont du Gard which spans the river Gardon. Take the D4 (west) out of Tavel and at the T-junction with the N86 turn left, through Valliguières, then right onto the D981 and turn off left towards the river. Follow the footpath underneath the bridge on the right bank which will take you to the Ch de St-Privat which has a breathtaking view of the aqueduct. Beautiful as well as awe-inspiring the Roman aqueduct (built in about 20 BC) formed part of the engineering system designed to bring water from Uzès to Nîmes.

From the Pont du Gard join the N100 for Avignon crossing the A9 then take a left fork on the D976 and follow this road through Rochefort-du-Gard parallel to the A9 to Roquemaure and then left, across the Rhône to Orange. The Roman theatre is one of the finest to have survived from the ancient world and is still used for performances in summer. Other remains include a statue of the Emperor Augustus, a Roman temple and a triumphal arch.

Take the D975 (to Vaison-la-Romaine) heading NE out of Orange. At Camaret-sur-Aigues, a left turn through Sérignan-du-Comtat will take you on the D172 and then turn right on the D11 to Uchaux and the impressive Ch St-Estève estate. Retrace your steps to the D975 and a left turn on the D8 takes you to Cairanne, another fortified hilltop village, and one of the Côtes du Rhône villages. Continue along the D8 and take a right turn on the D117 at Rochegude to Suze-la-Rousse, the home of a university of wine in the restored château. Return to the D975 and a little further along you come to Rasteau on a hilltop to the left. Most famous for its Côtes du Rhône Villages wines – red, dry white and rosé, it also produces an Appellation Contrôlée Vin Doux Naturel which is interesting rather than exceptional. The Domaine de Beaurenard (on the road to Roaix outside the village) has a Musée du Vigneron.

On the way to Vaison-la-Romaine, still on the D975 you pass the quaint medieval village of Roaix itself. The road then curves to the right following the Ouvèze river (it is said that Hannibal came this way with his elephants) into Vaison-la-Romaine, a town rich in antiquity and is fascinating to visit. Essentially Roman its history dates back even further and extensive remains, including a Roman theatre, have been uncovered. The oldest part of the town is the Haute Ville, with 14th-century houses and castle ruins. You reach it by a 2,000-year-old bridge.

The Route now follows the D977 in the shadow of the jagged range of mountains called the "Dentelles de Montmirail" which forms part of the foothills of Mont Ventoux to the east. Up on the left of the D88 clinging to the cliff is the village of Séguret,

commanding spectacular views to the west, and through Séguret on the D88 or off the D977 is the medieval Sablet which is the home of the invention of a machine for grafting American rootstock onto French vines.

Turn off the D977 travelling se onto the D8, left onto the D80, then left again onto the D7, taking the right fork into the attractive wine village of Gigondas at the foot of the Dentelles de Montmirail. The main grape varieties are Grenache, Syrah, Mourvèdre and Cinsaut and the vineyards stretch across the hills and plateau to the west of the village. There is a tasting room in the village where wines from some 30 producers can be sampled. Return to the D7 and turn left onto the D8 which takes you to Vacqueyras. Currently only entitled to the Côtes du Rhône Villages appellation, but its elevation to full *appellation contrôlée* status in the next few years is almost guaranteed. A wine to watch out for is Clos de Cazaux near the town, incidentally, the birthplace of the 12th-century poet and minstrel, Rimbaud. Continuing on the D8, a left turn on the D21 takes you into Beaumes-de-Venise, one of the leading "villages" of the Côtes du Rhône producing dry red as well as a fortified Muscat dessert wine (Vin Doux Naturel).

Now return to the D7 and follow the road through Carpentras onto the D942 into Avignon; once the centre of the Christian world and the home of the Popes in the 14th century. Clement V (formerly Bertrand de Goth, Archbishop of Bordeaux – see Graves Wine Route) was the first to set up the papal court in Avignon, not Rome. Originally a prehistoric enclave, later a Roman city and later still an important early medieval town, its famous bridge, the 12th-century Pont St-Bénézet, is just one of the sights for tourists in this lovely old town. The papal palace and many of the other buildings are spectacular when floodlit during the summer months. Just across the river is Villeneuve-lès-Avignon, the home of many cardinals before the schism in 1378 when the papacy returned to Rome. From

Villeneuve the D980 heading n will take you towards Châteauneuf-du-Pape.

Follow the N570 through Avignon to Trascon whose castle gazes across the Rhône at that of Beaucaire. Continue on the N570, away from the river, then turn right onto the D33 and follow the road as it curves left to join the D17. Turn left into the hills to Les Baux-de-Provence, an unmissable diversion. Les Baux, perched precariously on the hillside with spectacular views down into the Val d'Esper. The ruined fortress seems to be part of the actual rockface and on a clear day you can see the Mediterranean.

Return to the D17 and turn left to Arles and in the town centre cross the river and take the N572 to St-Gilles and then through to Vauvert. Turn left at Amargues to join the D979. Turn left again to visit the fortified Aigues-Mortes and the area where the wines of Listel are made from vines grown near salt flats. Return along the D979 and turn right onto the N113. Turn left into Lunel, home of a very good Muscat, then continue on the N113 into Montpellier, the eastern gateway to the Languedoc.

WINE INFORMATION

AVIGNON
Maison du Tourisme et du Vin
41 Cours Jean-Jaurès
ST-PAUL-TROIS-CHATEAUX
La Maison de la Truffe et du Tricastin

HOTELS AND RESTAURANTS

LES ANGLES, 30133
l'Ermitage Meissonnier (B)
tel: 90 25 41 68
Food is much more exciting than setting. Good wine selection. Also a hotel.
AVIGNON, 84000
Brunel (A), 46 Rue de la Balance,
tel: 90 85 24 83
Restaurant serving inventive light dishes. Splendid desserts.

La Fourchette (C), 7 Rue Racine, tel: 90 85 20 93
Good value and popular (with the locals) restaurant. Regional accent to cooking.

Hiély-Lucullus (B), 5 Rue de la République, tel: 90 86 17 07
Renowned restaurant with wide range of dishes.

Les Trois Clefs (B), 26 Rue des Trois-Faucons, tel: 90 86 51 53
Good cooking in distinctive setting.

Le Vernet (C), 58 Rue Joseph-Vernet, tel: 90 86 64 53
Market fresh ingredients and good decor. Large garden.

BAGNOLS-SUR-CEZE, 30200
Château de Coulorgues (B)
Route d'Avignon, tel: 66 89 52 78
Small château set in a park with a restaurant and swimming pool.

BEDOIN, 84410
l'Oustau d'Anaïs (C)
tel: 90 65 67 43
Good country food at foot of Mont Ventoux.

CAROMB, 84330
Les Géraniums (C), Le Barroux, tel: 90 62 41 08
Generous helpings of Provençal dishes. Also good value hotel (B/C).

CARPENTRAS, 84200
Fiacre (B), 153 Rue Vigne, tel: 90 63 03 15
Quiet 18th-century hotel in the town centre.

Restaurant des Halles (C), Rue Gallone, tel: 90 63 24 11
Very reasonably priced authentic regional cooking.

l'Orangerie (C), 26 Rue Duplessis, tel: 90 67 27 23
Cooking of high standard. Expertly chosen regional wines.

Univers (B), Place Aristide-Briand, tel: 90 63 00 05
Businessman's hotel with solid reputation. Restaurant.

ENTRECHAUX, 84340
St-Hubert (B), tel: 90 46 00 05
Near to Vaison-la-Romaine with shady terrace and good-value regional cuisine.

FONTAINE DE VAUCLUSE, 84800
Hotel de Parc (B), tel: 90 20 31 57
Hotel near river Sorgue. Functional

rooms and good restaurant.

GIGONDAS, 84190
Les Florets (B), tel: 90 65 85 01
Hotel in very peaceful countryside location. Restaurant (C).

GRIGNAN, 26230
Hotel Sévigné (B/C)
tel: 75 46 50 97
Budget hotel with variable plumbing.

MONDRAGON, 84430
La Beaugravière (C)
tel: 90 40 82 54
The long wine list and good cooking at this restaurant helps you to forget the location. Also a hotel (B).

MONTEUX, 84170
Le Saule Pleurier (B), Quartier Beauregard, tel: 90 61 01 35
Good cooking and a terrace.

MONTFAVET, 84140
Les Frênes (A), tel: 90 31 17 93
Luxurious hotel in eastern suburb of Avignon. Good restaurant (B).

MORNAS, 84550
Le Manoir (B), tel: 90 37 00 79
Meticulous restaurant with rooms below ruins of an old castle.

NYONS, 26110
Le Petit Caveau (C)
tel: 75 26 20 21
Restaurant in old part of town.

La Picholine (B), tel: 75 26 06 21
Hotel in quiet setting. Swimming pool. Restaurant (B).

ORANGE, 84100
Hotel Arène (B), Place de Langes, tel: 90 34 10 95
Quiet hotel despite central location.

Le Parvis (B), tel: 90 34 82 00
Comfortable restaurant close to Roman theatre. Good service and long wine list.

LE POET LAVAL, 26160
Les Hospitaliers (A), Au vieux Village, tel: 75 46 22 32
Very good restaurant with good wine regional wine selection. Also a hotel.

LE PONTET, 84130
Auberge de Cassagne (B)
tel: 90 31 04 18
Very good restaurant in luxury hotel (A) near Avignon. *Demi-pension* in season.

RASTEAU, 84110
Bellerive (B), tel: 90 46 10 20
Modern hotel surrounded by vineyards. Restaurant (C).

SE

ROCHEGUDE, 26790
Château de Rochegude (A)
tel: 75 04 81 88
Castle dating back to 12th century
and now a comfortable hotel. Good
cooking. Well-stocked cellars.

LA ROQUE-SUR-CEZE, 30200
Le Mas du Belier (C)
tel: 66 82 78 73
Good cheap restaurant in village
northwest of Bagnols-sur-Cèze.

ROQUEMAURE, 30150
Château de Cubières (B)
tel: 66 82 64 28
Château hotel with park. Restaurant.

ROUSSILLON, 84220
David (C), tel: 90 05 60 13
In the Côtes du Ventoux, Provençal
cooking and interesting wine list.
Le Val des Fées (B)
tel: 90 05 64 99
Small, enthusiastic restaurant.

RUOMS, 07120
Savel (C), tel: 75 39 60 02
Standard hotel set in a park.
Restaurant has good wine list.

STE-CECILE-LES-VIGNES, 84290
Le Relais (B), tel: 90 30 84 39
Very congenial restaurant that
maintains high standard.

SEGURET, 84110
Domaine de Cabasse (B)
tel: 90 46 91 12
Friendly hotel that is part of a wine
estate. *Demi-pension* in season.
Restaurant (C).
La Table du Comtat (B)
tel: 90 46 91 49
Excellent cooking in a picturesque
wine village. Also a hotel.

SUZE-LA-ROUSSE, 26790
Relais du Château (B)
tel: 75 04 81 86
Modern hotel with restaurant and
swimming pool.

TAVEL, 30126
Auberge de Tavel (B)
tel: 66 50 03 41
Brilliant wine list at this hotel
restaurant. Swimming pool.

Hostellerie du Seigneur (C)
tel: 66 50 04 26
Agreeably priced wines and set
menus. Also a hotel.

VAISON-LA-ROMAINE, 84110
Burrhuss (B), tel: 90 36 00 11
Fairly modern hotel and restaurant in
centre of town. Attentive service.
Hostellerie Le Beffroi (A/B)
tel: 90 36 04 71
Situated in the old part of town, best
place to stay and eat. *Demi-pension* in
season.

VALLON-PONT-D'ARC, 07150
Le Manoir du Raveyron (C)
tel: 75 88 03 59
Pleasant place to stop for lunch in the
Ardèche.

VALREAS, 84600
Ferme Champ-Rond (B)
tel: 90 37 31 68
Charming old farmstead.

**VILLENEUVE-LES-AVIGNON,
30400**
l'Atelier (B), 5 Rue de la Foire,
tel: 90 25 01 84
Comfortable hotel in old centre of
town.
La Magnaneraie (A), 37 Rue
Camp-de-Bataille, tel: 90 25 11 11
Delightful old manor hotel with large
rooms. Good restaurant (B).

VINSOBRES, 26110
Auberge du Prieuré (C)
tel: 75 27 63 32
Country inn.

VIOLES, 84150
Le Mas du Bouvan (C)
tel: 90 70 94 08
Carefully prepared regional dishes.

VISAN, 84820
Les Troubadours (C)
tel: 90 41 92 55
Strictly regional cooking in cellar of a
château.

SE

CHATEAUNEUF-DU-PAPE

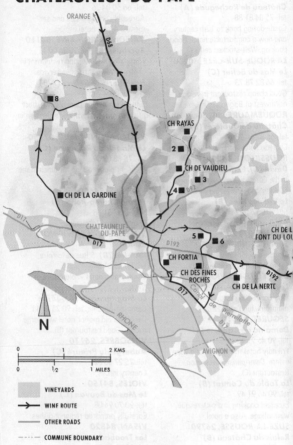

The vineyards of Châteauneuf are open and rolling, with wide woodlands on the hilltops. Much of the soil consists of large pebbles which absorb the heat of the sun, helping to bring the grapes to maximum ripeness. The wine of Châteauneuf-du-Pape can be made from 13 permitted grape varieties, and so what is actually planted differs from estate to estate. Classic Châteauneuf is "broad-shouldered" with plenty of alcohol; a wine in which the summer sun of Provence seems captured. It demands patience and often will not reveal its true class for eight to ten years. About three percent of Châteauneuf wine is white, and today can be an attractive alternative to white Burgundy.

THE WINE ROUTE

This wine tour can be approached via the D17 from Sorgues and Avignon in the south, or the D68 from Orange in the north.

From Orange take the D68 heading s, and as you cross the D72 you enter the rolling countryside of Châteauneuf – wide open plateaux and gentle hills make it seem like the roof of the world. Successive popes used the now ruined castle of Châteauneuf as a summer residence and avidly consumed the local wine. Planting was extensive and today there are some 3,000ha of vineyards.

Opposite a turning to the right is Domaine Trintignant **1** where a straightforward, soft, full red wine is made. Continue towards Châteauneuf then turn left along the D92 and left again as far as the small estate of Ch Rayas which is reached by a small track. Owned by the Reynaud family, this outstanding property produces well-structured, stylish wines, usually of a high quality. Return to the road and to the right is La Roquette **2**, planted principally with Grenache. Next on the right is the beautiful, late 18th-century Ch de Vaudieu, owned by the Meffres of Gigondas.

Over to the left is Domaine de Nalys **3**, an estate of some 49ha, followed by Domaine Sabon **4**, making almost exclusively red wine from a blend of predominantly Grenache and Syrah.

Return to the D68 and turn left following the road past Le Boucou **5**, then Domaine de la Solitude **6** which makes light, soft wines. The road curves to the right and then at a crossroads with the D192, the Ch des Fines Roches lies straight ahead. This is one of four estates, and probably the best (the others being Domaine de Clos du Roi, Domaine de la Font du Roi and Clos St-Michel) owned by the Mousset family. All the wines are made using the latest technology. Turn left onto the D192, and the road will lead you to Domaine du Vieux Télégraphe **7**, producing a full, dark tannic wine on the stony soil from old

vines (some aged up to 80 years).

Further n is Ch de la Font du Loup producing some excellent and rigorously selected wines. Back on the D192, turn left which takes you past Ch de la Nerte which was the first estate to do its own bottling in 1785. Restoration of the château is currently in progress. Follow the road to the D17 and turn right towards Châteauneuf-du-Pape itself.

The road passes the picturesque Ch Fortia on the right, home of one of the great wines of the area. Continue into the busy town, making sure to visit the ruined papal summer palace overlooking the vineyards which gives its name to the town, area and wine. Drive out of the town, still on the D17, and then take the right fork which takes you N and past Ch de la Gardine, producing a very good wine from light soil.

The road then continues N until a turning to the left on the high plateau leads to the renowned Domaine de Mont-Redon **8**, planted with nearly 100ha of vines. Follow the road back to the D68 and turn left heading N and back to Orange.

HOTELS AND RESTAURANTS

CHATEAUNEUF-DU-PAPE, 84230
La Garbure (C), tel: 90 82 75 08
Good value country cooking.
Hostellerie du Château des Fines Roches (A), tel: 90 83 70 23
Castle with seven luxurious rooms. Excellent cooking in restaurant (B).
Le Logis d'Arnavel (C)
tel: 90 83 73 22
Modern, comfortable hotel, west of Châteauneuf and belonging to grower.
La Mule du Pape (B)
tel: 90 83 73 30
Grat care is taken with the provençal-style cooking at this restaurant in the town centre.
Le Pistou (C), tel: 90 39 71 75
Traditional dishes of the region.

PROVENCE

The beautiful hinterland of the Côte d'Azur is perfect vineyard country, with a climate like California's and innumerable superb vineyard sites. The largest *appellation contrôlée* is Côtes de Provence. This is made up of 85 communes around the Massif des Maures and follows the coastline in a northeasterly direction from Toulon. This appellation has been known mainly for its dry, rather dull, rosé but efforts have been made to improve the quality of its red wine, which now makes up a third of the total harvest.

Two smaller wine districts are Aix-en-Provence and Les Baux-de-Provence. Red wines play a more important part here, with Cabernet Sauvignon giving them a quality that is rarely found in the Côtes de Provence. The first appellations to be created in Provence were the four small districts of Palette, Cassis, Bandol and Bellet. The biggest and undoubtedly the best is the largely red wine region of Bandol.

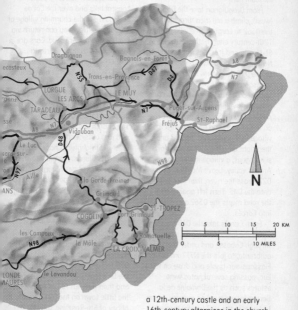

a 12th-century castle and an early
16th-century altarpiece in the church
of St-Jean-Baptiste.

Start the tour from the junction of
the N7 and N555: the Draguignan
junction on the A8 autoroute is close
by. Take the N7 heading E through Le
Muy and Puget-sur-Argens to the
outskirts of Fréjus. Be warned that the
surroundings of this coastal town
have been badly developed and it
suffers frequent traffic jams. In the
centre of town there is a group of
church buildings including a 13th-
century cathedral and an episcopal
palace with an archaeological
museum and also Roman ruins.

Turn left onto the D4, which climbs
through wooded country to Bagnols-
en-Forêt. Turn left again here onto the
D47, which runs w through woods to
La Motte and Trans-en-Provence. Join
the N555 to Draguignan, and passing
through the vineyards of the Nartuby
valley. Stopping off in this busy
market town, the *Café des Négociants*
on the market square is worth visiting

THE WINE
ROUTE

Visiting the Provence vineyards is a
sybaritic rather than intellectual
experience: a chance to visit beautiful
places, taste enjoyable wines and
perhaps catch up on some sunbathing
too. Wine is a natural part of the
civilized heritage of Provence, but
strangely there is little tradition of
excellence. However, with the aid of
modern equipment and more technical
know-how, there are signs of
improvement.

The Wine Route begins in the the
heart of the Côtes de Provence
appellation, the Argens valley w of
Fréjus. Here, at Les Arcs-sur-Argens,
is the *Maison des Vins* and the
headquarters of the CIVP, the
professional body in charge of testing
and controlling Côtes de Provence
wines. Also of interest are the ruins of

and you will also find the 17th-century Tour de l'Horloge and a town museum here.

From Draguignan take the D557 (west), climb a hill then turn left on the D562 to Lorgues. The village has a 12th-century church, the Collégiale St-Martin and frescoes in the chapel Notre-Dame-de-Benva. Leave Lorgues on the D10 driving NW and turning left very soon onto the D50, a minor road to Entrecasteaux. The castle towering above this village has been beautifully restored by its Scottish owners. Drive on to Cotignan and turn left into the village, left again onto the D13 and then right onto the D22 to Montfort-sur-Argens, a village in the upper Argens valley. Leave Montfort by the D22, cross the river, then turn left onto the D45. Turn left again where the road meets the D562 and drive into Carcés.

From Carcés take the D13 travelling s past the lake and on, passing through Cabasse and under the autoroute, to join the N7. Turn left to Flassans-sur-Issole and drive on to Le Luc, passing several noted wine estates such as the Domaine de la Bernarde (see over) on the way. From Le Luc take the N97 (south) through Gonfaron, Pignans and Carnoules to the outskirts of Cuers.

Halfway along the bypass around the town turn left off the N97, and take the D14 eastwards to Pierrefeu-du-Var. Turn right in the village onto the D12, which runs along the foot of the Massif des Maures, a range of rugged wooded hills which continues eastwards parallel to the coast as far as Fréjus. The D12 joins the N98 coastal road just outside Hyères. Turn left onto the N98, but in 2km turn right onto the old main road which takes you into La Londe-les-Maures. Follow the old rather than the new road up the valley to the east of La Londe, passing through St-Honoré. Where the two roads rejoin you can take a pleasant detour around a lake set in the hills. Rejoin the N98, driving E through the Maures to Cogolin.

Continue in the direction of the coastal resorts of Port Grimaud and St-Tropez but turn off to the right on the N559 to La Croix-Valmer. Turn left here onto a tortuous road, enjoying the panoramic views, through the coastal hills and over the Col de Collebasse to the charming village of Ramatuelle. Now you can return via the D61 to Port Grimaud. Cars are in fact banned from this striking harbour-village with a mooring for nearly every house. The best view is from the village tower.

Take the D61 across the plain to Grimaud itself which is built on a hillside at the foot of a ruined castle. The church is a Romanesque basilica and just outside the centre is the pretty 15th-century Chapelle des Pénitents Blancs. From the town drive into the Massif des Maures once more on the D558. The road climbs to La Garde-Freinet, then passes through the forest. Once at the foot of the hills, turn right onto the D48, which passes under the autoroute and eventually reaches Vidauban. Leave this village on the D48, crossing the river Argens, then turn right onto the D73 to Taradeau. Turn right here onto the D10 (east), go under the railway, and then turn left to Les Arcs. Leave the little town on the D91, passing the abbey of Ste-Roseline, a historic monument and home of a wine estate, then turn right onto the N555 back to the starting point and the A8 autoroute.

LOCAL PRODUCERS

Bandol
LE BEAUSSET
Domaine du Val d'Arenc: Well-made red wines that mature well. "Cuvée de la Gravière" is especially recommended.
LA CADIERE-D'AZUR
Moulin des Costes: Quality achieved by Paul and Pierre Bunan with their red, rosé and white Bandol is only occasionally matched by other local producers.
Domaine de Pibarnon: Highest wine estate in Bandol. Henri de Saint-Victor produces wines that are full of character and often win awards.

Bellet
BELLET-DE-NICE
Château de Crémat: Leading estate owned by the Bagnis family (who saved the Bellet appellation). Gently refreshing white, red and rosé wines.
ST-ROMAN-DE-BELLET
Château de Bellet: Excellent white wine. The red and rosé too, are very successful.

Cassis
CASSIS
Le Ferme Blanche: Attractive, refreshing white wines, from a blend of five grape varieties.
Château de Fontcreuse: This is the only Cassis château. The white Coteaux Cassidains is the best product.
Domaine du Paternel: An elegant Cassis.
Clos Ste-Magdeleine: Meaty, generous Cassis, made by François Sack.

Coteaux d'Aix-en-Provence
LANÇON-DE-PROVENCE
Château de Calisanne: A very good "Cuvée Prestige", as well as simpler wines.
LE PUY-STE-REPARADE
Domaine les Bastides: Sound red "Cuvée Spéciale" matured in wood.
Château La Coste
Château de Fonscolombe: Important property belonging to De Saporta family. Very successful red, white and rosé wines, especially the "Cuvée Spéciale".
RIANS
Château Vignelaure: Georges Brunet has done pioneering work here, e.g. by planting Cabernet Sauvignon. The elegant characterful red is one of the very best in Provence. Modern art can be admired in the château and cellars. In 1986 an American group acquired a majority shareholding and Brunet has left.
ST-CANNAT
Château de Beaupré: Baron Double's wines include a delicious pure rosé.
VERNEGUES
Château Bas: Since 1970 George de

Blanquet has produced red wines of a consistently improving quality; his "Cuvée Temple" deserves note.

Coteaux d'Aix-en-Provence-Les-Baux
ST-ETIENNE-DU-GRES
Domaine de Trévallon: Red wine, full of subtlety, the best in the district. The maker is Eloi Dürrbach.

Coteaux Varois
ST-MAXIMIN-LA-STE-BAUME
Domaine du Déffends/Clos de la Truffière: Estate producing exquisite red and rosé wines (including "Rosé d'une Nuit").
VILLECROZE
Domaine de St-Jean: Excellently equipped estate where American Alain Hirsch makes exemplary red and rosé wines from Cabernet Sauvignon and other grapes.

Côtes du Lubéron
APT
Domaine de l'Isolette: Owner Luc Pinatel repeatedly wins awards with his red and white wines.
BONNIEUX
Château La Canorgue: A fine estate of the Lubéron, with wines that include a red that could equal a *cru* from the Beaujolais. Jean-Pierre Margan is the owner.
PERTUIS
Château Val-Joanis: Large model estate created from nothing since 1978 by Jean-louis Chancel.

Côtes de Provence
ANTIBES
Domaines Ott: Head office of the very active Ott family, who own and successfully manage several well-known wine estates. Among them are Clos Mireille and Château de Selle in Côtes de Provence, and Château Romasson in Bandol.
LES ARCS-SUR-ARGENS
Domaine des Hauts de St-Jean: Henri Pawlowski's wines deserve their countless medals.
Château Ste-Roseline: This estate is a former convent, now listed as a historic monument. Generous red wine, in a striking bottle.

FREJUS
Domaine de Curebéasse: Jacques Paquette's white wine is one of the best in Provence, and his red and rosé are also good.

LA LONDE-LES-MAURES
Domaine St-André de Figuière: Intensely, fragrant, lively, red "Cuvée Spéciale".

LORGUES
Castel Roubine: M. Hallgren, a Dane, who bought this estate in 1979, has expanded the vineyards and improved quality.

LE LUC
Domaine de la Bernarde: Property with modern equipment producing admirable rosé and good red wines.

PIGNANS
Domaine de Rimaurescq: Estate owned by the Isnard family for three centuries.

PUYLOUBIER
Domaine Richeaume: An admirable estate both for its architecture and for its wines. Henning Hoesch is the owner.

SE ROQUEBRUNE-SUR-ARGENS
Domaine des Planes: The wine growers Christopher and Ilse Rieder make exemplary wines. The red Côtes de Provence comes in two styles.

VIDAUBAN
Domaine des Féraud: One of the leading estates: white, red and rosé are all excellent.

Domaine Peissonel: Pierre Lemaître is a fervent promoter of the wines of Provence. His own red wine is well above average.

Palette
MEYREUIL
Château Simone: Using a rich range of grape varieties, the Rougier family produces a red wine that in good years creates a veritable symphony of tastes. The château also produces a rosé and two styles of white.

WINE INFORMATION

LES ARCS-SUR-ARGENS
La Maison des Vins Côtes de Provence

HOTELS AND RESTAURANTS

AIX-EN-PROVENCE, 13100
Arbaud (B), 19 Cours Mirabeau, tel: 42 26 66 88
Beautifully furnished restaurant and tearoom food is good too.
Le Clos de la Violette (A/B), 10 Avenue Violette, tel: 42 23 30 71
Talented chef. Beautiful garden.
LES ARCS-SUR-ARGENS, 83460
Le Logis du Guetteur (B)
tel: 94 73 30 82
Hotel and restaurant in quiet location.
BANDOL, 83150
Auberge du Port (A)
tel: 94 29 42 63
Shellfish is popular at restaurant overlooking harbour.
Hotel Ile Rousse (A)
tel: 94 29 46 86
De luxe beach hotel with good food. Demi-pension only in season. Restaurant (B).
La Réserve (C), tel: 94 29 42 71
Pleasant restaurant with uncomplicated cooking.
LES BAUX-DE-PROVENCE, 13520
Bautezar et Musée (A/B)
tel: 90 54 32 09
Pleasant small hotel. Terrace.
La Cabro d'Or (A), tel: 90 97 33 21
Hotel and restaurant (same owners as l'Oustaù) surrounded by beautiful garden. Excellent food. Restaurant (B).
l'Oustaù de Baumanière (A)
tel: 90 54 33 07
Provençal cuisine of highest calibre. Impressive wine list. Also a luxury hotel.
BORMES-LES-MIMOSAS, 83230
La Tonnelle des Délices (B)
tel: 94 71 34 84
Extremely popular restaurant with regional dishes and wines.
LA CADIERE-D'AZUR, 83740
Hostellerie Bérard (B)
tel: 94 90 11 43
One of best and smartest hotels around Bandol. Food is worth a detour.
CASSIS, 13260
Chez Gilbert/Restaurant le Port (C), tel: 42 01 71 36
Busy harbour restaurant.

Le Flibustier (B/C)
tel: 42 01 02 73
Restaurant at harbour entrance.
La Presqu'île (B), tel: 42 01 03 77
Mediterranean fish creatively
prepared.
CASTELLET, 83330
Castel Lumière (B)
tel: 94 32 62 20
Cooking with a regional slant and an
impressive view from terrace. Few
rooms (*demi-pension* in season).
**CHATEAUNEUF-LE-ROUGE,
13790**
La Galinière (B), tel: 42 58 62 04
Hotel and restaurant close to N7.
COMPS-SUR-ARTUBY, 83840
Grand Hotel Bain (C)
tel: 94 76 90 06
Ideal place for lunch on way to the
Gorges du Verdon. Terrace.
LA CROIX-VALMER, 83420
La Brigantine (C)
tel: 94 79 67 16
One of the restaurants of the *Hotel
des Moulins de Paillas*, close to the
beach. *Demi-pension* only in season.
DRAGUIGNAN, 83300
Les 2 Cochers (C), tel: 94 68 13 97
Restaurant near to station and
offering reliable Provençal cooking.
EYGALIERES, 13810
Auberge Provençale (C)
tel: 90 95 91 00
Well-prepared simple meals and also
a few beautiful rooms. Terrace.
FREJUS, 83600
Auberge du Vieux Four (B)
57 Rue Grisolle, tel: 94 51 56 38
Small establishment with fine cuisine
and interesing wine list.
LA FUSTE, 04210
Hostellerie de la Fuste (A)
tel: 92 72 05 95
One of best places in Coteaux du
Pierrevert countryside. Restaurant (B).
GASSIN, 83580
Bello Vista (C), tel: 94 56 17 30
Magnificent view from well known
restaurant on promenade.
GRIMAUD, 83360
Au Café de France (C)
tel: 94 43 20 05
Adequate to good restaurant on
village square. Terrace.
**Hostellerie du Coteau Fleurie
(B)**, tel: 94 43 20 17

Charming hotel with views over valley.
Try good value "menu du marché".
Restaurant (C).
LES ISSAMBRES, 3380
La Réserve (B), tel: 94 96 90 41
Good value provençal cooking. Rooms
available. Large terrace.
LORGUES, 83510
Auberge Josse (C)
tel: 94 73 73 55
Good food served from the grill.
LE LUC, 83340
Hostellerie du Parc (B)
tel: 94 60 70 01
Prettily appointed hotel and
restaurant.
PERTUIS, 84120
Sevan (B), tel: 90 79 19 30
Modern complex with chalets. *Demi-
pension* in season. Restaurant (C).
PUYLOUBIER, 13114
Les Sarments (C), tel: 42 29 32 07
Provençal cooking with flair.
ST-TROPEZ, 83990
Café des Arts (C), tel: 94 97 02 25
Favourite eating place on Place de
Lices. Honest regional dishes.
Le Chabichou (A/B),
tel: 94 54 80 00
The best local restaurant with good
fish specialities.
La Romana (A), tel: 94 97 15 50
Très Tropézien Italian cuisine.
TOURTOUR, 83690
La Bastide de Tourtour (A)
tel: 94 70 57 30
Grand hotel with excellent restaurant
(B). *Demi-pension* in season.
Les Chênes Verts (B)
tel: 94 70 55 06
Small restaurant on road from
Tourtour to Villecroze.
Les Lavandes (B), tel: 94 70 57 11
Pretty hotel in wooded countryside.
Demi-pension in season.
TRETS, 13530
l'Oustau du Vin (C)
tel: 42 61 51 51
Attractive menu and wine list.
VIDAUBAN, 83550
Le Concorde (C), tel: 94 73 01 19
Good food and friendly service with
an extensive wine list.
VILLECROZE, 83690
Au Bien-Etre (C), tel 94 70 67 57
Restaurant and hotel (B) on road to
Lorgues. Talented *patron*.

SE

LANGUEDOC

APPELLATION CONTROLEE AREA
WINE ROUTE
OTHER ROADS
DEPARTEMENT BOUNDARY

The Languedoc is France's largest wine region, covering the départements of Aude, Garde and Hérault and comprising almost a third of all its vineyards. This is the traditional territory of Vin Ordinaire and in the past the sheer quantity of nameless wine produced has obscured the better-quality wines. However, during the 1980s several Languedoc districts have been awarded *appellation contrôlée* status: Faugères, St-Chinian, Coteaux du Languedoc, Corbières, Minervois, and Costières du Gard.

THE WINE ROUTE

The university town of Montpellier, seat of the most important wine school in France, is the eastern gateway to the Languedoc. Montpellier has been a wine town for centuries and some of the houses in the old part of the town still have cellars and winemaking equipment.

The Wine Route leaves the town via the N113, the main route to the west. As soon as you have left the suburbs, turn left onto the N112 for Frontignan. This road runs close to the coastal lagoons or *étangs* which are a feature of the Languedoc littoral. The town of Mireval, *en route*, is the centre of the Muscat de Mireval appellation for Vin Doux Naturel (VDN). It is soon succeeded by the AOC Muscat de Frontignan, also a VDN and the largest of the four districts for Muscat. It is worth stopping in the town to visit the museum which contains wine-related exhibits and in Frontignan-Plage, the cellars of Noilly Prat are open to the public. Continue on the N112 towards Sète, but turning right onto the D2 (a new road) along the eastern shore of the Bassin de Thau. Rejoin the N113, turning left to Mèze. After leaving Mèze turn left on the D51 to the wine village of Marseillan where the Domaine de la Fadèze makes excellent

Vins de Pays (Syrah). Return to the D51, shortly turning left onto the D18, then immediately right onto a minor road (D161 E) to Pinet. This is the centre of the Picpoul de Pinet district (Coteaux du Languedoc), where refreshing, tart white wines are made. From Pinet continue on the D161 E, crossing the autoroute, to Castelnau-de-Guers, a commune which also belongs to the Coteaux du Languedoc. This AOC covers a large tract of country from N of Montpellier across to N of Narbonne.

From Castelnau head NW (D32 E) for Pézenas, a fascinating old town with some beautiful old houses in the centre. Leave on the D13 to Roujan, another Coteaux du Languedoc commune. By now you will be able to see the hills of the Haut-Languedoc ahead. The French authorities are encouraging viticulture in this hill country and discouraging the growing of vines on the flat, over-productive land of the coastal plains.

The D13 is your route from Roujan to Faugères, the centre of an appellation for vigorous red wines. Much of the area is also entitled to use the AOC Coteaux du Languedoc: many Languedoc wine districts have these intertwining – and confusing – appellations. Leave Faugères on the D13 again and turn left onto the D909 for a short distance before turning right onto the D154. In the village of Cassiniojoules turn left onto the D154 E, which joins the D136 and continues through to Lenthéric and St-Nazaire-de-Ladorez. Here you leave the Faugères district and enter St-Chinian, another red-wine AOC in the Languedoc foothills.

At a junction past St-Nazaire-de-Ladorez (still on the D136) turn right onto the D19, which runs beside the river Orb to Roquebrun. Leave the village on the D14, along the west bank of the river, turning left on the D179 to follow the winding road through wooded countryside. Go through the wine villages of Berlou and Ferrières-Poussarou and join the main road (the N112), turning left for St-Chinian with its 9th-century monastery. Leave St-Chinian on the

SE

N112 in the direction of Béziers, but turn right after passing through Cébazan onto the D36. This road runs through AOC St-Chinian as far as Cruzy. Follow the D36 through Cruzy to the junction with the D5, where you turn right. You now enter the large Minervois appellation, which runs w almost as far as Carcassonne. The D5 crosses in and out of the Aude département and thus its number changes to the D11. Continue on this road and just before Olonzac, cross the bridge over the Canal du Midi and turn left onto the D611 to Lézignan-Corbières. This town has a very interesting Musée de la Vigne et du Vin with winemaking equipment etc. It is here that the large Corbières appellation begins, stretching across a range of hills to the southern border of the Languedoc.

From Lézignan-Corbières take the N113 (west) towards Carcassonne. The road runs along a wide valley, with the hills of the Minervois to the right and the stark ranges of the Corbières to the left. Take the minor D2113 through Moux and Douzens, rejoining the rather busy route nationale through Capendu to Carcassonne. The most famous part of the town is the restored old Cité built on a hill, a medieval stronghold, complete with walls, turrets and a moat.

Leave Carcassonne on the N113 again, but on the outskirts of Trèbes turn right onto the D3, which crosses the autoroute and immediately climbs into the Corbières hills. The D3 snakes through the hills, passing a string of wine communes which make increasingly impressive red wines. Continue through the Sou gorge (still on the D3) to Lagrasse with its ancient abbey, then on to Tournissan and St-Laurent-de-la-Cabrerisse. Here, join the D611, either continuing on this road to Thézan-des-Corbières and on southwards to link up with the Roussillon tour, or join the D613 across a wide vineyard valley eastwards. Where the D613 meets the N113, turn right into Narbonne. This ancient city has a fine 13th-century cathedral as well as a wine museum

(Rue Flatters) illustrating the history of winegrowing in the Aube.

From Narbonne take the D32 towards the coast. The line of coastal plains is broken here by the limestone massif of La Clape, which is rapidly gaining a name as a wine district. Elegant reds and good, fresh whites are made here, with Chardonnay among the grapes which flourish. The Wine Route ends at the coastal town of Gruissan.

WINE INFORMATION

BEZIERS
Maison Régionale des Vins
18 Rue de 4-Septembre
CARCASSONNE
Caveau des Vins d'Origine
Porte Narbonnaise
LEZIGNAN-CORBIERES
Les Coteaux Occitans (on the N113)
MONTPELLIER
Hotel Montpellierain des Vins du Languedoc
7 Rue Jacques-Coeur
OLONZAC
Maison du Minervois
Boulevard Blazin
ST-CHINIAN
Maison des Vins

HOTELS AND RESTAURANTS

BEZIERS, 34500
Hotel Imperator (B), 28 Allées Paul Riquet, tel: 67 49 02 25
Very comfortable hotel in the centre of town.
L'Olivier (B), 12 Rue Boïeldieu, tel: 68 25 22 17
Small bistro-style restaurant, clever and creative cuisine.
Au Trou Normand (B), 13 Allées Paul Riquet, tel: 67 28 53 01
Good restaurant with the prettiest dining room in Béziers.
CARCASSONNE, 11000
Domaine d'Auriac (A)
tel: 68 25 72 22
Luxury hotel surrounded by a park. Excellent restaurant (B).
Le Languedoc (B/C), 32 Allée d'Iéna, tel: 68 25 22 17

Good menu with regional dishes.
Logis de Trencavel (B), 2986 Avenue Général-Leclerc, tel: 68 71 09 53
Good cooking and wide range of regional wines. Rooms.
Auberge du Pont Lévis (B) tel: 68 25 55 23
Excellent restaurant just east of Cité (on the first floor).
Pont Vieux (B), 32 Rue Trivalle, tel: 68 25 24 99
Correct small hotel near Cité.

LEZIGNAN-CORBIERES, 11200
Le Tassigny (B), tel: 68 27 11 51
Hotel with classically furnished rooms. *Le Tournedos* restaurant (C) popular with locals.

LIMOUX, 11300
Maison de la Blanquette (C) tel: 68 31 01 63
Winegrowers' wives serve food and cooperative-produced wine.

LUNEL, 34400
Hostellerie du Palais (C) tel: 67 71 11 39
Traditional food in a rustic setting. Garden and hotel (B/C).

MINERVE, 34120
Les Aliberts (C), tel: 68 91 14 18
Old fortified farm high above Minerve: the wines of the abbey of Fontfroide used to be aged here.
Relais Chantovent (C) tel: 68 91 14 18
Delicious inexpensive food. Good views from balcony.

MONTPELLIER, 34000
Hotel Montpellierain des Vins du Languedoc (C), 7 Rue Jacques-Coeur, tel: 67 60 42 41
Promotional and information centre for wine, where you can also eat.

NARBONNE, 11100
l'Alsace (C), 2 Avenue Pierre-Semard, tel: 68 65 10 24
No specialities from Alsace but excellent *bouillabaisse*.
Le Floride (B), 66 Boulevard Frédéric-Mistral, tel: 68 32 05 52
Relaxed eating place with *fruits de mer* a speciality.

La Résidence (B), 6 Rue du 1er Mai, tel: 68 32 19 41
Very pleasant hotel in town centre.
La Réverbère (B), 4 Place des Jacobins, tel: 68 32 29 18
Highly regarded restaurant with inventive and high-quality food.

NIMES, 30000
Hotel du Cheval Blanc (B) tel: 66 67 20 03
Renovated hotel near Roman arena. Restaurant.
Mapotel Imperator/l'Enclos de la Fontaine (B), tel: 66 21 90 30
A pleasant restaurant in an old restored house with charming garden. Also a hotel (A/B).

ORNAISONS, 11200
Le Relais de Val d'Orbieu (B) tel: 68 27 10 27
Very quiet high-class hotel. Good restaurant (B).

PEYRIAC-MINERVOIS, 11160
Château de Violet (A/B) tel: 68 78 10 42
Beautifully-furnished château-hotel with park and pool. Restaurant (B).

PEZENAS, 34120
Hotel Genieys (B/C) tel: 67 98 13 99
Small, renowned town hotel with country style food. *Demi-pension* obligatory in season.

POILHES-LA-ROMAIN, 34310
La Tour Sarrasine (B) tel: 67 93 41 31
Former smithy with modern paintings and stylish cooking.

ST-CHINIAN, 34360
Lou Flambadou (C), tel: 67 38 13 02
Inn with regional dishes and wines.

SETE, 34200
La Palangrotte (C), Quai Général-Durand, tel: 67 74 80 35
Probably the best fish restaurant in the area.

VIC-LA-GARIOLE, 34110
Le Balajan (B/C), tel: 67 48 13 99
Functional hotel standing amongst Frontignan vineyards. Restaurant (C).

SE

ROUSSILLON

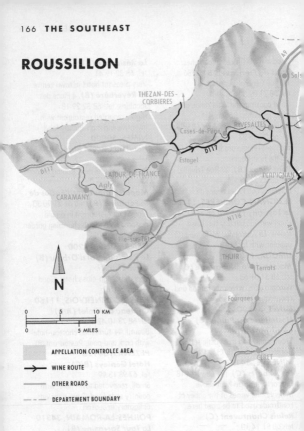

Roussillon only became part of France in 1642, and it is still a distinct province, with more in common with the rest of Catalonia, across the Spanish border, than with France. Spanish influences are still clearly present: the language spoken in this area (now the département of Pyrénées-Orientales) is Catalan and old fortified villages still mark the former frontier with France.

The wines, however, are similar to those of Languedoc to the north and are of a consistently good quality. *Macération carbonique* (the traditional method of Beaujolais) is widely used to make fresh, fruity red wines and ageing in wood is also gaining ground. Côtes du Roussillon is the overall appellation, with Côtes du Roussillon Villages for the superior northern part of the zone. In volume, the Côtes du Roussillon is France's largest producer of Vin Doux Naturel, a fortified apéritif and dessert wine.

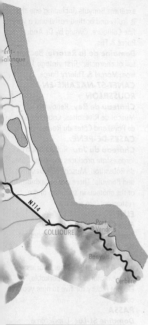

From Estagel follow the river Agly E, still on the D117, passing through the heart of the Côtes du Roussillon Villages country. Turn left on the D614 into Rivesaltes, the capital of the VDN appellation. Rivesaltes is made in red, white and Muscat styles: the latter is generally considered the best. Leave the town on the D12 going N, then turn right on the D83 to cross the autoroute and join the N9. Turn right (and south) towards Perpignan.

Perpignan is the capital of Roussillon, an ancient city with many fine monuments. The old centre is still surrounded by medieval walls, and in the heart of the city is the palace of the kings of Mallorca, who ruled Roussillon until 1642. Also in the city centre is the cathedral of St-Jean dating from the 14th to 16th centuries and well worth seeing. The 1397 Loge de Mer was formerly a courthouse for maritime cases. In Perpignan in summer you can see the dancing of the Sardana, a graceful folk-dance celebrated in sketches and paintings by Picasso and indigenous to Catalonia. Perpignan is also the centre of the Côtes du Roussillon wine industry and the site of the big cooperative group, Vignerons Catalans, which unites some 50 producers and makes much of the region's best wine.

Continue S from Perpignan on the N114 across a wide plain where fruit, vegetables and grapes are grown. Grapes are in fact the most common fruit in Roussillon – some 40% of all agricultural lands is planted with vines. In summer, the farmers sell fruit – especially, peaches, cherries and plums – at the roadside. Bypass Elne, another historic fortress town which for centuries was more important than Perpignan. The town has a beautiful early-medieval cathedral with fine cloisters, which are among the most famous architectural treasures found in the Romanesque abbeys and churches of Roussillon.

South of Elne you can see the easternmost mountains of the Pyrenees rising ahead of you, and vineyards extend W into the beautiful

THE WINE ROUTE

The Wine Route begins in the north, linking with the Languedoc Route on page 162. (To connect the two, follow the D611 southwards from Thézan-des-Corbières through Villeneuve-les-Corbières, Tuchan and Paziols.) Enter Roussillon on the D611, driving S from Paziols through the gap in the frontier hills carved by the river Verdouble. The road follows the river into the valley of the Agly, one of the main east-west rivers draining the foothills of the Pyrenees. On reaching the main road between Maury and Estagel, turn left, joining the D117 to Estagel. This countryside falls within the Maury appellation, a district making Vins Doux Naturels – mostly red – from the Grenache and other grapes. The area, and indeed most of the winegrowing in Roussillon, is within the VDN appellation of Rivesaltes, and many growers use this better-known name rather than Maury.

countryside of the foothills. To the east is the coastal plain, most of which is outside the Côtes du Roussillon appellation. The flat, sandy coast, much of which is backed by salt-water lagoons, has been developed as a string of modern holiday resorts. This development was only made possible by a major campaign to eradicate the mosquitoes which until the 1960s made the area almost uninhabitable.

An interesting detour leads inland from Argelès-sur-Mer on the D618 to the little town of Ceret, set in a valley in the foothills and surrounded by cherry orchards. The town has an attractive small museum of modern art which houses some treasures by Picasso and Matisse.

Return to the main Wine Route heading s. Past Argelès the N114 begins to climb and the sea comes into view: this is the Côte Vermeille, so-called for its red cliffs. The next town you come to is the port and holiday village of Collioure, with its fortified church on a harbourside quay, and gives its name to an appellation for strong red wines grown on terraces behind the town. Collioure is a favourite haunt of early 20th-century artists such as Matisse. The AOC extends beyond Port-Vendres, further s on the N114, then comes the Banyuls appellation. The steep slaty hillsides and an obligatory period of ageing make Banyuls one of the better VDNs.The best (and most mature) is Banyuls Grand Cru.

The dramatic coast road leads on to Cerbère, beyond which is the Spanish frontier. The road can be followed into Spain for a visit to some of the least-spoilt fishing villages of the northern Costa Brava. Alternatively, a dramatic and steep minor road, the D86, leads from Banyuls through the hills back to Collioure.

LOCAL PRODUCERS

BANYULS-SUR-MER
Domaine du Mas Blanc: Produces

excellent Banyuls (including one that is fruity and bottled early) and a very fine Collioure. Owned by Dr André Parcé & Fils.
Domaine de la Retorie: Banyuls full of character (first vintage 1984) from Marcel & Thierry Parcé.
CANET-ST-NAZAIRE-EN-ROUSSILLON
Château de Rey: Renowned Muscat de Rivesaltes, Cabernet (Vin de Pays) and Côtes du Roussillon.
CASES-DE-PENE
Château du Jau: Robert Doutres' large estate produces excellent Côtes du Roussillon, Muscat de Rivesaltes and Banyuls. There are art exhibitions at the château in summer, and a restaurant (see over).
ELNE
Mas Chichet: Paul Chichet's speciality is a wood-aged Cabernet Vin de Pays.
MAURY
Mas Amiel: The owner Charles Dupuy, matures his remarkable, elegant Maury for five to nine years in cask.
PASSA
Domaine St-Luc: Luc-Jérôme Talut's best wine is his Muscat de Rivesaltes.
PERPIGNAN
Vignerons Catalans: A group set up in 1965. Some 50 cooperatives and various individual estates are now associated with it. More than any other concern, Vignerons Catalans has striven to raise the standard of quality of Roussillon wine – with great success. The group's large range includes red Villages from Caramany, Latour-de-France and from Château Cap de Fouste, Château St-Martin and Mas de la Dona. Many of the white wines are also to be recommended, for example the Taïchat, and the rosé from Rasiguères is one of the best in the district.
PORT-VENDRES
Cellier des Templiers/GICB: Group of five cooperatives that produce more than half of all Banyuls (and Collioure). The group has a good range of many excellent wines.
RIVESALTES
Cazes Frères: André and Bernard

Cazes make a wide range of good wines, notably, Muscat de Rivesaltes, Côtes du Roussillon Villages and both red and white Vins de Pays.

WINE INFORMATION

La Commende Majeure de Roussillon and Les Maîtres-Tasteurs du Roussillon.
(Both of these bodies promotes Roussillon wines.)
Les Templiers de la Serre
(Promotes the wines of Banyuls.)

HOTELS AND RESTAURANTS

BANYULS-SUR-MER, 66650
Le Catalan (A/B), tel: 68 88 02 80
Modern hotel, built in a semicircle on the rocks. *Demi-pension* in season.
Les Elmes (B), tel: 68 88 03 12
Comfortable beach hotel where you can eat well. Restaurant (C). *Demi-pension* in season.
Le Sardinal (C), tel: 68 88 30 07
Good seafood dishes and a fine wine list.
CASES-DE-PENE, 66600
Château de Jau (C),
tel: 68 64 11 38
You can lunch here in summer by prior arrangement. (See Local Producers also.)
CASTELNOU, 66300
l'Hostal (C), tel: 68 53 45 42
Famous for *cargolade* and other regional dishes.
CLAIRA, 66530
Le Baroque (C), tel: 68 28 23 17
Excellent selection of Roussillon wines at this restaurant.
COLLIOURE, 66190
La Bodega (B/C), tel: 68 82 05 60
Regional cooking of good standard in a former wine cellar.
La Casa Païral (A/B)
tel: 68 82 05 81
Luxuriously appointed hotel in a park

full of flowers. Swimming pool.
La Frégate (C), tel: 68 82 06 05
Restaurant with garden-like interior and terrace outside. Also hotel (B).
Les Templiers (C), tel: 68 82 05 58
Great artists such as Dufy, Matisse and Picasso paid their bills at this restaurant with their art. Some 3,000 works hang in the premises. Also a hotel (B/C).
MAURY, 66460
Le Quéribus (C), tel: 68 59 10 26
Game and local wine.
PERPIGNAN, 66000
Athéna (B/C), 1 Rue Queya,
tel: 68 34 37 63
Central but reasonably quiet hotel. Swimming pool.
Le Festin de Pierre (B/C), 7 Rue du Théâtre, tel: 68 51 28 74
Restaurant noted for fish and poultry.
Le François Villon (C), 1 Rue de Four-St-Jean, tel: 68 51 18 43
Inspired regional cuisine.
Le Mas des Arcades (B), Rue d'Espagne/RN 9, tel: 68 85 11 11
Modern complex on edge of town with swimming pool and restaurant.
Park Hotel/Le Chapon Fin (B)
18 Boulevard Jean-Bourrat,
tel: 68 35 14 14
Progressive cooking in quite luxurious hotel.
Le Rallye (C), 8 Place des Variétés, tel: 68 35 16 16
Authentic regional cuisine.
Relais St-Jean (B), 1 Cité Bartissol, tel: 68 51 22 25
Contemporary cuisine in the shadow of cathedral. Good wine list with wines by the glass.
Le Vauban (C), 29 Quai Vauban, tel: 68 51 05 10
Busy, brasserie-style bistro.
RIVESALTES, 66600
Alta Riba (B/C), tel: 68 64 01 17
Pleasant and very adequate hotel and restaurant.

SE

CORSICA

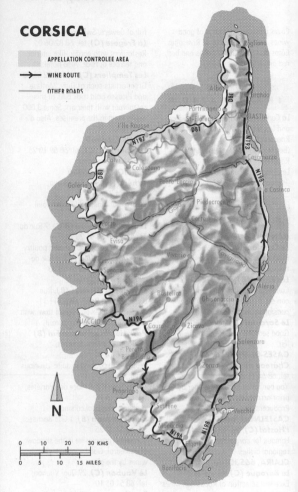

APPELLATION CONTROLEE AREA

WINE ROUTE

OTHER ROADS

Traditionally the greater part of winemaking in Corsica has been concentrated on cheap Vins de Table, and for many years *appellation contrôlée* wines represented less than three percent of the total output. However, the island does produce a respectable amount of very good wines from independent growers and the proportion of appellation wines is on the increase.

THE WINE ROUTE

Starting from Bastia in the north, follow the coastal road through the scattered vineyards that make up the appellation Coteaux du Cap Corse. These most northerly vineyards specialize in dessert wines including sweet Muscat. The best dry white

wine of the island (100% Vermentino), Clos Nicrosi, is also made at the tip of this wild limestone peninsula.

In the southwest of the peninsula is the beautiful little district of Patrimonio which produces some excellent red wines, made primarily of Nielluccio, with one degree higher minimum alcohol (12.5%) than the rest of the island's wine. The top grower is Dominique Gentile in St-Florent.

Continue along the scenic west coast on the N197 and you enter La Balagne, the largest quality wine district with its wines being sold under the name Calvi. Principal producers of the area include Domaine de Cantone and Couvent d'Alzipratu. From Calvi take the D81 through Galéria to Porto, near to which the vineyards of the Ajaccio appellation begin. The Coteaux d'Ajaccio, around the capital, is one of the most active wine districts with the classic Corsican red grape, the Sciacarello, grown principally here and in the Sartènais area around Propriano.

From Ajaccio take the N196 to the little port of Proriano itself, dating back to classical times and now a thriving seaside resort. Continue into the medieval town of Sartène which is the centre for another Vin de Corse appellation. Keep on the N196 to Bonifacio, an old fortress-port on a spectacular site at the very south of the island. The N198 leads from Bonifacio through the vineyards of the Porto-Vecchio appellation. The town is a busy holiday resort and the fact that it is still numbered among the wine districts is largely due to one dynamic grower, Christian Imbert (Domaine de Torraccia).

The east coast is dominated by its low-lying area, where the best wines are offered under the name Vin de Corse. Large estates and a number of cooperatives set the pace. Considerable advances have been made in quality so that today there are pure, pleasant red and rosé wines to enjoy. In central Corsica, near Ponte Leccia, there is a tiny district that also produces Vin de Corse.

To return to Bastia, continue up the east coast by the N198 and N193.

WINE INFORMATION

AJACCIO
CREPAC
Casa Corsa,
22 Boulevard Dominique Paoli
BASTIA
GIVC
6 Rue Gabriel Péri

HOTELS AND RESTAURANTS

AJACCIO, 20000
Columbia (C), 2 Avenue de Paris, tel: 95 21 12 66
Simple, pleasant hotel for budget-conscious visitors.
Eden-Roc (A), Routes des Sanguinaires, tel: 95 52 01 47
By the sea. *Demi-pension* only.
Fesch (B), 7 Rue Cardinal-Fesch, tel: 95 21 50 52
Comfortable hotel in town centre.
Palm Beach (B), Routes des Sanguinaires, tel: 95 52 01 03
Small hotel restaurant owned by winegrower. Modern Corsican cuisine.
Pardi (C), 60 Rue Cardinal-Fesch, tel: 95 21 43 08
Corsican cooking in a traditional setting.
BASTIA, 20200
Chez Assunta (B), 4 Place Fontaine-Neuve, tel: 95 31 67 06
Renowned restaurant in large vaulted room with a terrace.
Lavezzi (B), 8 Rue St-Jean, tel: 95 31 05 73
The best classic and local cuisine in Bastia by the old harbour.
CALVI, 20260
l'Abbaye (B), Route de Santure, tel: 95 65 04 27
Conveniently and comfortable hotel in a former monastery.
Comme Chez Soi (C)
tel: 95 65 00 59
Fish restaurant with a view over the harbour.

SE

INDEX

Latour, which if the local boundaries had not been rearranged would still be in St-Julien.

Continue on the D2, past Ch Fonbadet to your left and Ch Bellegrave to your right (not visible from the road), but then take the left-hand fork off the D2 which takes you past Ch Lynch-Bages **7** down a small road to your left.

At the next junction turn right, then left again towards Pauillac back on the D2. 250 metres on turn right, then take the left fork which, by taking another left turn onto the D2 E6, will take you into Pauillac via the river quay past Ch Grand-Puy-Ducasse. Follow the road around to the left then turn right at the next T-junction away from Pauillac onto the D2.

Follow the road (ignoring the D205) to your left into Le Pouyalet. Go straight through the village. The road curves to the left, then straightens. Take the next left to Ch Lafite-Rothschild.

Continuing on the D2 will take you onto the St-Estèphe Wine Route.

SW Retrace your steps to Le Pouyalet, then turn right, passing Ch Mouton Rothschild, elevated in 1973 to the status of Premier Cru, to your right. Take the next left which goes past Ch Mouton Baronne Philippe **8** and at the T-junction with the D20, turn right.

Follow the road eastwards for about a km and at the next junction take the second left through vineyards and then through woodland in the direction of Labrousse. After nearly 2km the road curves to the left, then bends to the right where the vineyards begin again. Just past Ch Fonpiqueyre down to your left, take a left turn. The road goes straight for nearly 500m, then turns sharply to the left; as it joins the D104 E1 turn left.

Follow the road, with woodland on your right, vineyards to your left, over a hill, past Ch le Fournas. Take a left turn at the next crossroads, then a sharp right at Ste-Croix along the D104 E3 following the road to a crossroads. Turn right. The road bends sharply and Ch Grand-Puy-Lacoste owned by the Borie family lies to the left. Continue to a crossroads

with the D206 and turn right, following the road past Ch Batailley to your left, with its wonderful park, towards St-Laurent-et-Benon.

About 3km down the road you pass Ch Larose-Trintaudon, which has the biggest vineyard in the Médoc. Continue for about 2km and the road forks with the right-hand turn taking you to the N215 to Lesparre-Médoc, which enables you to join up with the Northern Médoc wine tour. To continue through the St-Julien area take the left fork and join the N215 (south) for a short distance, then the first left – the D101 back towards Beychevelle.

As you follow the road you pass successively on your right: Ch la Tour-Carnet, Ch de Camensac, then Ch Belgrave and as the road turns to the right, Ch Lagrange again to your right. Continue on the D101 into Beychevelle, and as the road bends to the right, then to the left, Ch Gruaud-Larose lies to the south.

The D2 joins from the left; turn right to return to Lamarque.

THE CHATEAUX

St-Julien-Beychevelle (Appellation St-Julien)
Château Beychevelle
4e Grand Cru Classé
Much-needed improvements have been made by the civil service organization that owns the estate.

Château Branaire-Ducru
4e Grand Cru Classé
An immaculate château, set well back in grounds, opposite Beychevelle.

Château Ducru-Beaucaillou
2e Grand Cru Classé
This château is set majestically against the east slope of the southerly St-Julien gravel plateaux.

Château Gruaud-Larose
2e Grand Cru Classé
The large château with its extensive park and vineyard belongs to the Cordier family.

Château Lagrange
3e Grand Cru Classé
Large estate that has been renovated by its owners, Suntory.

St-Julien wines are among the most celebrated and most sought after in the world. Grand Crus predominate with no fewer than 11, which between them occupy 85 percent of the vineyard area. Nearly all the rest of the St-Julien wines are also of a high standard and in terms of quality this is one of the most homogenous Bordeaux appellations.

The provincial town of Pauillac, with some 6,500 inhabitants is the capital of the Médoc. Most of the châteaux are spread out over the commune, often around small hamlets such as St-Lambert and Bages south of the town and Le Pouyalet to the north. Latour, Lafite and Mouton, three of the five first-growths of the 1855 classification are found here and 15 more classed growths, with Rothschild a recurring theme. Pauillac's great estates are less split up than those in Margaux. This is a countryside of broad vineyards under single ownership surrounding their proprietors' châteaux.

THE WINE ROUTE

Take the D2 N from Lamarque to Beychevelle crossing the Cheval du Despartins and passing the beautiful 17th-century Ch Beychevelle on your right opposite Ch Branaire-Ducru **1**. Turn left as the D101 joins from the right and take a right-hand turn N again up the D2.

Just before going over a small crossroads, Ch Gloria **2** lies on the left-hand side of the road. Continue up the D2 through Cru Classé vineyards – a km along the road to the left, Chx Langoa-Barton **3** and Leoville-Barton, face each other both owned by the Barton family.

Drive through St-Julien-Beychevelle, past Ch Léoville-las-Cases on your right: its winery is on the village street and a good proportion of its vineyards is in Pauillac opposite Ch Latour. A few dozen steps across the street lies Ch Léoville-Poyferré **4** with its recently improved wines, cellars and garden.

Continue on the D2. As you cross the Ruisseau de Juillac you pass from St-Julien to Pauillac.

Just before Ch Pichon-Longueville Comtesse de Lalande **5** on the right side of the road and Ch Pichon-Longueville Baron **6** on the other, there is a small entrance to the right. This leads to the first-growth Ch

THE
WINE ROUTE

The river Loire heads s from the vineyards of Touraine through Orléans to the last of the important Loire vineyards: Sancerre and Pouilly-Fumé. The Wine Route begins in Sancerre itself. It can be reached via the N7 to Cosne-sur-Loire where you cross the river to pick up the D955

Ménétréol-sous-Sancerre. Gitton Père & Fils is an important local grower with a family estate of 30ha producing a range of balanced Sancerre and Pouilly-Fumé. Turn right onto the D307 crossing under a viaduct and heading w from the village through Les Garennes. At the next T-junction turn left for a short while on the D307E then take the next right turn to pass La Moussière vineyard on the left of the road. Turn left at the T-junction with the D955

through Bannay and St-Satur to approach the far side of the village. Strategically positioned on a steep hill high above the peaceful landscape of the Loire, the village dominates the neighbouring countryside. Sancerre has no Maison du Vin, but it does have enormous rock cellars, the Caves de la Mignonne, where information is available and wine can be tasted. These are situated just off the D955 on the road to Amigny on the southwest side of the village.

Take the D920 into Sancerre itself. The ancient village exudes genuine charm with its many old houses, separated from each other by narrow, winding, steep little streets. In the centre of the village is the attractive market square surrounded by cafés, shops and restaurants. Continue on the D920 as it takes a twisting route through vine-covered slopes to

towards the hamlet of Bué. Continue on this road until you reach the crossroads where a right turn on the D85 will take you into the village.

Some of Sancerre's best wines have their origins in the vineyards surrounding Bué. Among the most notable vineyards are Le Chêne Marchand and Le Grand Chemarin (with Le Clos du Roy beyond) on either side of the D85 heading into Bué. Follow the D85 through the village and take the D923 right before you reach the hamlet of Venoize. Shortly after passing the resevoir, turn left (still on the D923) to pass one of the most impressive vineyards in the region, the Clos de la Poussie which forms a natural amphitheatre with slopes of 60 degrees or more in places. Continue along this road driving through the middle of the Poussie vineyard until you reach the

crossroads with the D7.

Turn left heading back towards Sancerre, but turn off the main road at Amigny. Through the village, turn right and continue climbing up the vine-covered slopes. Turn left at the 1-junction onto the D183 to the charming village of Chavignol in the valley. Among the producers found in this commune is the small and prestigious firm owned by the Cotat brothers who continue to produce Sancerre by traditional methods.

From the village continue along the D183 following the steep contours of the Côte de Montagne. Turn right on the D134E and follow the road as it passes the Monts Damnés and the Côte de Verdigny vineyards to the village of Verdigny itself. It is worth making a stop at the village to visit the Sancerre Musée du Vigneron. Important growers based in the village include Paul Prieur & Fils, Jean Reverdy and Paul & Claude Fournier. From Verdigny take the D134, passing vineyards to the left of the road, to Chaudoux. Growers based here inlcude the mayor of the village, the old-style grower, André Dezat.

Head SE from Chaudoux through La Perrière vineyard towards St-Satur. When you reach the crossroads with the D54 turn left towards Ste-Gemme-en-Sancerrois but then turn right on the D57 through the Bois de Charmes. Follow the road which skirts Les Ports du Clos vineyard on the right back to the D955 for Sancerre. Turn left on the D955 to cross over to the eastern side of the river Loire on the D2 (becoming the D4) at St-Thibault. At the next junction turn right on the D553 to Tracy-sur-Loire. Turn right in the commune to pass the Ch de Tracy on the left. This château has been owned by the family of the Comte d'Estutt d'Assay since the 16th century and continues to produce Pouilly-Fumé by traditional methods.

Take the D553 through the hamlet of Bois Gibault, crossing the N7 on the D247 and then onto Bois Fleury where you turn right and then left through the start of the Pouilly vineyards to Les Cassières. The next hamlet on the Wine Route is Les Berthiers which has

some of the best vineyards in the Pouilly-Fumé appellation, with most of the growers living either here or in Les Loges. Wine can be tasted in some of the houses – look out for "vente directe" signs. The district also has its own signposted wine route. Among the leading producers based here are Jean-Claude Châtelain and Serge Dagueneau.

Take the D553 from Les Berthiers to the next wine village, St-Andelain, where you turn right on the D153. Keep on this winding road and you will come to Ch de Nozet on the right of the road. This stylish château, owned by the Baron Patrick de Ladoucette, is the major producer of Pouilly-Fumé with a production of over 85,000 cases from some 65ha of the firm's vineyards and must is also bought in from other growers. Turn left back on the D553 at the next crossroads to visit (via Bouchot) Pouilly-sur-Loire itself. For many years the N7 ran through the centre of the village, but peace has been returned to this former Roman settlement with the completion of the bypass. You can join the N7 here to head north via Gien to the historic old town of Orléans.

Leave Pouilly on the D153 for the hamlet of Les Loges where important local producers include Paul Figeat and Bailly Père & Fils. Continue on the D153 to Bois Gibault where you can retrace your route back across the Loire to Sancerre.

LOCAL PRODUCERS

Sancerre
BUE
Bailly-Reverdy: One of the rare estates where both the white and the red Sancerre are excellent.
Lucien Crochet: Excellent Clos du Chêne Marchand and a good Clos du Roy.
Pierre Girault
Lucien Picard
Clos de la Poussie: Belongs to the Cordier firm of Bordeaux.
Jean-Max Roger: Elegant wines from an energetic grower. Jean-Max

also makes an excellent Menetou-Salon.

SANCERRE
Cave Coopérative
Alphonse Mellot: Quality-minded merchants.
Château de Sancerre: Belongs to the Marnier-Lapostolle family (of Grand Marnier fame).
Domaine Vacheron: White and red wines of high standard.

Pouilly-Fumé
POUILLY-SUR-LOIRE
Pascal Jolivet: A small négociant with impeccable wines.
De Ladoucette: At Château du Nozet, built in 1850, Patrick de Ladoucette makes more than half of all Pouilly-Fumé. Part comes from the firm's own vineyard of some 65ha, and must is also bought in from other growers. The Pouilly-Fumé is exquisite, but the special, very expensive Baron de L selection is of even higher standard.
Domaine J.M. Masson-Blondelet: Small family estate with expertly made wines that has repeatedly won awards.

WINE INFORMATION

SANCERRE
Caves de la Mignonne

HOTELS AND RESTAURANTS

BEAUGENCY, 45190
l'Abbaye (A), tel: 38 44 67 35
Hotel in an old abbey in this lovely little town west of Orléans. Restaurant (B).
Ecu de Bretagne (B)
tel: 38 44 67 60
Quiet hotel on main square. Modern annexe. Also has a restaurant (C).

LES BEZARDS, 45290
Auberge des Templiers (A)
tel: 38 31 80 01
Eminent restaurant and hotel north of Gien. Well-stocked wine cellar.
CHAVIGNOL, 18300
Auberge La Treille (C)
tel: 48 54 12 17
A good eating place. Try the Crottin de Chavignol cheese.
COSNE-SUR-LOIRE, 58200
Auberge a la Ferme (B)
tel: 86 28 15 85
Quiet hotel in the countryside, just outside Cosne on D114 to Cours. Restaurant (C).
La Sévigné (C), 16 Rue du 14-Juillet, tel: 86 28 27 50
Regional cooking in an atmospheric setting.
POUILLY-SUR-LOIRE, 58150
L'Espérance (B)
tel: 86 39 10 68
Conservative restaurant near the river and vineyards. Also has rooms.
Le Relais Fleuri (B)
tel: 86 39 12 99
Pleasant little village hotel with a terrace by the river. Regional cooking in *Le Coq Hardi* (C).
ST-THIBAULT, 18300
l'Auberge (C), tel: 48 54 13 79
Old village inn near Sancerre. Also a hotel.
l'Etoile (B/C), tel: 48 54 12 15
Hotel and restaurant. *Demi-pension* obligatory in season.
SANCERRE, 18300
Auberge Alphonse Mellot (C)
tel: 48 54 20 53
Joseph Mellot owns this simple restaurant. Also a display of old winemaking equipment.
Hotel Panoramic (B)
tel: 48 54 22 44
Functional hotel for overnight stay.
La Tour (B), tel: 48 54 00 81
The best local restaurant, offering dishes with a regional touch.

BORDEAUX AND THE MEDOC

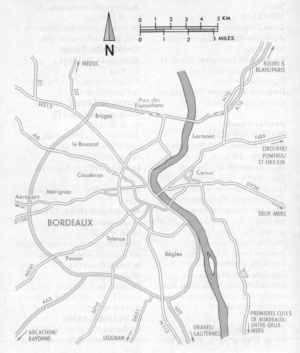

Bordeaux is perhaps the most famous wine city of old, hub of the Médoc, Pomerol, St-Emilion, Sauternes and Entre-Deux-Mers, but it gives little away of its vinous character.

Not a jolly city, but solid, handsome, secure in its position, commercially successful and expanding continually. If you want to feel close to the vines, follow one of the Wine Routes, particularly St-Emilion and Castillon, where the town of St-Emilion seems to grow out of the soil. Bordeaux city shows the businesslike face of wine, the port through which the barrels of wine have been bought and sold for maybe two thousand years.

Bordeaux is the home of merchants, "courtiers", "négociants", whose business was, and is, dealing in the wine of the surrounding regions. Many have their main offices in the city and many are still based around the area of the Quai des Chartrons. Ranged along the quayside in 18th-century buildings, their vast cellars are warrens below ground.

Bordeaux, whilst being perhaps the most renowned vinous centre in the world, is also France's fourth city, and therefore is the home

to the biennial Vinexpo, the largest, and best, wine trade fair in the world. On the north of the city Vinexpo dominates the entire area when staged in June (the next in 1989, followed by 1991): accommodation and flights to Bordeaux are like gold dust. Some exhibition and trade visitors even commute from Biarritz.

Bordeaux is the home of the airport Bordeaux-Mérignac and the route to, not only wine, but holiday and coastal destinations. The N250 and A63 take you to Arcachon where many Bordeaux city-dwellers escape to (perhaps second or holiday) homes on the Bassin d'Arcachon. The D2 out of Bordeaux is the main route through the Médoc and Bordeaux is pivotal to all the wine tours, especially, using it as a specific starting point for Margaux and the Southern Médoc, Graves and Sauternes, and Between the Rivers (Entre-Deux-Mers and the Premières Côtes de Bordeaux).

Central to Bordeaux itself is the Place de la Comédie adorned by the Grand Théâtre designed by Victor Louis, completed in 1780, a beautiful classical structure. On the Cours du 30-Juillet is the Maison du Vin available for advice on visiting châteaux and areas. For other information the Maison du Tourisme is across the street.

Bordeaux is not just a city of wine but also a commercial and industrial centre with a bustling port on the Garonne. Busy and businesslike Bordeaux perhaps shows best the trade aspect of wine, that to reach the consumer's table, a bottle needs to be bought, sold, shipped. Wander through the wine districts then return to Bordeaux to remind yourself that wine, although a pleasure is also, for the producers, a way of life and a business.

SW

HOTELS AND RESTAURANTS

BORDEAUX, 33000

Le Bistrot du Clavel Centre (B)
7 Rue Montesquieu, tel: 56 51 28 81
Owned by the master chef Francis Garcia. Mainly regional menu. (M. Garcia has moved his splendid restaurant, Clavel, into *Le Chapon Fin*.

Le Chapon Fin (A/B)
tel: 56 79 10 10
Adjoining the *Bistrot*.

Le Cellier Bordelais (C), 30 Quai de la Monnaie, tel: 56 31 30 30
Good cooking and interesting and affordable wines.

La Chamade (A/B), 20 Rue Piliers de Tutelle, tel: 56 48 13 74
Attractive atmosphere and food. Lower-priced lunch menu.

La Ferme St-Michel (C), 21 Rue des Menuts, tel: 56 91 54 77

Market-fresh ingredients.

Grand Hotel (A), 2 Place de la Comédie, tel: 56 90 93 44
Fine old hotel but has been cheaply renovated and rooms are cramped.

Chez Joël (c), 12 Rue Piliers de Tutelle, tel: 56 52 68 21
For oyster lovers.

Lou Magret (C), 62 Rue St-Rémi, tel: 56 44 77 94
Good, inexpensive and always busy.

Normandie (B), 7 Cours du 30-Juillet, tel: 56 52 16 80
Large, traditional hotel.

Novotel-Bordeaux le Lac (B)
Parc des Expositions,
tel: 56 50 99 70
One of the modern hotels in the exhibition area north of the city. Swimming pool and restaurant.

Le Pavillon des Boulevards (A/B), 120 Rue de la Croix-de-Seguey, tel: 56 81 51 02

Venturesome cooking with occasional hints of the Oriental and a charming courtyard where you can dine in summer. Lower-priced lunch menu.
Ramet (A/B), 7 Place Jean-Jaurès, tel: 56 44 12 41
Distinctive atmosphere and fine cuisine.
Le Rouzie (B), 34 Cours de Chapeau Rouge, tel: 56 44 39 11
Inventive menu and stylish setting. A small restaurant on the first floor (*Le Bolchoi*) serves dinners and suppers.

Royal Médoc (B), 3 Rue Séze, tel: 56 81 72 42
Central, friendly and not too noisy. Much used by wine writers and buyers. Perhaps the best of a disappointing lot.
Hotel de Sèze (B)
23 Allées de Tourny, tel: 56 52 65 54
Functional hotel.
La Tupine (B), 6 Rue de Porte-de-la-Monnaie, tel: 56 91 56 37
The cooking of the French southwest at its best.

THE MEDOC

The Médoc is a region that every wine lover associates with fine wines and superb châteaux. However, wine growing is practised in only small part of the Médoc: a relatively narrow strip that follows the Gironde from the outskirts of Bordeaux almost to the northern tip of the peninsula. Only in one place do the vineyards reach about 12 kilometres (7 miles) inland from the river, usually the distance from the Gironde is less than 5 kilometres (3 miles). The D2, the "Route des Châteaux" runs from south to north linking the communes.

There are eight appellations: Margaux (the largest and including the southern Médoc communities Arsac, Cantenac, Labarde, and Soussans); Moulis and Listrac (in the central Médoc); St-Julien; Pauillac; St-Estèphe; the Haut-Médoc (which covers wines not included in the previous six); and Médoc (the northern or Bas-Médoc).

WINE INFORMATION

LESPARRE
Maison du Médoc
MARGAUX
Maison du Vin
PAUILLAC
Maison du Tourisme et du Vin
Château Mouton Rothschild Museum
ST-ESTEPHE
Maison du Vin

HOTELS AND RESTAURANTS

ARCINS, 33460
Le Lion d'Or (C), tel: 56 58 96 79
Atmospheric restaurant serving tasty food. Popular with the locals.

BLANQUEFORT, 33290
Auberge des Criquets (B)
tel: 56 35 09 24
Specializing in game, friendly service. Also offers 8 rooms.
LAMARQUE, 33460
Le Relais du Médoc (C)
tel: 56 58 92 27
Strictly regional cuisine and a few hotel rooms. Excellent value.
LESPARRE, 33340
Hotel de Paris (C)
tel: 56 41 00 22
Accommodation without frills.
La Mare aux Grenouilles (B)
tel: 56 41 03 46
Popular family restaurant.
LISTRAC, 33480
Hotel de France (C)
tel: 56 58 03 68

Small hotel in middle of town with neat clean rooms.

MARGAUX, 33460

Auberge le Savoie (C)
tel: 56 88 31 76
Friendly village restaurant. Good wine list and traditional cooking.

Relais de Margaux (A)
tel: 56 88 38 80
Hotel set in large park close to Château Margaux and overlooking the river. Seasonal regional specialities in restaurant.

PAUILLAC, 33250

Hotel La Coquille (C)
tel: 56 59 07 52
On the quay, do not expect too much.

Château Cordeillau-Bages (A/B), tel: 56 59 18 92
Pauillac's first quality hotel and restaurant, to be opened in Spring 1989, close to Château Lynch-Bages. Managed by a former *sommelier* who also runs the Ecole de Bordeaux, an organization that arranges tastings and excursions etc. in the area. 18 comfortable rooms.

La Salamandre (C)
tel: 56 59 08 68
On the quay with bar and a tearoom.

QUEYRAC, 33340

Vieux Acacias (B), tel: 56 59 80 63
Hotel in a peaceful setting, a few kms north of Lesparre on the D102 E, with its own small park.

ST-JULIEN-BEYCHEVELLE, 33250

Bar-Restaurant du Square (C)
tel: 56 59 08 26
Country cooking with no frills.

ST-LAURENT-ET-BENON, 33112

Hotel-Restaurant le Lion d'Or (C), tel: 56 59 40 21
Simple and acceptable regional dishes.

Hotel-Restaurant de la Renaissance (C)
tel: 56 59 40 29
The patron supplies meals to the

châteaux (and to pickers). Nourishing regional fare.

ST-SEURIN-DE-CADOURNE, 33250

Hotel du Midi (C), tel: 56 59 30 49
Only recommended if no other accommodation available. No restaurant.

ST-YZANS-DE-MEDOC, 33340

Château Loudenne (B)
tel: 56 09 05 03
Lunch in the Cuisine des Vendanges at the beautiful old Gilbey château (reservations at least 48 hours in advance). The price includes a choice of two wines.

SALAUNES, 33160

Le Domaine des Ardillières (B)
tel: 56 05 20 70
Hotel and restaurant about 20km west of Margaux on D105 and N215. Swimming pool and tennis court.

SOULAC-SUR-MER, 33780

Hotel-Restaurant des Pins (B)
tel: 56 09 80 01
Restaurant in typical seaside resort at the northern end of the D101. Try the lamprey or *confit de canard* Interesting wine list.

SOUSSANS, 33460

Larigaudière (B), tel: 56 88 74 02
Fashionable restaurant that is an extension of the wine estate of Château Haut Breton Larigaudière.

VENDAYS-MONTALIVET, 33930

La Clef des Champs (B)
tel: 56 41 71 11
Eccentric establishment but worth a visit for regional dishes. Village of Vendays-Montalivet lies outside the actual wine area, 14km from Lesparre.

LE VERDON-SUR-MER, 33123

Le Côte d'Argent (B)
tel: 56 09 60 45
Near the tip of Médoc peninsula on the N215. Seafood is a speciality.

SW

MARGAUX AND SOUTHERN MEDOC

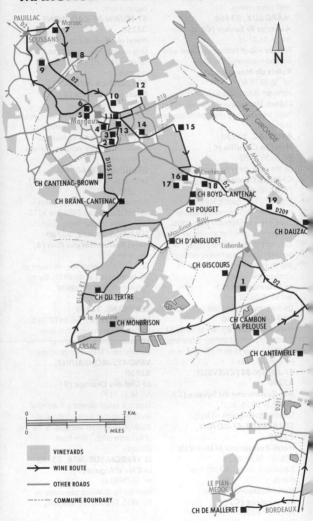

Margaux is the largest of the Médoc appellations, covering some 1,150 hectares (2,850 acres) of vineyards and with more Crus Classés (21) than any other. As well as Margaux itself, the appellation includes Arsac, Cantenac, Labarde and Soussans, a quartet of adjoining communities.

Traditionally Margaux and the surrounding villages were the territory of only a few wealthy *seigneurs* who lived in the châteaux of Margaux, d'Issan (in Cantenac) and La Tour de Mons (in Soussans). Today the township of Margaux (population is little under 1,400 inhabitants) is more a village than a town and the other villages of the appellation are little more than hamlets. Almost everyone in Margaux makes their living from wine and many of the châteaux are in a neighbourly cluster around and in the centre of the town, their vineyards divided into small plots that intermingle in the surrounding countryside.

THE WINE ROUTE

Head N from Bordeaux on the D2 towards Blanquefort. A small river called the Jalle de Blanquefort marks the start of the Médoc, but you don't begin to see any châteaux until you have been through Blanquefort itself.

Appropriately, the first château you come across, set back off the road to the left is Ch Dillon, an agricultural college where winemaking is taught and a highly agreeable red and crisp, fruity dry white (Ch Lirias) are produced.

Your map starts 4.5km N of Ch Dillon with a small diversion w to Ch de Malleret just outside Le Pian-Médoc, whose stables have racetracks for training their thoroughbreds. Back to the D2, turn left and continue N to the crossroads with the D210 E2, the right-hand turning leading to Ch La Lagune a reliable third-growth Haut-Médoc.

Still on the D2 and just before the road curves w Ch Cantemerle is hidden on the left. Its peaceful parkland conceals a lake and reveals the fairytale château a good distance from the main road. At the next crossroads a detour to the left will take you to Ch Cambon la Pelouse but the main route carries on over the next crossroads, taking the left fork (away from Labarde). Ch Canteloude **1** to your left is situated just within the Margaux side of the boundary with

the Haut-Médoc appellation.

Turning left at the next junction, southwards you can see the large estate of Ch Giscours on your right. At the crossroads turn right, climbing towards Arsac and on one of the small hills to your right is Ch Monbrison. In Arsac turn right along the D105 E1 through La Mouline, then right to Ch du Tertre whose name derives from its hilly situation: "tertre" meaning knoll. The estate dates back as far as the 12th century.

Turn NE with the stream and wooded country to your right. Turn right then right again to Ch d'Angludet whose proprietor, Peter A. Sichel (also a co-owner of Ch Palmer) was elected in 1988 the President of the Union des Grands Crus de Bordeaux – the first Englishman to hold the post.

Cross the stream again and turn left inland. At the next crossroads turn right onto the D105 E1. Take the right-hand fork which leads you directly to the second-growth Ch Brane-Cantenac (in 1820 the Baron de Brane sold Brane Mouton, now known as Ch Mouton-Rothschild, to concentrate on Brane-Cantenac). Follow the D105 E1 past Ch Cantenac Brown on the left.

Cross the railway and turn immediately to the right towards Margaux to discover a remarkable concentration of châteaux. Be warned, however: a little sign in a vineyard proclaiming a château's ownership does not mean that that is the name of the adjacent splendid winery – vineyards can be far-flung.

Follow the road as it bears to the

left and next door to each other on the left-hand side of the road are Chx Rausan Ségla **2** and Rauzan-Gassies **3** which used to share ownership. Turn left, then immediately right at the next crossroads, and immediately left, leaving Ch Marquis de Terme **4** on the corner, created from the amalgamation of a number of growths and bearing the name of a previous 18th-century owner, the Marquis de Terme who acquired it on his marriage to the niece of M. de Rauzan.

Take the next right turn. On your right is Ch Ferrière **5**, once the property in the 18th century of Gabriel Ferrière, the King's Huntsman, then to his cousin, Jean, later Mayor of Bordeaux. Round the corner is the ivy-covered Ch Lascombes **6** with traditional outbuildings but a brand-new "state-of-the-art" winery. It has British owners.

The road now winds to the right and meanders N towards Soussans where you can break into the Wine Route of the Central Médoc along the D2. Turn right, out of Soussans, E towards Marsac turning right in the village just after passing Ch Marsac Séguineau **7**.

Turn right opposite Ch Labégorce-Zédé **8** whose vineyards straddle the communes of Soussans and Margaux to Ch Labégorce **9** whose vineyards date back to 1332 with a château dating from the 18th century designed by Courcelles.

Turn left onto the D2 returning to Margaux where you find the Maison du Vin on the left and Ch La Gurgue hidden on the right, before coming to the grand château of Marquis d'Alesme Becker **10** set in a large park. Follow the road to find Ch Malescot St-Exupéry **11** which was once owned by the St-Exupéry family (the same family as the author of "The Little Prince"); now the proprietor is Roger Zuger whose father, Paul bought the château in 1955.

The road continues ahead, past the right-hand turn to the D2 until on your left, a vision opens up along a leafy drive of the most impressive château of the Médoc: Ch Margaux

12. Magnificent and manicured and wonderfully well-ordered. Do not miss it.

Retrace your route and turn left along the D2 to Cantenac. Turn right then left, and as you do so, facing you is Ch Durfort-Vivens **13** owned by Lucien Lurton (also proprietor of Ch Brane-Cantenac). Turn left in Issan and in the bend of the road is Ch Palmer **14** partly owned by Englishman Peter Sichel, of Ch d'Angludet (with French and Dutch co-proprietors). Continue past Ch Vincent, Montbrun (once part of the Palmer estate) and Pontac Lynch, then turn right, which takes you past Ch d'Issan **15** a very old estate and château producing an excellent, elegant wine.

Follow the road at the edge of the vineyards to the next crossroads and turn right, then left when you come to the D2, past Ch Prieuré-Lichine **16**. The vineyard changed its name from Prieuré-Cantenac in 1953 after its acquisition two years previously by Alexis Lichine, author of "The Encyclopaedia of Wines and Spirits". Beyond it can be seen a characteristic grand plateau.

Drive through Cantenac, where a turning to the right takes you across the railway line to first Ch Kirwan **17** which was acquired in the 18th century by the Irish family of Kirwan; later changing hands to the City of Bordeaux and later still, the firm of Schröder et Schÿler. Further down are Ch Boyd-Cantenac (and Ch Pouget across from it). Both are owned by the Guillemet family. Now go back to the D2. Just past the crossing, to your right is a courtyard that houses the renovated Ch Desmirail **18**. Follow the D2 running parallel with the railway, as it follows the river Gironde over to the left past the flat coastal land.

Take the left fork onto the D209 and the next château on the left will be, Ch Siran **19** in the Labarde commune. Keep heading towards the river and just as the road starts to curve away towards Macau, Ch Dauzac appears on your left. The château's vineyards occupy grand

plateaux on the other side of the road dating back to the 13th century. In the 18th century, the property belonged to the Irishman, Count Lynch, later Mayor of Bordeaux. It was at Dauzac that pioneering work was done on "Bordeaux Mixture".

Follow the road straight through coastal Macau onto the D210, a continuation of the D209, passing on the left as the road straightens, Ch Maucamps **20** which is entitled to the appellation Haut-Médoc. The road now passes vineyards and woodlands. In Ludon-Médoc it goes past Ch d'Arche with its museum of tools used in viticulture and winemaking.

As you journey s the last château of the route is fittingly enchanting, Ch d'Agassac poised above its medieval moat, and surrounded by woods and vineyards.

THE CHATEAUX

Margaux
(Appellation Margaux)
Château Durfort-Vivens
2e Grand Cru Classé
A Lucien Lurton estate: the cellars are across the road from the château.
Château Ferrière
3e Grand Cru Classé
A miniature property.
Château Lascombes
2e Grand Cru Classé
Excellently managed and maintained estate, one of the largest in the Médoc, with a rather ungainly Victorian château.
Château Malescot St-Exupéry
3e Grand Cru Classé
The comfortable château, dating from 1885, is in the main street in Margaux; the vineyards (typically for Margaux) are scattered.
Château Margaux
1er Grand Cru Classé
The most impressive château of the Médoc: an avenue lined with tall trees leads up to a large country house with the air of a palace.
Château Marquis d'Alesme Becker
3e Grand Cru Classé
A neighbour of Malescot St-Exupéry,

in the same street in Margaux.
Château Marquis de Terme
4e Grand Cru Classé
During the 1980s a great deal has been invested in equipment.
Château Rausan-Ségla
2e Grand Cru Classé
Older than most well-known Médoc estates, dating back to 1661.
Château Rauzan-Gassies
2e Grand Cru Classé
The balance of the old Rausan estate.

Cantenac
(Appellation Margaux)
Château Boyd-Cantenac
3e Grand Cru Classé
The wine used to be identical to that of Pouget, but is now vinified and bottled separately.
Château Brane-Cantenac
2e Grand Cru Classé
Large, well-run Lucien Lurton property with vineyards in a prime site on Cantenac's plateau.
Château Cantenac Brown
3e Grand Cru Classé
Imposing structure (it has more than 350 windows) that looks more like an English country house than a château.
Château Desmirail
3e Grand Cru Classé
A low grey building on the left before the crossroads in Cantenac. The Brane-Cantenac team makes the wine.
Château d'Issan
3e Grand Cru Classé
Beautifully restored (by the Cruse family) 17th-century moated castle.
Château Kirwan
3e Grand Cru Classé
An 18th-century manor with a beautiful show of flowers in summer.
Château Palmer
3e Grand Cru Classé
This picture-book château produces splendid, balanced wine.
Château Pouget
4e Grand Cru Classé
The château where the wine of Boyd-Cantenac was made until early 1983.
Château Prieuré-Lichine
4e Grand Cru Classé
Visitors are always welcome at this hospitable Grand Cru château.

SW

THE CENTRAL MEDOC

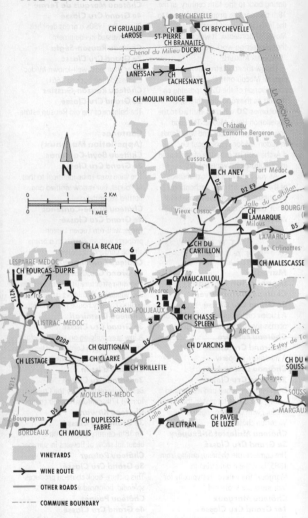

Unlike the neighbouring communes of Margaux and St-Julien, their
are no Grands Crus in the Central Médoc. This is Crus Bourgeois
territory — but there are several estates producing wines that can
match the Grands Crus. The communes of Moulis and Listrac have
their own appellations, whereas the other commune of the Central
Médoc are entitled to the appellation Haut-Médoc. The hamlet of

Moulis itself is little more than one main street. As to concerned the more important estates are grouped arou. hamlet Grand Poujeaux, a few kilometres to the northeast, e.g Châteaux Chasse-Spleen, Maucaillou and Poujeaux. Visitors are particularly welcome between June and September at Château Clarke, Baron Edmond de Rothschild's spectacular and technically advanced estate in Listrac.

THE
WINE ROUTE

This Route can be entered from a variety of directions and is a useful departure point of tours in other areas. The full circuit, with numerous diversions off the beaten track, begins at Soussans, which is reached from Margaux and the Southern Médoc on the D2.

Follow the D2 out of Soussans and after almost a km take the left fork off the road into the commune of Avensan Pass Ch Paveil de Luze on your left through woodland on both sides of the road representing part of the 400ha estate belonging to Ch Citran whose vineyards you will see before reaching the château itself, just over 2km from the D2. The moat is all that remains of the original 13th-century château – the building you see is 18th-century.

Retrace your route back to the D2, turn left and head N once more. Just past the junction is Ch Tayac, entitled to the appellation of Margaux, as is the entire commune of Soussans.

As you follow the road N to Arcins you cross the Estey de Tayac with Moulis to the west beyond areas of wooded countryside and the Gironde to the east. Just before you enter the village, the late 19th-century, well-maintained Ch d'Arcins lies to your left. The road forks in the village. Take a right-hand turn off the D2 over the small crossroads, right, then immediately left northwards through vineyards all the way to Lamarque. To the east the land becomes flatter as it slopes to the river.

About 1.5km along the road you pass Ch Malescasse on your right, built in the early 1800s and bought in 1979 by the owner of both Pauillac's

Ch Pontet-Canet and St-Estèphe's Ch Lafon-Rochet.

Follow the road into Lamarque. By turning right onto the D5 you will reach the car ferry for Blaye where you can join the wine tours of Bourg and Blaye; otherwise, turn left, still on the D5. By turning right, off this road; you can visit the wonderfully picturesque Ch de Lamarque.

At the next crossroads, turn right. The road bends sharply to the left and at the next crossroads, turn right, rejoining the D2.

Well worth the detour is an excursion to the Fort Médoc, part of the fortifications of the Gironde. To reach it take the right-hand turn at the crossroads and head eastwards on the D2 E9.

After visiting Fort Médoc retrace your steps and continue the Wine Route by turning right onto the D2. Follow the road past Ch Aney on your right, through the village of Cussac-Fort-Médoc and shortly, again on your right, is the entry road to Ch Lamothe Bergeron. The château dates back to the reign of Napoleon III and has been restored after a fire in 1957. The surrounding property once belonged to the Lord (known as Captal) of Buch who, when captured by the French during the Hundred Years War, was ransomed with ten future crops of wine from Lamothe.

Next on your left, on the edge of woodland is Ch Moulin Rouge situated on the final gravel slope before you enter St-Julien.

Take the next turn to your left which takes you past Ch Lachesnaye on the road to Ch Lanessan which has been owned by the same family since 1790. It has a Musée du Cheval (with old carriages, stables and saddles etc).

return to the D2, back through Cussac, and just past Ch Aney take the right-hand fork towards the village of Grand Poujeaux. To the right the land rises and the road takes you to a small crossroads. Turn left, then immediately right, over the Ruisseau du Cartillon and right again at the T-junction. Leaving Ch du Cartillon on your left, head s with vineyards to your left and woodlands to your right. Go over the crossroads with the D5, and Ch Maucaillou is on the right whose vineyards slopes are covered in pebbly soil reflecting the sun onto the vines. Cross the railway line to reach Grand Poujeaux. In the village there is a number of châteaux of note, some bearing the name "Poujeaux". First as you enter the village, on your right, is the large estate of Ch Poujeaux **1**, owned in the mid 16th-century by Gaston de l'Isle. It was also a satellite of La Tour St-Lambert, now known as Ch Latour in Pauillac. This is followed by Ch Grand Poujeaux **2** and Ch Dutruch Grand Poujeaux **3**.

SW
Take a left turn off the D5 past Ch Gressier Grand Poujeaux **4** to Chasse-Spleen. Follow the road past a left turn to Arcins and rejoin the D5 where you cross the Ruisseau de Larrayaut as you enter the commune of Moulis-en-Médoc.

Past Chx Guitignan to the right and Brillette to the left the road continues straight towards Moulis, crossing the Ruisseau du Pont d'Eysson before entering the village. Here you can make a small detour from the main Route by going straight over at the crossroads with the D208. Off the D5, along the same turning to the left are two châteaux. Ch Duplessis-Fabre once made up part of the family estate of Armand Duplessis, Cardinal de Richelieu, and was originally used as a hunting lodge. The other is Ch Moulis, characterised by rose bushes at the end of the rows of vines. Back to the D208 and turn left NW to Listrac-Médoc. A small crossroads leads left to Ch Lestage and its parkland whereas the next right turning takes you to Ch Clarke whose first vines were planted in the 12th

century by the Cistercian monks. The name comes from the family who arrived in Bordeaux in 1692 in the reign of William of Orange having backed the losing side of James Stuart.

Return to the D208 and continue your journey to Listrac-Médoc. Turn right in the village, then left to join the N215.

If you should wish to visit another part of the Médoc or curtail your journey, a left turn will take you back to Bordeaux. On the way you will pass several châteaux: Semeillan, Fonréaud and Ch Moulin à Vent.

Retrace your steps to Listrac, then go N through Le Tris, to Ch Fourcas-Dupré. Following the N215 enables you to link up with the Wine Route for the Northern Médoc at Lesparre-Médoc.

To explore further in the Central Médoc, backtrack to Le Tris and turn left. At the T-junction turn right then left again along the D5 E2. The first turn on the left takes you to Ch Saransot-Dupré **5** with its own flock of sheep (an important source of fertiliser). Turn right back on the D5 E2, then right and take the first right again which crosses the country eastwards, eventually to Lamarque. On the left is Ch La Bécade, whose motto is "Traditiori Fidelis", and is followed by Ch Lafon **6** situated in woodland on the slopes of an area called Les Marcieux.

Just before the railway line turn right to Médrac. Then turn left, past Ch Maucaillou to pick up the D5 to take you s to Soussans.

THE CHATEAUX

Moulis
(Appellation Moulis)
Château Chasse-Spleen
Cru Grand Bourgeois
Exceptionnel
Indeed an exceptional Moulis that has repeatedly shown itself to be the equal of a Grand Cru. The wine is matured in oak and usually half the casks are replaced each year. A small part of the vineyard is in Listrac.

Château Dutruch Grand Poujeaux
Cru Grand Bourgeois Exceptionnel
Wine with a good deal of tannin, demanding long maturing.

Château Maucaillou
Cru Bourgeois
The name of the estate comes from an old description of the soil: *mauvais cailloux*, "bad pebbles", from the days when it was too gravelly to grow corn (but proved later, of course, to be excellent for vines). At blind tastings the supple, subtly nuanced wine is hardly distinguishable from a Grand Cru.

Château Moulin à Vent
Cru Grand bourgeois
Although a third of the vineyard is in Listrac, all the wine is sold as Moulis.

Château Poujeaux
Cru Grand Bourgeois Exceptionnel
This is the largest estate in Moulis after Chasse-Spleen and, thanks to the efforts of the Theil family, the wine is well enough known to be sold directly from the château instead of via the Bordeaux trade. Dark and long-lived, it usually needs time to lose its reserve, but patience is richly rewarded.

Listrac
(Appellation Listrac-Médoc)
Château Clarke
Cru Bourgeois
Since 1973 Baron Edmond de Rothschild (of the Château Lafite-Rothschild family) has spent millions of francs in making this the most spectacular and technically advanced estate in Listrac. No other property has produced, and received, so much publicity. The wine does not yet have quite the depth and length to be at the top in Listrac, but this can only be a matter of time.

Clos des Demoiselles
This small estate lies along the D2 on the vine-clad hill at Listrac. Brilliant and well-balanced wine of which, alas only 2,000 cases a year are made.

Château Fourcas Dupré
Cru Grand Bourgeois Exceptionnel
A concentrated Listrac of the highest standard. The vineyard lies about 1km north of the village centre on the D2 and has ample parking space for visitors.

Château Fourcas-Hosten
Cru Grand Bourgeois Exceptionnel
A fine wine with plenty of fruit and tannin and the class of a Grand Cru. The château is opposite Listrac's 13th-century church and the splendid park at the back was designed in 1830 by an Englishman.

Château Lestage
Cru Bourgeois
An imposing château set in a park of tall old trees, with the same owners as Château Fonréaud on the other side of the hill at Listrac. The wine is an out-and-out Listrac that has improved in quality since the early 1980s.

Avensan
(Appellation Haut-Médoc)
Château Citran
Cru Grand Bourgeois Exceptionnel
Sound, supple wine that at the moment seems to lag a little behind the other *exceptionnels*. The vineyard is part of a well-wooded estate of some 400ha.

Château de Villegeorge
Cru Bourgeois Supérieur Exceptionnel
A Lucien Lurton (owner of ane-Cantenac among other properties) estate on very gravelly soil, producing well-rounded wine with plenty of colour, a long finish and outstanding ageing potential.

Cussac-Fort-Médoc
(Appellation Haut-Médoc)
Château Lanessan
Cru Bourgeois Supérieur
Classic, traditionally made, intense wine that approaches a Grand Cru in quality. There is also a carriage museum at the château.

SW

ST-JULIEN AND PAUILLAC

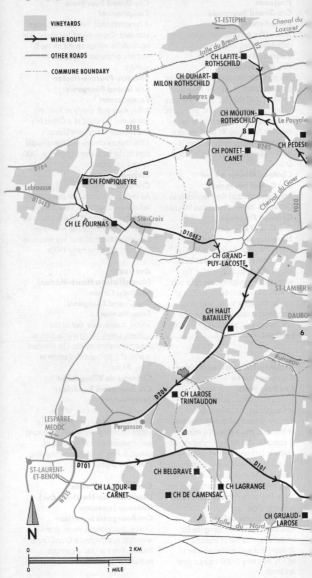

VINEYARDS

→ WINE ROUTE

OTHER ROADS

COMMUNE BOUNDARY

ST-ESTEPHE

Chenal du Lazaret

Jalle du Breuil

CH LAFITE-ROTHSCHILD

CH DUHART-MILON ROTHSCHILD

Loubegres

CH MOUTON-ROTHSCHILD

Le Pouyale

8

D205

CH PEDESC

CH PONTET-CANET

D205

D104

Chenal du Goer

D206

CH FONPIQUEYRE

Labrousse

D104E3

Ste-Croix

CH LE FOURNAS

D104E3

CH GRAND-PUY-LACOSTE

ST-LAMBERT

CH HAUT BATAILLEY

DAUBO

6

Ruisseau

D206

CH LAROSE TRINTAUDON

LESPARRE-MEDOC

Perganson

D101

ST-LAURENT-ET-BENON

D101

CH BELGRAVE

CH LAGRANGE

D101

N215

CH LA TOUR-CARNET

CH DE CAMENSAC

CH GRUAUD-LAROSE

Jalle du Nord

N

0   1   2 KM

0   1 MILE

Château Langoa Barton
3e Grand Cru Classé
This is the only Cru Classé owned and inhabited by the same family as when the 1855 Classification was made.

Château Léoville-Barton
2e Grand Cru Classé
The smallest Léoville is owned by the Barton family.

Château Léoville-las-Cases
2e Grand Cru Classé
The largest of the three Léoville châteaux. A large part of the vineyard is opposite Ch Latour.

Château Léoville-Poyferré
2e Grand Cru Classé
The Cuvelier family have made great improvements at Poyferré.

Château St-Pierre
4e Grand Cru Classé
Good deal of original vineyard has been reunited with the château.

Château Talbot
4e Grand Cru Classé
With more than 100ha this is the largest property in St-Julien.

Pauillac
(Appellation Pauillac)
Château Batailley
5e Grand Cru Classé
It is worth visiting this estate to see the park.

Château Clerc Milon
5e Grand Cru Classé
Modest house serves as the château.

Château Croizet-Bages
5e Grand Cru Classé
This estate seems to have been going through a difficult period.

Château Duhart-Milon-Rothschild
4e Grand Cru Classé
There is a *chai* but no château.

Château Grand-Puy Ducasse
5e Grand Cru Classé
Château is on the quay at Pauillac.

Château Grand-Puy-Lacoste
5e Grand Cru Classé
This estate is owned by the Borie family of Ducru-Beaucaillou.

Château Haut-Boges-Libéral
5e Grand Cru Classé
The wine of this medium-sized estate improves steadily.

Château Haut-Batailley
5e Grand Cru Classé
Unpretentious estate managed by Jean-Eugène Borie of Ducru-Beaucaillou.

Château Lafite-Rothschild
1er Grand Cru Classé
As you drive north from Pauillac, this is the last château before St-Estèphe.

Château Latour
1er Grand Cru Classé
Latour is a thoroughbred Pauillac that can only be described in superlatives, and so can its reliability. Latour produced successful wines even in such notoriously bad years as 1963 and '65.

Château Lynch-Bages
5e Grand Cru Classé
The château has been completely renovated by Jean-Michel Cazes. Lynch-Bages is a complete Pauillac, strong, often with a suggestion of mint in its perfume and an aroma of small red fruits. It is far better than its classification.

Château Lynch-Moussas
5e Grand Cru Classé
Replanting and modernization is now showing results

Château Mouton Baronne Philippe
5e Grand Cru Classé
The château, actually a half-completed villa, stands beside the Mouton Rothschild drive.

Château Mouton Rothschild
1er Grand Cru Classé
Mouton is today one of the most respected and most visited wine estates in the world.

Château Pédesclaux
5e Grand Cru Classé
The vineyard of this château is scattered around the commune.

Château Pichon-Longueville Baron
2e Grand Cru Classé
The wine has regained its former glory under new owners.

Château Pichon-Longueville Comtesse de Lalande
2e Grand Cru Classé
"The Comtesse" is the larger portion of what was once a single estate.

Château Pontet-Canet
5e Grand Cru Classé
A very typical Pauillac and far superior to its fifth-growth status.

ST-ESTEPHE

ST-YZANS

CH COUFRAN

CH VERDIGNAN

ST-SEURIN-DE-CADOURNE

LA GIRONDE

Estey d'Un

St-Corbian **6** Chenal de Calon CH CALON-SEGUR

St-Estèphe

Pez **5** CH MEYNEY

7 **4**

VERTHEUIL CH LE BOURDIEU

Leyssac CH MONTROSE

D204 Marbuzey **3 2**

8 D2 **1**

CH LANDAT CH COS D'ESTOURNEL Chenal du Lazaret

CH CISSAC CH COS LABORY CH LAFITE ROTHSCHILD

CISSAC-MEDOC **9** CH LAFON-ROCHET MARGAUX

CH DUHART-MILON ROTHSCHILD Jalle du Breuil

▨	VINEYARDS
➤	WINE ROUTE
—	OTHER ROADS
- - -	COMMUNE BOUNDARY

N

0 ___ 1 ___ 2 KM
0 _____ 1 MILES

St-Estèphe is the biggest wine commune of the Médoc, with some 1,100 hectares (2,700 acres) under cultivation. The landscape is different from the rest of the Médoc, a scattering of six hamlets with some steepish slopes and only a few isolated châteaux. This is Cru Bourgeois country. There are only five classed growths, led by Cos d'Estournel.

THE WINE ROUTE

Driving N on the D2 from Pauillac with Ch Lafite-Rothschild on your left crossing a culvert called a "jalle" you enter the commune of St-Estèphe.

A sharp bend in the road reveals Ch Cos d'Estournel with its astonishing Eastern architecture.

Turn right immediately onto the D2

E3, downhill over a railway line then take the next turn right through the hamlet of Marbuzet. Go right at the crossroads then immediately left. At a small crossroads you will find Ch de Marbuzet **1** and Ch Tour de Marbuzet **2** facing each other. Ch Haut-Marbuzet **3** is off the road to the left.

Retrace your steps back onto the D2 E3 and turn right. Drive over the crossroads, straight on at a fork in the road, then turn right to Ch Montrose.

Retrace your steps again back to the D2 E3 and turn right following the road towards St-Estèphe. On your right you will see the low silhouette of Ch Meyney, perched on a hill. Follow the D2 E3 past Ch Tronquoy-Lalande **4** to your left then take the first left leaving Ch Phélan-Ségur **5** to your right. Then you enter St-Estèphe.

At the junction with the D2 E2 turn right to travel past Ch Calon-Ségur. Take the next right turn, the D2E, into St-Estèphe again, turning left along the river at the next crossroads. The road bends and then continues straight for ¾km close to the Gironde; a sharp turn left is followed by another to the right. Cross the Chenal de Calon, pass Ch Sociando-Mallet and follow the road to St-Seurin-le-Cadourne. In the village the D2 joins from the south. Turn right and head northwards through the vineyards to Ch Coufran.

Return down the D2 passing Ch Verdignan on the left after about 1km. At St-Seurin-de-Cadourne turn right continuing on the D2 over the Estey d'Un and as the road climbs to the left, turn right, still on the D2 into St-Corbian. On your left, past Ch Morîn lies Ch Beau-Site **6** at the highest point in the commune. Follow the road into Pez where the road bends sharply but turn off the road on the corner onto the D204 E3. The road turns to the right and just before it curves to the left; Ch Les-Ormes de-Pez **7** is situated on the left.

Now follow the D204 E3 through vineyards and woods, across the railway line into Vertheuil. On the way you drive past Ch le Meynieu. East of the village is Ch le Bourdeiu.

Drive through the village, go straight over the crossroads with the D204 onto the D104 crossing the boundary between Vertheuil and Cissac just before Ch Landat on the right.

In Cissac-Médoc take the left turn to Ch Cissac leaving it on your left. Continue for about 1km taking a small left fork past Ch Larrivaux, through Bas Queyron and at the junction with

the D204 turn right. The road descends from Ch Hanteillan **8** and curves to the left with Ch Puy Castéra **9** about 1km to the south. The road climbs again along the Cru Classé vineyards of Ch Lafon-Rochet to the right. At a T-junction go straight onto the D2 past Ch Cos Labory. A right turn still on the D2 now takes you back into Pauillac.

THE CHATEAUX

St-Estèphe
(Appellation St-Estèphe)
Château Calon-Ségur
3e Grand Cru Classé
The château now belongs to the Capbern-Gasqueton and Peyrelongue families.

Château Cos d'Estournel
2e Grand Cru Classé
Perfectly maintained château owned by the Prats family. Visitors welcome.

Château Cos Labory
5e Grand Cru Classé
A fairly soft St-Estèphe.

Château Haut-Marbuzet
Cru Grand Bourgeois
Exceptionnel
Much-visited wine estate in Marbuzet.

Château Lafon-Rochet
4e Grand Cru Classé
The château was built in the 1960s. Carefully made but, austere wines.

Château de Marbuzet
Cru Grand Bourgeois
Exceptionnel
Wine from this small vineyard with its fine Louis XVI château is blended with Cos d'Estournel *cuvées*.

Château Meyney
Cru Grand Bourgeois
Exceptionnel
A former abbey, prefectly preserved and now a flourishing wine estate.

Château Montrose
2e Grand Cru Classé
Montrose, the "pink hill" is today under the dynamic management of its owner, Jean-Louis Charmolüe.

Château Les Ormes-de-Pez
Cru Grand Bourgeois
A very characteristic St-Estèphe.

THE NORTHERN MEDOC

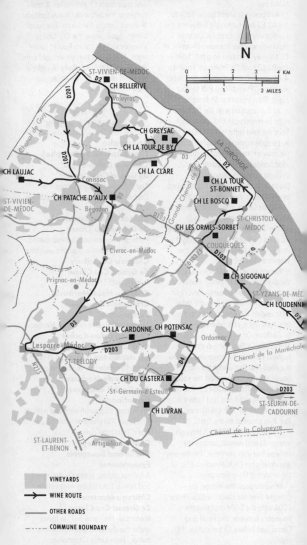

This part of the Médoc should strictly be called Bas-Médoc ("Lower Médoc") because it is downstream on the Gironde. The wine growers however, prefer to simply use the appellation Médoc to refer to wines from this northern part of the peninsula. The landscape is flatter, with more meadowland and fewer vine-clad slopes. The villages seem sleepier and quieter than farther south.

As a result of the rather heavy clay and chalk soil, the wines are slightly less fine, less complex than those from the southern Médoc. Cooperatives play an important part and produce about 40 percent of all the wine. But increasingly it is the individual estates that are giving the appellation a good name and many of today's Médocs are of very high quality.

THE WINE ROUTE

Take the D2 from St-Seurin-de-Cadourne in St-Estèphe towards St-Yzans-de-Médoc.

Just after crossing the Chenal de la Maréchale take the first right turn to the beautiful, pale pink Ch Loudenne and its wine museum.

Retrace your steps to the D2, turn right and head towards St-Yzans-de-Médoc. Drive straight through the town still on the D2. The road bends to the right and in the curve lies Ch Sigognac. The D2 swings off to the right to St-Christoly-Médoc, but continue straight ahead on the D103. At the crossroads with the D103 E5 turn right, into Couquèques past Ch Les Ormes Sorbet.

Continue on this road into St-Christoly-Médoc over a crossroads, then the D2 joins from the right – follow this through the village, taking a sharp left turn as the D2 runs alongside the Gironde. To the left off the road lie Chx Le Boscq and La Tour St-Bonnet not far from the river. The road runs parallel to the Gironde for 2½km then crosses the Grand Chenal de By where the D3 joins from the left. Immediately afterwards, turn left and take the left fork to Ch La Tour de By which lies to the right.

Turn left, then right onto the D3. Once through the town of By, the road forks with Ch La Clare on the D3 to the left. Take the right-hand fork and as it curves to the right, Ch Greysac is on your right. Cross the Chenal de Troussas, and continue through Troussas with the Bois de Troussas on your left. Turn right at the crossroads for Valeyrac and turn left

onto the D2 when you get to the village.

Follow the road past Ch Bellerive to the next junction. Ahead the D2 continues towards St-Vivien-de-Médoc. Turn left onto the D201 heading s. About 4km down the road go straight over the crossroads, then onto the D103 as it joins from the right. At a meeting of five roads turn right and 2km further on you will come upon Ch Laujac.

Retrace your steps back to the D103 in the direction of Bégadan and Couquèques. In the centre of Bégadan is Ch Patache d'Aux. Turn right on the D3 for Lesparre-Médoc through Civrac-en-Médoc, past Prignac-en-Médoc to the west. Continue into the town of Lesparre-Médoc. At the junction with the N215 turn left and at the crossroads with the D204 turn right, then left at the next crossroads and finally right, doing a square in the town. Go straight over the crossroads with the N215 and continue for about 1 km to where the road turns to the left and joins the D204. Turn right into St-Trélody and left onto the D203. Drive straight ahead for nearly 4km through woodland, and the vineyards of Ch La Cardonne will appear on your left.

The road goes through the hamlet of Potensac and past Ch Potensac with its cellar-church. Take the left fork and in Plautignan turn right taking the D4 to St-Germain d'Esteuil.

Just before you reach the town, take the left turn opposite Ch du Castéra to Boyentran. Turn right then left, and right again onto the D203. Follow this road back to St-Seurin-de-Cadourne in St-Estèphe.

BOURG AND BLAYE

Although Bourg and Blaye do not aspire to the heights reached by the great châteaux across the Gironde, wine was being shipped from here long before winegrowing developed in the Médoc.

Bourg's wine district, the Côtes de Bourg, lies mainly along three valleys parallel with the Dordogne. The district makes a majority of red wines (97 percent). Some sparkling Bordeaux is also produced. Although the winegrowing district of Blaye covers an area five times that of Bourg, much of the district is unsuitable for vines and production of *appellation contrôlée* wine is roughly equal in both areas. About 85 percent of wines are red and the best carry the appellation Premières Côtes de Blaye.

THE WINE ROUTE

Head N from Bordeaux on the D911 crossing the river Dordogne at St-Vincent-de-Paul via Eiffel's bridge.

Turn left off the D911 onto the D669 and follow the road towards Bourg with the river Dordogne on your left. Cross the river Moron, ignoring the right turn (D133) to Tauriac and continue on the D669 to Bourg-sur-Gironde.

Drive through Bourg taking the left fork onto the D669 E1 running parallel with the D669. At a T-junction turn left towards the river then fork left driving past Ch Tayac, distinguished by a wooden watch tower dating from the time of the Black Prince.

Follow the loop in the road away from the river, turn left at the next junction, through Bayon and over the crossroads. At the next crossroads turn left towards the Gironde, then right onto the D669 E1 along the waterside. When you come to the crossroads with the D669 go straight over towards Villeneuve and branch left in the village, driving past Ch de Mendoce.

At the junction with Ch Bellevue facing, turn left towards Plassac. At the junction with the D669 turn right and 3km N you enter Blaye. Turn right into the centre of this citadel-town, then left over the railway line onto the D255 ignoring signs for St-Martin-Lacaussade (D937).

Turn right along a small road through Segonzac then over the next crossroads. At a T-junction turn right then cross the D937 onto the D133. Go straight over the next two crossroads. At the next junction with the D937 turn right, then first left to Ch Barbé. Turn left, then left again onto the D133 E3 which shortly brings you back to the D133. Turn right, then take the D135 over the river Brouillon, with Ch Loumède to your left and Ch La Tuilerie to your right as you drive into the tiny Berson.

Take the first turn right (the D251) in the centre of the village. Turn left at the crossroads with the D250, then fork left, over the next crossroads and the road joins the D134 in Teulllac. Once through Mombrier turn right, then shortly left off the road in Lansac and go straight over the next crossroads. Follow the road as it curves left over a small stream. Continue to a T junction then turn right to Tauriac.

From Tauriac take the D133 which will bring you back to the D669. Turn left for Bordeaux.

WINE INFORMATION

BLAYE
Maison du Vin
BOURG
Maison du Vin
Place de L'Eperon

HOTELS AND RESTAURANTS

BLAYE, 33390
Hotel Bellevue (B)
tel: 57 42 00 36
Country-style hotel in the town of Blaye with simple restaurant (C).
Hotel La Citadelle (B)
tel: 57 42 17 10
Modern hotel in Blaye's citadel with a panoramic view over the Gironde. Restaurant.
Château La Grange de Luppé (B), tel: 57 42 80 20
A château in its own park just ooover a km north of Blaye along the D255.

GRAVES AND SAUTERNES

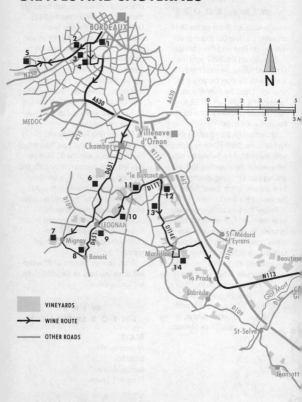

Wine growing has flourished in Graves since the 14th century and this area was first responsible for giving the Bordeaux region its reputation for quality wines. The largest and best known estates and all the Crus Classés are situated on the gravelly soils directly south of Bordeaux.

The small district of Sauternes is renowned for its strong sweet white wines. Sauternes were the only white wines to be included in the 1855 classification.

THE WINE ROUTE

GRAVES

The Route begins in the suburbs of Bordeaux, on the N250 heading for

Archachon and the Atlantic Coast.

Whilst still in the built-up area you will see to your left Ch La Mission Haut Brion **1** and to your right, Ch Haut-Brion **2**. This was the only Graves estate to be included in the

GRAVES AND SAUTERNES 53

famous 1855 classification, as a Premier Cru. To the left of the road is Ch Laville Haut Brion **3** whose vineyards abut Ch La Mission Haut Brion and Ch La Tour Haut Brion **4**.

Take the right-hand fork off the N250 through Baraillot to arrive at Ch Pape-Clément **5**, the wine estate established in 1300 by an archbishop who was later Pope Clement V.

Now retrace your steps to the N250 and just past Ch La Mission Haut Brion on your right, turn right and follow the road due s for some 500m, passing Ch La Tour Haut Brion. At the next crossroads turn left, which takes you, after a right turn at the next junction, to the N10 in Talence.

Turn right, heading s on the road that would eventually take you to Bayonne on the southwest coast. However, at the major intersection with the A630 choose the eastbound route to Villenave d'Ornon and Bordeaux. Approximately 2.5km towards Villenave d'Ornon, just before the intersection with the N113 turn right on the D651 to Chambery and Léognan. On the outskirts of Chambery you can take a detour right to Ch Brown which sells apples grown in its own excellent orchards. The next turn right leads to Ch Olivier **6**, a splendidly medieval moated fortress. Follow the D651 in attractive woodland and hilly countryside through the commune of Léognan. Cross the D109 and turn sharply to the right as the road becomes the D214. Turn left along vineyards to the modest Domaine de Chevalier **7** in the middle of woods. Enter the hamlet of Mignoy and cross over following the road to the D651. Turn left and past Ch de Fieuzal **8** on the left, and as the road curves to the right, Ch Malartic-Lagravière **9** whose vineyards extend across a 20ha plateau.

Follow the road up the hill towards Ch Haut-Bailly **10** on one of the highest points on this side of the Garonne. The road, now the D657E3, winds its way across the hill past Ch Coucheroy on the right towards the famous old estate of Ch Carbonnieux **11** where the road changes into the D111. Ch Carbonnieux was taken over by the Benedictine monks in 1741 who planted white grape varieties, with remarkable success.

As the road descends towards the N113 take the D111 E4 right in the direction of Martillac, travelling past Ch Bouscaut **12** and to the right, Ch Valoux. Cross the Rau de Bourran and you can see to the right Ch Smith-Haut-Lafitte **13** whose wines are improving under the influence of the firm of Louis Eschenauer. Continue through the commune of Martillac, still on the D111 E4, and about 3km down the road is Ch Rochemorin, with a history dating back to the Saracens when a fortress was built as part of the defence of Bordeaux against possible attack from the Moors.

Cross the D214, then turn right, and take the second left which leads to Ch La Tour Martillac **14** whose name derives from the tower in the courtyard.

Turn left, then right onto the D214 and follow the road through woodland until it reaches the N113. Turn left for Bordeaux or right for Sauternes and to continue the tour.

SAUTERNES

The *Circuit du Sauternais* is a signposted route that takes you past many of the châteaux and their cellars that can be visited. Ask at the *Maison du Vin* and look for *vente directe* on roadside signs.

The N113 heading s from Bordeaux runs parallel to the A62 Autoroute des Deux Mers then curves to the left before crossing the motorway and heading for Beautiran and the Garonne.

In the centre of the bend is a right turn to Labrède which is worth a detour to visit the Ch de Labrède, a gloriously idyllic castle once the home of Montesquieu. Take the D108 through Labrède and the château is on the outskirts of the village.

Keep on the D113 as it follows the route of the river: Podensac is the home of the *Maison des Vins de Graves* and the apéritif producers, Lillet. The old windmills you see were once used to grind corn.

Through Cérons you are at the start of the southern Sauternes

section of the Wine Route. Just before you enter Barsac, you will see on the right Ch Nairac **15** and opposite Ch Prost whose walled vineyard encircles the village.

The ancient village of Barsac is worth a visit but continue on the N113, passing on your right Ch Suau **16** which once belonged to the Lur Saluces family. Past the right turn, and just before the small river Ciron (a tributary of the Garonne) is Ch Rolland which caters for tourists with a parking area and vineyard visits and tastings.

Halfway between the road and the railway line on your right is Ch St-Armand, once the home (in the 5th century) of the Bishop of Bordeaux.

In the village of Preignac turn right along the D109, taking the left turn to the station, and following the railway track which runs parallel with the road, turn right at the junction with the D8E4. Go immediately left and follow the road close to the railway to Ch de Malle **17**, a beautiful, 17th-century national monument worth visiting for its gardens alone – try the dry as well as the sweet white wine.

After this inspirational detour, go back to the D8E4 and turn left. Immediately after crossing the A62, the Autoroute des Deux Mers, as the road rises to the region's clay and gravelly hills, you will see on your right, Ch Bastor-Lamontagne.

Through wooded, hilly countryside the road climbs past Ch Suduiraut **18** on the right, remarkable for its beautiful park designed by Le Nôtre, the creator of the gardens at Versailles. Cross over the D116 and to the right is Ch d'Yquem, owned by the Count Alexandre de Lur Saluces, the château as glorious as its golden wine. In a class of its own: ruthless selection and attention to detail combined with the château's position result in a yield per year of one glass of nectar per vine.

Turn left along the D8 past Ch Rieussec **19** to your left, on one of the highest hills in the district: the dry white (called "R") is also impressive. The road bends to the left, then curves to the right: turn right to Fargues on